Politics, Identity and Education in Central Asia

Focusing on the areas of politics, identity and education, this book looks at some of the most pressing and challenging issues that Kyrgyzstan faces in the post-Soviet era. It argues that Kyrgyzstan is challenged with oscillations between the old and the new on the one hand, and domestic and international on the other.

The book analyses the process of post-Soviet transition in today's Kyrgyzstan by focusing on the political elites, some of the major identity problems and educational issues. It discusses how Kyrgyzstan's first president in the post-Soviet era had already been an exceptional leader even prior to the collapse of the Soviet Union in terms of his democratic and liberal tendencies. The book goes on to look at how identity is a major factor in the country, shaped to a large extent by genealogical factors and patron–client mechanisms on the one hand, and religious considerations on the other. Finally, it highlights how education has been perceived as a very influential agent of socialization that develops not only literacy and other skills, but also common attitudes and values that are considered essential to any society.

By evaluating these three areas, the book argues that Kyrgyzstan cannot isolate itself from the demands, priorities and pressures of international actors, which sometimes are in conflict with the country's domestic conditions. It is of interest to students and scholars of Asian Studies, Politics and International Relations.

Pınar Akçalı teaches in the Department of Political Science and Public Administration at the Middle East Technical University, Turkey. She has published widely on Central Asian identity issues and post-Soviet transition.

Cennet Engin-Demir teaches in the Department of Educational Sciences at the Middle East Technical University, Turkey. She has published widely on education in Central Asian countries.

Routledge advances in Central Asian studies

Politics, Identity and Education in Central Asia

Post-Soviet Kyrgyzstan

Edited by Pınar Akçalı and Cennet Engin-Demir

Routledge
Taylor & Francis Group

LONDON AND NEW YORK

First published 2013
by Routledge
2 Park Square, Milton Park, Abingdon, Oxon OX14 4RN

Simultaneously published in the USA and Canada
by Routledge
711 Third Avenue, New York, NY 10017

Routledge is an imprint of the Taylor & Francis Group, an informa business

British Library Cataloguing in Publication Data
A catalogue record for this book is available from the British Library

Library of Congress Cataloging in Publication Data
Politics, identity and education in Central Asia : post-Soviet Kyrgyzstan /
edited by Pinar Akcali and Cennet Engin-Demir.
    pages cm. – (Routledge advances in Central Asian studies ; 3)
    Includes bibliographical references and index.
    1. Kyrgyzstan–Politics and government–1991– 2. Nationalism–
Kyrgyzstan. 3. Education and state–Kyrgyzstan. I. Akçali, Pinar,
editor of compilation. II. Engin-Demir, Cennet, compilation.
    DK918.875.P65 2013
    958.43'085–dc23   2012039091

ISBN: 978-0-415-81613-7 (hbk)
ISBN: 978-0-203-38561-6 (ebk)

Typeset in Times New Roman
by Wearset Ltd, Boldon, Tyne and Wear

Contents

Figures, maps and tables

Figures

Maps

Tables

Notes on contributors

Pınar Akçalı is a graduate of the Department of Political Science and Public Administration at Middle East Technical University, Ankara, Turkey. After her graduation, she went to the Bologna Center of the John Hopkins University in Italy for a one-year Diploma programme in international relations. Upon completing the programme, she finished her master's degree at Middle East Technical University's Department of Political Science and Public Administration. In August 1991, she went to the United States for her Ph.D. degree and completed her master's and Ph.D. degrees at Miami University's Department of Political Science in Oxford, Ohio in August 1998. The title of her Ph.D. dissertation was "Identity Politics and Political Mobilization in Central Asia: The Case of the Islamic Renaissance Party". Since December 1998, she has been working at the Department of Political Science and Public Administration at Middle East Technical University. She has published in Turkish and in English on Central Asian identity issues, nationalism, Islamic revival, post-Soviet transition and Eurasianism.

Düishön Alievich Shamatov is a Research Fellow at the University of Central Asia. He received his Master of Education in Teacher Education from the Institute for Educational Development of the Aga Khan University (AKU-IED) and his Ph.D. from the Ontario Institute for Studies in Education at the University of Toronto. Düishön has taught at Osh State University, AKU-IED, American University in Central Asia and International Atatürk-Alatoo University. He has served as an education consultant for the World Bank, Aga Khan Education Service, Care International and USAID. Düishön's research interests include teacher education, curricular reforms, assessment and examination, educational policy and research. Düishön has extensive teaching and research experience in Kyrgyzstan, Tajikistan, Pakistan and Yemen. He has presented his work at many conferences on primary, secondary and higher education. His publications have appeared in the *Encyclopaedia of Language and Education*, *International Journal Citizenship Teaching and Learning*, *Inner Asia*, *Journal of Transformative Education*, *Central Asian Survey*, *International Perspectives on Education and Society* and *International Handbook on Teacher Training*. Düishön is a member of the

Comparative and International Education Society (CIES), Central Eurasian Studies Society (CESS), and Central Inner Asia Studies (CIAS).

Alan J. DeYoung, Ph.D., is Professor and Chair of the Department of Educational Policy Studies and Evaluation at the University of Kentucky. His formal training is in the Sociology and Anthropology of Education, where his particular interest is in rural education and education and social change. Dr. DeYoung's Central Asian research has spanned 14 years, during which time he was a Fulbright Scholar to the Abai Pedagogical University in Almaty, Kazakhstan (1995–1996), and to the Arabaev Pedagogical University in Bishkek, Kyrgyzstan (2000–2001). He was also an advisor to the Kyrgyz education ministry in 2001–2002, and administered a US Freedom Support Act university partnership between the University of Kentucky and three Kyrgyz universities from 2003 to 2006. Dr. DeYoung has published over two dozen articles and book chapters on education reform in Central Asia during this time. He has also co-edited a book with Dr. Steve Heyneman (*Challenges to Education in Central Asia*, 2004); co-authored a book on rural Kyrgyz secondary schools (*Surviving the Transition? Schools and Schooling in the Kyrgyz Republic since Independence*, 2006); and just published *Lost in Transition: Redefining Students and Universities in the Contemporary Kyrgyz Republic* (Information Age Publishing, 2011).

Cennet Engin-Demir is currently an associate professor of Curriculum and Instruction at Middle East Technical University (METU). Her areas of interest include education in Central Asian countries, citizenship education, child labour and education, hidden curriculum, Turkey's educational policies on Central Asian countries, gender and education and social foundations of curriculum. Some of her authored and co-authored articles and chapters have appeared in the *International Journal of Educational Development, Central Asian Survey, Encyclopedia of Women and Islamic Cultures, The World of Child Labor: An Historical and Regional Survey* and *Educational Research and Evaluation*. She has taught teacher preparation courses at METU's Faculty of Education, as well as graduate courses in Curriculum and Instruction. She was a visiting scholar at the University of Minnesota in 1999–2000. She was awarded a Fulbright Senior Research scholarship and conducted research at the University of Wisconsin, Madison in 2010–2011.

Aksana Ismailbekova completed her Ph.D. dissertation titled "Social Poetics of Patronage-Patron and Kinsmen in Rural Kyrgyzstan" at Max Planck Institute for Social Anthropology, Germany. Her academic interests stem from research projects in Kyrgyzstan on kinship, informal economy and rural development. In 2005, she was awarded the joint Chevening/Open Society Institute/Edinburgh scholarship in order to complement her existing BA with the MS. She studied Social Research in Edinburgh, Scotland. She received her first BA degree in Cultural Anthropology at American University-Central Asia (AUCA), Kyrgyzstan. Currently, she is a research fellow at Zentrum Moderner Orient, Berlin.

Svetlana Jacquesson is an associate researcher at the Max Planck Institute for Social Anthropology (Halle, Germany) and the Centre d'études turques, ottomanes, balkaniques et centrasiatiques (Paris, France). She has conducted long-term field work in Northern Kyrgyzstan, as well as in Karakalpakstan and western Uzbekistan. Her research interests focus on identification, classification and categorization as fundamental processes linking nature and society and conditioning all aspects of social relations. She has published on the economic, social and symbolic aspects of human-animal relations and their transformations, kinship and genealogy, funerary ritual and ritual change. Between 2000 and 2003, she held a fellowship from the French Institute for Central Asian Studies (Tashkent, Uzbekistan) and from July 2006 until December 2009 she has been a senior research fellow at Max Planck Institute of Social Anthropology with a research project on the social dynamics of kinship in Northern Kyrgyzstan.

Martha C. Merrill worked on higher education reform in the Kyrgyz Republic from 1996 to 2001, and made return visits in 2005, 2006, 2009, 2010 and 2011. Currently Associate Professor of Higher Education at Kent State University in the US and Coordinator of the program's International Education Certificate, Dr. Merrill previously was the Dean of Academic Programs at the International Partnership for Service-Learning and Leadership, taught intercultural communication and international education to master's students at the School for International Training (Vermont), and was a Visiting Scholar at the Inner Asian and Uralic National Resource Center at Indiana University. She has published ten articles and book chapters and presented many conference papers on higher education in Central Asia, and also writes on other topics in international and comparative education. Her degrees are in Russian literature (BA, Michigan), Liberal Studies/Creative Writing (Master's, Boston University), College and University Administration (Master's and Ph.D., Michigan) and Islamic Studies (Master's, Columbia University). She continues to research educational reform in Central Asia, as well as the globalization of quality assessment standards in higher education and, in particular, the effect of such globalization in Central Asia.

Irina Morozova is a research fellow in Central Asian history at the International Institute for Asian Studies, Leiden University and a lecturer at Moscow State University, Institute of Asian and African Studies. In 2007–2009, she was a Humboldt fellow at the GIGA Institute of Middle East Studies in Hamburg. She is the author of *The Comintern and Revolution in Mongolia* (White Horse Press, 2002) and *Socialist Revolutions in Asia* (Routledge 2009) and the editor of *Towards Social Stability and Democratic Governance in Central Eurasia* (IOS Press, 2005).

Seçil Öraz is a research fellow in Social, Economic and Political Relations in Turkic World at the Institution of Turkic World Studies, Ege University, İzmir, Turkey. After taking her bachelor's degree from the Department of

International Relations at Ege University, she completed the MA programme in Eurasian Studies at Middle East Technical University, Ankara, Turkey. She is currently a Ph.D. candidate in European Studies at Dokuz Eylül University, İzmir, Turkey. Her areas of interest specifically include Central Asian Republics, Central Asian political culture and the transition process of Central Asia countries.

David Radford is currently a lecturer in International Relations at Flinders University (Adelaide, Australia). He completed his Ph.D. degree in the department of Sociology, Flinders University, in 2011. The title of his dissertation was "Religious Conversion and the Reconstruction of Ethnic Identity: An Investigation into the Conversion of Muslim Kyrgyz to Protestant Christianity in Kyrgyzstan, Central Asia". His areas of academic interest include the Central Asian, West Asian and South Asian regions; nationalism and national identity; religion and ethnic identity; religious fundamentalism; religion and the state; secularisation and religious revitalization; and the role of ideas in social movements. He has published articles in the *Indian Social Science Review* and the *International Sociological Association E-Bulletin*.

Anita Sengupta is a fellow at the Maulana Abul Kalam Azad Institute of Asian Studies, Kolkata. She has contributed articles on boundaries and state formation, the question of minorities and minority identity, gender, problems of transitional polities and culture in the Central Asian region to several national and international research journals, such as the *Central Asian Survey, Journal of Central Asian Studies* and *Central Asia and the Caucasus*. Dr. Sengupta has been a guest speaker at various national and international seminars. She is the author of *Heartlands of Eurasia: The Geopolitics of Political Space*, Lanham, Boulder, New York, Toronto, Oxford: Lexington Books, 2009; *Russia, China and Multilateralism in Central Asia*, New Delhi: Shipra Publications, 2005; *The Formation of the Uzbek Nation-State: A Study in Transition*, Lanham, Boulder, New York, Toronto, Oxford: Lexington Books, 2003 and *Frontiers into Borders: The Transformation of Identities in Central Asia*, Delhi and London: Hope India Publications and Greenwich Millennium Press, 2002. She was Issue Editor of *Asia Annual 2007*, Special Issue on "Envisaging Regions", New Delhi: Manohar, 2008.

Acknowledgements

The authors wish to thank first and foremost Prof. Dr. Ayşe Güneş-Ayata, the Chair of the Center for Black Sea and Central Asia (KORA) at Middle East Technical University, Ankara, Turkey, for her valuable guidance for our book project, as well as her help in allocating financial sources from KORA for the process of editing the manuscript of the book.

We also owe many thanks to our colleagues for agreeing to contribute to our book and for their willingness to revise the earlier versions of their texts. Without their cooperative and flexible attitudes, this book would not have been published.

Finally, we wish to thank Thomas Bonnenfant for his punctuality, seriousness and patience in the process of editing the first manuscript of the book, and Gülçin Tan Şişman, Leyla Sayfutdinova and Rasul Osmonov for their help in the process of checking and organizing the endnotes, references and transliteration of Kyrgyz and Russian names and words.

Introduction

Pınar Akçalı[1] *and Cennet Engin-Demir*[2]

This book primarily aims to look into some of the most pressing and challenging issues that Kyrgyzstan faces in the post-Soviet era. It also intends to focus on three specific areas that are in fact quite related to each other: political leadership and constitutional reform, reconstruction of Kyrgyz identity and educational reform. These three areas are believed to be among the most basic in realizing the process of post-Soviet transition. In the post-Soviet era, similar to other Central Asian countries, Kyrgyzstan is challenged by various conflicts between the old and the new on the one hand, and domestic and international on the other. In all these areas, the legacy of the past meets with the requirements of the post-Soviet transition, and domestic conditions and priorities of Kyrgyzstan are also shaped or influenced to some extent by certain international actors and their priorities. The Kyrgyz case, however, seems to be unique, as this country has suffered more than the others in recent years from political tensions and instability, as well as economic problems.

As for political leadership and constitutional reform, Kyrgyzstan is a striking case in Central Asia, since the first president of the country in the post-Soviet era, Askar Akaev, had already been an exceptional leader even prior to the collapse of the Soviet Union in terms of his democratic and liberal tendencies. His role in the process of democratic transition (as well as his later switch to more authoritarian rule) was obvious. We see a similar pattern for the relatively shorter period under the second president of Kyrgyzstan, Kurmanbek Bakiev. Kyrgyzstan has so far been the only Central Asian country in which the two post-Soviet leaders were forced to leave power as a result of public demonstrations and protests. Kyrgyzstan is also the only country in the region to have a woman president and to have switched to a parliamentary democracy. These developments were, in part, due to elite-level fragmentations on a variety of domestic and international issues, resulting in shifting political alliances.

Reconstruction of a new Kyrgyz identity under post-Soviet conditions has turned out to be another major factor in the country, shaped to a large extent by genealogical factors and patron–client mechanisms on the one hand and religious and regional considerations on the other. But here too we see fragmentations which are basically the result of both domestic and international conditions and pressures. Some of the most basic identity factors are renewed, reshaped and redefined with new justifications that seem to be in close contrast with the previous ones.

The educational reform process, which has always been perceived as a very influential agent of socialization that develops not only literacy and other skills, but also common attitudes and values that are considered essential to any society, is another major area that needs to be looked into. In this sense education plays a vital role in the post-Soviet transformation of Central Asian countries, including Kyrgyzstan. As such, new trends and policies that aim to develop a post-Soviet curriculum to promote the necessary attitudes and values to cope with the economic, social and political changes taking place both in the domestic and international spheres are emerging.

In this general framework, the first part of the book focuses on political leadership and constitutional reform in Kyrgyzstan and its role in post-Soviet transition. This part consists of three main chapters. Irina Morozova's chapter, "Patterns of elite consolidation and rivalry in Kyrgyzstan between 1960 and 2010", provides both a historical analysis and an account of the recent developments, and concentrates on the formation of elites within a broader socio-cultural context as well as the international environment. According to Morozova, there are continuously repeated or reproduced patterns of elite consolidation and rivalry in Kyrgyzstan, the roots of which can be traced back to regional and/or kinship affiliations. Whenever there are radical social transformations (such as *perestroika* and post-Soviet transition), new alliances and networks are formed and the "existing normative social order launches mechanisms of resistance". Under such conditions, the priority of elites would be to manage material assets. This was the case during the Soviet era in which the regional elites were in competition with each other over the distribution of political, social and economic resources. The general pattern also did not change in the post-Soviet era in which the former elites of the upper *nomenklatura* made a shift and adapted to the conditions of the post-Soviet era by emerging as the new business elite. Morozova concludes that the tension that shook the country in the spring of 2010 was yet another "new stage of struggle for resources" among the elites.

Seçil Öraz, in her chapter entitled "The impact of Askar Akaev's political leadership in the process of democratization in Kyrgyzstan", looks into the relationship between the process of democratization in the Akaev era and suggests that between 1991 and 2005 this process was shaped to a large extent by Akaev's attitude and priorities as a leader. As such, the three stages of his leadership corresponded to the three phases in Kyrgyzstan's political transition, which started out as an initial democratic leap (1990–1995), followed by a reversal (1995–2000) and ending with a shift to authoritarianism (2000–2005). By referring to the literature on both political leadership and democratic transition, Öraz concludes that the political leadership of Askar Akaev, which shifted from a "transactional-democratic leader depending on a legal-charismatic base of authority to a transformational-authoritarian one depending on traditional authority", had a major impact on the process of the post-Soviet transformation of Kyrgyzstan from its initial democratic path to an authoritarian one. The chapter sheds some light on the attitudes and preferences of the first president of the country and, as such, aims to portray a picture of the challenges presented by leadership patterns in terms of transition to democracy.

This part of the book also contains Anita Sengupta's chapter, "Colour revolutions and constitutionalism: the case of Kyrgyzstan". The author analyses Kyrgyzstan from the perspective of colour revolutions and "the complex process of constitutionalism" by looking at the process of adaptation of the 1993 Constitution, as well as the amendments introduced to this document, with a specific emphasis on the political events and developments since the Tulip Revolution. Sengupta also focuses on the emergence of new political actors in Kyrgyzstan who are instrumental in introducing changes. The chapter concludes that the real challenge for Kyrgyzstan is "to develop institutions and practices that would uphold the values of the constitution". As such, various constitutional amendments, including the ones in 2010, were attempts to find a balance between different powers of the state.

The second part of the book, which consists of three chapters, focuses on identity issues, with a specific emphasis on kinship mechanisms and genealogical identification, as well as religious conversion, that (re)shape certain identity attachments. Aksana Ismailbekova's chapter, entitled "'Circles of trust': functions and mechanisms of patron–client relations in the private farm", analyses the internal dynamics of the new private farm and its importance for the local Kyrgyz by specifically looking at the conflicts that emerged after the dissolution of the former *kolkhoz* structure within the small village of Orlovka in the Kara-Balta *raion* in Northern Kyrgyzstan. Ismailbekova focuses on the "circle of trust" that is shaped within the general framework of "patron–client relations" in these farms that are neither forced nor voluntary. The chapter suggests that, although the management process in these new economic units is disorganized, it nevertheless has its own internal logic. As such, the private farm emerges as a complex arena in which visible patterns of patron–client relations can be observed. These patterns are basically shaped by manipulative strategies used by both the patrons and the clients and they are justified by kinship ties and transformed into circles of trust.

Svetlana Jacquesson's chapter, entitled "From herd breeding to land farming: social uses of descent and kinship in a Kyrgyz village", looks at the recent patterns of interaction among the members of a village community in the Aktalaa region that specialized in sheep breeding during the Soviet era. By basing her analysis on ethnographic data and field research, Jacquesson looks into the role of kinship (in its "official" and "practical" forms) and descent in the (re-)emerging patterns of cooperation after the dismantling of the *kolkhozes* and the establishment of private agricultural enterprises in the post-Soviet era. By analysing three such enterprises, Jacquesson focuses on the social use of kinship and descent that accounts for the distribution of tasks, obligations and activities among kinship categories. The chapter concludes that the social practices of kinship emerge as a result of the interaction of official kinship and practical necessities of life.

The final chapter of the second part, written by David Radford and entitled "Religious conversion and its impact on ethnic identity in post-Soviet Kyrgyzstan", analyses religious conversion among the ethnic Kyrgyz to Protestant Christianity in the post-Soviet era and suggests that this conversion has challenged the assumption that "to be Kyrgyz is to be Muslim". Basing his analysis on field interviews, Radford points out that the converts (*mashayakche*) do not see themselves as any "less Kyrgyz" than other Kyrgyz people, as they have found ways of reconciling their new faith within traditional Kyrgyz values. The chapter concludes that for many Kyrgyz Christians, to be Kyrgyz is also to be a *mashayakche*, not just a Muslim.

The third and the final part of the book focuses on the issue of education in post-Soviet Kyrgyzstan. In the first chapter, entitled "Everyday realities of a young teacher in post-Soviet Kyrgyzstan: a case of a history teacher from a rural school", Düishön Alievich Shamatov provides insight into the impact of socio-political upheaval on the life of a young history teacher in the context of post-Soviet Kyrgyzstan. Using the data drawn from an ethnographic case study, he explores the challenges a beginning teacher in a village school faces in the process of transition. Shamatov's analysis is based on the detailed descriptions of an educational context in relation to social, economic and political context from a historical perspective. Shamatov argues that although some of the challenges that Kanybek (the history teacher) has to face are typical for any beginning teachers in any part of the world, his challenges are compounded and enlarged by the specific socio-political and economic changes that Kyrgyzstan has been facing since 1991.

In his chapter entitled "Redefining students and universities in the Kyrgyz Republic", Alan J. DeYoung, makes an overview of the educational inputs and outcomes visible in Kyrgyzstan. His interviews conducted with students, teachers, parents and administrators, as well as his participant observation in several faculties involved with international languages in a Kyrgyz university, provided him with an opportunity to explore and explain the contradictions in the higher education sector from an "insider" perspective. DeYoung argues that there is a gap between the expressed wish for higher education at the level of both ministry and university presidents and what actually takes place in Kyrgyz universities. According to DeYoung, although academic quality and rigour have decreased in state universities, higher education demand remains high for reasons that are other than academic or professional in nature in Kyrgyzstan.

Martha C. Merrill's chapter, "Higher education in Kyrgyzstan: the inevitability of international actors", highlights the geographical, historical, demographic, political, cultural and economic factors that influence higher education in Kyrgyzstan in its specific context. She specifically focuses on the internationalization of higher education in Kyrgyzstan and outlines a dozen different reasons in this field that prevent Kyrgyzstan from isolating itself from the demands, priorities and pressures of international actors. Merrill classifies both factors influencing the internationalization of higher education in Kyrgyzstan over which the country has little or no control, and also factors which are under its direct control. The chapter suggests that Kyrgyzstan needs to improve academic integrity, curricular independence and transparency in order to strengthen its own universities in an effort to meet the challenges of internationalization and globalization.

Within this general framework, this book, which is mostly composed of some of the revised and updated papers presented at the Tenth ESCAS (European Society for Central Asian Studies) Conference organized by the Center for Black Sea and Central Asia (KORA) of Middle East Technical University in Ankara, Turkey, between 13 and 15 September 2007, is expected to make a contribution to the existing body of studies by bringing together several scholars from different disciplines working on different aspects of this small but fascinating country. It also aims to put Kyrgyzstan within an international context around some critical themes and looks at the interaction between domestic and international issues and actors. As such, it highlights the case of Kyrgyzstan, a small Central Asian country that has attracted increasing attention in recent years.

Notes

1 Middle East Technical University, Department of Political Science and Public Administration.
2 Middle East Technical University, Department of Educational Sciences.

Part I
Politics

1 Patterns of elite consolidation and rivalry in Kyrgyzstan between 1960 and 2010[1]

Irina Morozova

Kyrgyzstan is often characterized as a "failing" or "failed" state, revealing conflict potential for further disintegration along territorial and clan lines. In 1990, social and economic development in the Kyrgyz SSR was not sufficient to meet the challenge of increased rural migration into the cities, causing social deprivation. Against such a background of a collapsing economy and social deprivation, ethnic diversity was exploited to divide rather than consolidate several communities living in the country, and bloody clashes occurred among Uzbek, Kyrgyz and Slavic populations living in the south of the republic, specifically in Osh and its surrounding territories. Despite a number of pessimistic prognoses, further escalation of ethnic conflict did not take place, although the drastic systemic change that came with the USSR's disintegration and dismantling of socialism in December 1991 caused disorientation and apathy among the people, and the socio-economic ground for conflict escalation remained acute and even deepened throughout the 1990s. Against this background and the sharp competition for resources, institutional voids and coup d'états became typical for Kyrgyzstan's political life in the first decade of the new millennium. In June 2010, violence again erupted in the cities of Osh, Jalalabad and Bishkek. Ethnicization of the conflict was encouraged by major input from various international and local media agents, who suggested that ethnic differentiation had been the main cause of the conflict.[2] The subsequent alarming predictions of a further increase in bloody clashes "on an ethnic basis" proved to be baseless, as the legitimizing process of the new government went ahead peacefully. However, the large of number of deaths and victims and the brutality of the conflict deepened polarization between the Uzbek and the Kyrgyz, the two major groups in Osh, and increased the probabilities of the continuously discussed and imagined disintegration of the country. In people's narratives, the massacre of June 2010 is imaged as the "war" and is often dangerously justified by one side of the conflict against the other as a struggle for social space.[3] As long as three specific conditions continue to exist in Kyrgyzstan, the possibilities for further escalation of the conflict remain acute: (1) Kyrgyzstan's current situation in the middle of a complex multi-level competition among various global, trans-regional and trans-local actors, (2) persistence of social polarization and deprivation and (3) the reproduction of memories of the "war".

Historically having been largely dependent on the Soviet budget, after proclaiming independence, Kyrgyzstan, a country with few resources, was in need of foreign assistance to cope with its collapsing economy and a drastic fall in living standards in the post-Soviet era. The adoption of IMF reforms in 1991 led Kyrgyzstan to experience shock price liberalization and hyperinflation, and soon the country found itself in the list of states with high levels of poverty. In July 1998, the country became the first of the former Soviet republics to acquire membership of the WTO. The Kyrgyzstani government was forced not only to let the international markets, financial institutions and companies in, but also to open the public domain to international human rights organizations and various NGOs. With a high degree of interference from the external powers and a vivid coverage of its domestic affairs by national as well as international media, Kyrgyzstan had become one of the most favourite transition cases to be studied.

The overthrow of President Askar Akaev with the so-called Tulip Revolution in March 2005 was perceived by other Central Asian governments (and certain groups in China and Russia) as a destabilizing and threatening power transition scheme and a turning point in the course of the economic reform process. The new president of the country, Kurmanbek Bakiev, fostered yet another privatization campaign and attempted to join the new millennium energy boom by bargaining with Kyrgyzstan's strategic resources, mainly gold, water and hydroelectricity. In April 2010 President Bakiev, accused of serious corruption and increasing his family's fortunes, had to leave his post in Bishkek as a result of civil unrest against his rule. The scenario of his removal was reminiscent of the overthrow of his predecessor Akaev.

This chapter aims to trace the continuously repeated (or reproduced) patterns of elite consolidation in Kyrgyzstan before and after independence. Viewing the formation of elites within a broader social and socio-cultural context, as well as the changes in the international environment, it is possible to trace the continuity of power models and to depict how rapid social transformation happens in periods of crisis (such as the social disarray during the time of *perestroika* and after the disintegration of the USSR). When exogenously generated change causes disruption to social systems by breaking traditional economic ties and social networks, and threatens certain groups with marginalization or elimination, the existing normative social order launches mechanisms of resistance. Social systems undergo a process of restructuralization in which certain latent elements, such as a basic mode of production and communal institutions, including social hierarchies, albeit modified, are preserved. As such, the establishment of a new political elite accompanies a radical social transformation and both individual and collective actors search for new alliances and networks.

For the purposes of this chapter, a distinction is made between the elite groups in power that directly control and/or participate in the process of accumulation and redistribution of wealth within the society on the one hand, and other competing groups that also seek legitimacy from various sources, including ethnic, national and religious identities on the other. I focus on the ruling elites and analyse their claim for additional, non-essentialist sources of power that include, above all, noble lineages, kinship and various local identities. I argue that in a crisis period of radical social transformation, the priority of the elites is often to manage material assets (as was the case during privatization campaigns). Thus, the chapter will focus on, first, the patterns of elite adaptation in terms of the shift from the high *nomenklatura* (those holding key administrative posts in the Soviet power structure) positions to the new business elite; second, the ways in which this newly transformed elite secures its access to and distribution of national resources; and, third, the ability or strength of the elites in centralizing resource redistribution in the country.

The legacy of the Soviet rule: formation of regional elites

Among the power-regulating schemes that have had the most impact on the current development of Central Asian political institutions and the composition of elites, the Soviet supra-legal institutions of political control and police, whose activities could not be constrained by any legal code,[4] centre-periphery relations and state-party hierarchies still remain the basic factors both at the national and regional levels. The mechanisms of redistributing wealth and authority between the capital and the regions with their four-level administration structures – republic, province (*oblast*), region (*raion*) and local authorities (*ail*) – are either a copy or a deviation from the previous Soviet model.

During the Soviet era, the competition among the elite groups inside the Central Asian republics often went along regional lines, and, although alliances were often made at trans-regional and trans-local levels, various agents as heads of *oblast* and *raion* party committees and industrial-economic departments were reproducing rivalry by claiming or emphasizing their territorial and kinship affiliations. The centre-periphery power conflict was essential, but not structural, in Soviet Central Asian republics. The complex mosaic picture of peoples, ethnicities (or what was believed to be ethnic), migrated groups and religious elites was an object for positivist case studies of modernization with its scientific classifications applied to local communities by the Soviet policy makers (as well as by the Russian Tsarist administration in earlier periods). The already existing conflicts were not only consciously and unconsciously being escalated, but also modelled by means of socio-political and socio-economic reforms that were launched by the Soviets, and spurred social disarray in the 1920s–1930s. These reforms, on the one hand, followed the pattern of relationships that had been practised during tsarist times: outside authority, preservation of local identities and normative social order. During the first decades of Soviet rule, the new political centre in Moscow was perceived as something foreign and distant to the people at local level. On the other hand, Soviet reformist politics in Asia was based upon a stronger idea of modernization, scientific progress and internationalism, and in many ways contrasted to the tsarist policies, for instance, in relation to the indigenous population of Central Asia and the migrants from the European part of the Empire. The new social model developed by Soviet architects aimed at the construction of new social groups and identities, regardless of ethnic origins and previously existing social hierarchies. However, these goals of the Soviet reformers were never achieved. The introduction of a new taxation system by the Soviet government in the early 1920s and the land reform of 1926–1928 followed by collectivization led not only to the elimination of the formerly privileged social groups and elites, but also to the destruction of social relations and networks at grass-roots level. Analysis of the recently published documents from the political police (OGPU) archive (*"Sovershenno Sekretno"* 2001, 2002, 2003) shows that the reform purposely intensified social and ethnic conflict to hasten the process of formation of the new classes, while the selectiveness of the OGPU data itself reflected an attempt by the policy makers to frame the ongoing social processes as a suitable concept to continue the reform.[5] In this general framework, Soviet Kyrgyzstan also became an example of a society integrated along titular-national lines in an affirmative way. The Bolsheviks locally rooted the new type of republican nationalism by promoting Kyrgyz *national* communist cadres and by creating the new ruling strata – the *national nomenklatura*.

During the first Soviet five-year plan (1928–1932) monetary aid from the centre flew to the "underdeveloped" republics, accompanied by a strong modernistic ideology. The Central Asian republican elites successfully appropriated the rhetoric of backwardness to secure special financial help (Martin 2001: 130–131). The greatest progress of *korenizatsiya* (affirmative indigenizing cadres) and *vydvizhenie* (promotion), as proved with references to archival sources by certain scholars (ibid.: 24) was achieved in that period. In 1932 the percentage of titular nationals in positions of authority increased; however, in 1933, following the immediate devastating effects of appointing unqualified cadres for the ideologically imposed policy of ethnic group representation in administration and industry, as well as Stalin's politically motivated and repressive attitude in the quick rotation of cadres, there was an evident regress once again. As the local elites also adopted and used the political lexicon of *korenizatsiya* in their political competition, campaigns against "local nationalism" were rapidly alternated with campaigns against "great chauvinism" that had been first launched in Central Asia by the Bolsheviks at the start of the 1920s (ibid.: 137–138).[6] Thus, *korenizatsiya* was run not solely by the policy makers from the Soviet political centres, but was principally supported by those whom it targeted – the newly promoted local cadres, who adapted this policy to compete against each other.

Soviet plans for Central Asia were clearly of a modernizing nature and the goal of creating a communist and/or socialist society was implicit in the views of its architects, although the definitions of such a society could change, depending on the political situation. In the 1920s, it was believed that social discontent rooted in ethnic conflict had to be produced in the masses in order to stimulate the creation of new social classes.

In the early 1920s, and especially before 1924, competition among political groups within the prospective Kyrgyz SSR (Soviet Socialist Republic) resulted in some sort of regional separatism. On the one hand, there were the leaders from the Bishkek, Karakol and Naryn regions who historically had had more interactions with the Russian settlers and managed to develop better cooperation with the Soviets; on the other hand, there were groups from the south, especially from Osh, Andijan and Namangan, who considered themselves to be closer to the former "centre" – the capital of the Turkestan *krai*, Tashkent.[7] First, an attempt was made by a group of northern communists to establish the "Mountainous Kyrgyz *Oblast*", which excluded the Fergana region; later, the same people were employed to work on drafting the proposals for national delimitation within the Central Asian Bureau attached to the Russian Communist Party of Bolsheviks (RCP(b)) Central Committee. These northern communists would have preferred ceding some southern territories of the prospective Kyrgyz ASSR to Uzbekistan in order to rid themselves of political competitors. However, this could not have been accomplished, as the central concern for the Bolsheviks was to liquidate any potential for consolidation among the regional elites who lobbied for the formation of a bigger Turkestan republic (the so-called "Turkestan project") (Haugen 2003: 117–118, 206–209; Abashin 2007: 179–195). The Fergana area was therefore "divided" between the Uzbek SSR, Tajik ASSR and Kyrgyz ASSR. The Kyrgyz republic was finally mapped in its present borders, encompassing Issyk-Kul, parts of Semirechie, Tianshan and the Fergana valley, as well as adjacent mountainous areas. Immediately after the delimitation and establishment of the republican capital in Frunze (previously Pishpek) the northern groups found themselves in a more privileged position in comparison with the southerners and the authorities in Frunze were in charge of economic planning for the southern regions of the newly formed republic.[8]

Soviet rule and external control from Moscow introduced centralized structures[9] into the newly formed Central Asian republics, as a result of which some regional and local groups gained better bargaining positions in terms of participating in decision-making processes and redistribution of resources as compared to others. The territorial-administrative reforms were targeted either at making smaller administrative units or re-merging them into larger units – the policy that was closely connected with the regular course of new elite formation.

The key line in Soviet cadres policy was the creation of a native political elite and consequent integration of wider sections of the local population into the new political system. In the decades following the Second World War, the new republican *nomenklatura* took a more clear-cut form, further institutionalized and developed. The isolation of the Soviet population from the outside world as a consequence of the Cold War led to belated post-colonial protest in Central Asian republics. On the wave of the decolonization process, the native *nomenklatura* in the 1960–1980s discovered ways to avoid the simple process of adjusting to the communist ideology believed to be universal as it had done between the two world wars. In contrast to the previous pattern, the native elite was learning to adapt the Soviet state and party institutions to the remaining social cults and normative order in such a way that those institutions supported the elite's rule over the population. Thus, in the second part of the twentieth century, institutions introduced from above were not only subject to major impact from regional and local actors, but the latter sometimes also changed the nature of these institutions.[10] As for the traditional groups identified in various categories, such as kinship, family, territory, religion, culture and occupation, it is possible to observe that they never vanished or dissolved completely in Central Asia, but mutated under the impact of the external factor of socialist state building. The upper layers of the republics' *nomenklatura* also did not completely break with the noble kinship lineages, which by themselves saw that those "unofficial identities" helped them to maintain positions of leadership. For instance, the First Secretary of the Kyrgyz Communist Party, Tudarkun Usubaliev, who held power from 1961 to 1985, is believed to have a noble lineage.[11] As such, the institutions became a means of adaptation in the political and social sense. Local elites in many ways utilized centralization schemes. Mechanisms of decentralization also existed and began to play a larger role with Nikita Khrushchev's reforms and later, once again, came to the forefront under Mikhael Gorbachev.

Khrushchev's decentralization along party lines was accompanied by the increasing importance of ministerial branches in running the Soviet economy. The ministerial networks involved such economic actors as directors of enterprises and *kolkhozes*, ministerial officials and organs of party control, and united them not only horizontally, but also vertically. During the long rule of Leonid Brezhnev certain concealed mechanisms were created within those networks to manage a part of the Soviet economy in a hidden and illicit way via corruption, fraud and stealing from the factory.[12]

At the time of *perestroika*, a deeper separation of economic interests and political jurisdiction was seen between the central (the republican-level state administration) and provincial (*oblast-* and *raion*-level) authorities, as local authorities and industrial companies received wider rights to manage their local economic resources with the introduction of the Law on State Entrepreneurship in 1987. Furthermore, the policy of *glasnost* would permit them to emphasize their reasserted local identities, to use these to claim recognition for their socio-economic problems at the all-union level, and to ask affirmatively for assistance from the republican centre vis-à-vis Moscow. The disintegration of the USSR hastened the "rise of the provinces" (and simultaneously the "rise" of the illegal economy and criminal groups). Managing limited local resources, including the "shadow criminal economy", and running privatization campaigns became the basic means of survival for the late-Soviet provincial elites and a matter of constant dispute with the republican authorities who did not want to lose their former monopoly over managing the largest shares of resources in their republics vis-à-vis Moscow. The dynamics of this "transitional bargaining game" between the groups wanting to regain their position or to acquire access to major resources developed while alternately favouring one side or the other (Luong 2002: 25).

The Soviet Kyrgyz *nomenklatura* and academia

Up until the end of the 1990s, the Akaev regime in Kyrgyzstan was advertised in the public domain as the least autocratic in Central Asia. Akaev was a representative of the Kyrgyz intelligentsia and was actively engaged in politics. This social stratum was formed by the end of the Soviet era; some its representatives took the lead in the nation-building process after the disintegration of the USSR. The contribution of academicians, especially in the field of humanities, as well as of writers and artists, in defining the post-Soviet ideological shift and in determining the course of reforms was especially noteworthy in Kyrgyzstan, where academicians and specialists from the European Republics of the USSR were dominant in hard science and technical spheres,[13] while nominal scientists were predominantly working as in humanities departments.[14]

The Kyrgyz intelligentsia involved in framing nation-building projects at the beginning of the 1990s did not have to start with an empty page, since the rhetoric of national independence had its roots in the 1924 delimitation and the fundamental projects on writing the history of the Kyrgyz SSR and the Kyrgyz nation dated back to the establishment of the republic's Academy of Science in the 1940s. The developmentalist "national liberation" rhetoric was employed practically unanimously by Kyrgyz historians, following mainstream Soviet social science. As such, projects on writing the national histories of the titular nations were launched in the USSR on a large scale in the 1940s. Based on extensive ethnographic field material collected by regional ethnographers, many of them remain unknown to the public as they were retained by the local authorities; the massive volumes of the histories of the Kazakh SSR, Uzbek SSR, Kyrgyz SSR, Turkmen SSR and Tajik SSR were produced and filled the shelves of central and municipal libraries in the 1950s and 1960s (*Istoriya Kirgizii* 1963). The first volumes of those histories were devoted to the ethno-genesis of the Kyrgyz from ancient times, reflecting on archaeological and written historical sources, as well as the oral histories of the groups that had inhabited the territory of the Kyrgyz Republic since time immemorial, up until modern times and the October Revolution of 1917. At the time, no one paid any sincere scholarly attention to the second volumes of those histories, which were disproportionally devoted to a period of socialist revolutions, national liberation and people's achievements under socialism. As for the first volumes, they were developed in the works of native historians in the republican academies of science. Such an academic career was considered to be elitist and granted a person great social prestige, comparable to the social cult of the families of saints[15] or belonging to a noble lineage.

A substantial proportion of members of the national intelligentsia who had also been educated within the Muslim intellectual tradition before the Bolshevik revolution were purged in the 1930s; however, those who survived were often the most receptive to socialist educational campaigns and, re-establishing their alliance with the central party organs, started working on issues in their nations' cultural development under the new communist regime.

The 1940s brought a principle change to intellectual and religious elites in Central Asian societies, both at republican and municipal levels. Soon after the beginning of the Second World War, Soviet leaders realized the importance of raising patriotic feelings among the people and they started to address ethnic and religious groups, diasporas and wider sections of the population by calling them to a fight against fascism under the banner of Islam and national awakening (Poujol 2005: 50–63). The policy of tight party control over the population, particularly those who might had have contacts with foreigners (for instance, in the southern border regions), was strictly adhered to by the authorities in the Kremlin, who at the same time tried to supervise the revolutionary work among the oppositional groups in neighbouring countries, especially Iran and Afghanistan, both during and after the war (Morozova 2005a: 85–120). As more Asian leaders decided to ally with the victorious USSR and a new wave of communist parties' activities coincided with the post-war de-colonization process, Soviet Muslims and Central Asian intellectuals had an intention (that soon became an illusion due to the emergence of the Cold War) to transnationalize and build up new networks at international level, using the winners' advantages, considering not just contributing to, but guiding post-war ideological trends in the Orient.

As soon as the Central Asian *ulama* (Muslim scholars) acquired an opportunity to institutionalize within the newly established Spiritual Directory of the Muslims of Central Asia and Kazakhstan (SADUM) in 1943, national intellectuals who had now learned to adopt a secular rhetoric in the public sphere after the political campaigns and repressions of the 1930s, also got a better chance to consolidate and form a new stratum of Soviet republican national intelligentsia. Lucrative positions in academia, especially in the USSR's Academy of Science, and the opportunity to work on national history or national literature and form their own research groups, albeit within the Soviet mainstream, gave these people additional motivation to cooperate with the state and party authorities, rather than oppose them, either openly or covertly.

The new intelligentsia of the Soviet Central Asian republics developed in unison with mainstream policies dictated from Moscow, although with some room for deviation. As these intellectuals and the upper layers of *nomenklatura* cadres often shared the same educational background and had been exposed to the same ideological propaganda, transition from one group to another was very easy and quite normal. As such the representatives of the intelligentsia were appointed to high *nomenklatura* positions, or officials joined the academia after retirement. Due to the importance given to education and knowledge among Central Asian elites, a university education was a matter of social prestige for a high ranking official.

The sphere of higher education had been broadened in the 1960s and 1970s as a part of the socialist welfare system. The improvement of living conditions in parallel with the development of Soviet state and party institutions worked positively for the new social identities and for the wider involvement of educated national cadres, also from rural areas, in the public life of the republics. At the time of the Khrushchev's "thaw" and during the *perestroika* years several people, although they were not professionally involved in any type of intellectual work and education, also started to identify themselves as "intelligentsia" on the grounds that they opposed the existing political regime and wanted reforms. Against the background of rising living standards and general educational levels, the prestige of higher education obtained in the republican capitals or European parts of the USSR became even more significant and framed a new "elite cast" which consisted of certain representatives of the national intelligentsia and educated *nomenklatura* apparatus. In the Central Asian context "intelligentsia families" tended to maintain their circle of elitist relatives and acquaintances, which also helped them occupy higher and prestigious positions in the state and party structures.[16]

The intelligentsia, and to a greater extent the *nomenklatura*, of Central Asian republics differed from their counterparts in the Slavic republics by a tighter commitment to and dependency on their networks at republican, regional and local levels. New ideological trends that penetrated Soviet society during the *perestroika* years from the West (such as ideas of democracy and civil society) and from the Middle East (such as Islamic reformist movements) were equally unwelcomed by the upper *nomenklatura* circles. Nevertheless, these circles, together with the national intellectuals from the Academy of Science, approached the liberal rhetoric of market economy and democratic institutions in an apologetic way, as a new line of the CPSU (Communist Party of the Soviet Union): the newly rediscovered liberal rhetoric was meant to be instrumental for the ideological legitimization of the on-going political and socio-economic course. During *perestroika* creation of the link between social scientific knowledge and political reform (and later political independence) was already being called for (Amsler 2007). In the post-Soviet era, while not officially refusing liberal market rhetoric, the newly independent governments would frame social consolidation within the discussions on national awakening and liberation; such discussions had been learned and practised exensively among the national intelligentsia during the former decades of Soviet rule.

The biography of Roza Otunbayeva, the third president of Kyrgyzstan, is very exemplary in this sense: since her formation as a politician started during *perestroika* and the first years of independence, she followed the typical path of combining her career within the communist party with being promoted in academia. Obtaining scientific degrees in dialectical materialism from the philosophy faculties of Lomonosov Moscow State University and Kyrgyz State University, she was climbing the Soviet hierarchical party administration ladder, starting from the position of the secretary of *raikom* (regional committee) in Bishkek and after a while the capital *gorkom* (town committee). Under Gorbachev she became the deputy chairperson of the Council of Ministers and Minister of Foreign Affairs. As a member of the Ministry Board in the USSR's Foreign Office, she was the representative of the USSR in the UN and UNESCO in 1989–1991, acquiring international recognition as a messenger of *glasnost* and *perestroika*.[17] Her participation in the so-called Issyk-Kul Forum organized by Chinghiz Aitmatov in October 1986[18] can also be seen as a proof of her being selected as a promoter of the new *perestroika* course not only domestically, but also in the international arena. Later, Akaev's government used Otunbaeva's diplomatic experience: she served as the Minister of Foreign Affairs (1992, 1994–1996) and the first Kyrgyzstani Ambassador to the United States and

Canada (1992–1994), as well as to the United Kingdom (1998–2001). In fact, Otunbaeva was a much more typical representative of the Soviet *nomenklatura* than Akaev, whom she began accusing of corruption after she lost her post in his government, or Bakiev, with whom she allied during the "Tulip Revolution" and whom she also accused of corruption and intrigues afterwards. Following the ousting of Bakiev in April 2010 and the widespread violent riots in the country, Otunbaeva became President of the interim government for the short period till 31 December 2011.

The outcomes of building a *nomenklatura* in Central Asian republics vary significantly. Although the *nomenklatura* was the ruling stratum in the USSR and its socio-economic interests bound its agents together not only at the union level but also internationally as they directed the foreign policy of the USSR, the Central Asian *nomenklatura* did not usually serve outside their own republics. The Kyrgyz *nomenklatura* had its own characteristic: it turned out to be less monolithic than the others, which determined the rapid political transition of this republic at the beginning of the 1990s, in contrast to other Central Asian states, with the exception of Kazakhstan. The sharp competition among various Kyrgyzstani political players in the post-Soviet era demonstrates little continuity of *nomenklatura* structures and identity, but rather more regional, territorial and clan loyalties. This pattern is also reflected in the situation with political parties in the country: there have been many parties but none has become a truly leading institution.

It must also be kept in mind that the Soviet welfare system, which had started with Khrushchev's reforms and was developed during the Brezhnev era with his "stability of cadres" policy, presented the people with the opportunity to run small private businesses based on households, and hence increased the quality of life through trading at local bazaars and black markets (Friedman and Vidiasova 1996: 20–22). Such small private businesses in a socialist economy were run more vigorously by those layers of the population who did not belong to, or were distant from, the intelligentsia stratum. Elites from Bishkek, Chui and Issyk-Kul regions happened to have better access to prestigious education and advantageous career paths. As the key educational institutions were concentrated in the north of the republic, the south of Kyrgyzstan remained industrially less developed and more agrarian (and in addition lacked adequate connection with the north, except for one mountainous road), despite the fact that it was not less, but, perhaps, even more active in small-scale entrepreneurship. Due to the frequent recruitment of the Soviet Kyrgyz *nomenklatura* from academia in the final years of the Soviet era, the existing stratification in social status and profession drew a dividing line between the former "northern intelligentsia" (with which Akaev's group became associated) and the new "southern business groups". The rise of a "shadow and criminal economy" during the time of *perestroika* and further criminalization at the beginning of the 1990s became evident with the beginning of and increase in drug, weapon and human trafficking throughout Central Asia, in which southern groups became actively involved due to their geographical location, thus gaining additional assets over the northern groups.

This did not create a dichotomy of north versus south, in fact, there have been large business groups and influential "oligarchs" in the north as well, while the southern groups' involvement in the social and cultural life of the country was no less essential. As is further argued below, the north–south opposition was often artificially overemphasized and framed by Kyrgyzstani political groups themselves.

Regionalism and social adaptation: does the "south–north" conflict really exist?[19]

The regional factor has played a rather deconsolidating role in the newly independent Kyrgyzstan, since the so-called "south–north opposition" is interpreted as following not only geographical and economic lines, but also socio-cultural, ethnic and religious divisions. As such, it is believed to be a potential factor for the country's splitting into two parts.

The tendency to maintain control over the strategic assets and the mechanisms of resource redistribution by Askar Akaev (the former deputy in the USSR Supreme Soviet and the first President of the Kyrgyz SSR), who was associated with the "northern" groups, became more visible with time.[20] Analysts divide Akaev's term of office into two periods. The first years of his presidency were highly praised by Western policy makers and journalists,[21] as he not only opened the country to international financial institutions and accepted the IMF reforms on transition to a market economy, but also seemed to behave as an intellectual democrat who granted his fellow citizens more liberties than any other president in post-Soviet Central Asia. Akaev's scientific background[22] granted additional legitimacy to his presidency from the perspective of his people, who perceived a scientific career, especially pursued in the central research institutions of Leningrad and Moscow, as a highly rewarding social status. The general attitude towards his presidency, however, had been changing by 2000, as some Kyrgyz and Western media institutions launched campaigns to accuse him of increased authoritarianism and corruption. The puzzling question here is whether Akaev's ruling principles had really changed or whether the change in attitude happened only in the eyes of foreign politicians and media consumers.

Akaev's first term in office was marked by consolidation of his group's rule, leading in the second period to fragmentation of the group itself as well as accumulation of more wealth in his family and among close personal allies. The "privileged inner circle" was narrowing, provoking negative aspiration and dissatisfaction even among the members of the "northern clans" that were believed to be more loyal to the Akaevs,[23] although still deprived from accessing key resources at national level. A very frequently heard populist justification for the political upheaval in March 2005 was the perception that "only Akaev's family members could afford a good life". This perception was shared by the representatives of both "southern" and "northern" elites as well as the common people in Bishkek. Even if people acknowledge the illegality of the transfer of power to Kurmanbek Bakiev, they remain convinced of the "fair" removal of Akaev's "clan".

The way that the "northerners" and "southerners" perceived the situation under the presidency of Bakiev differed. The surveys conducted by a number of research institutes studying public opinion in Bishkek and Osh (in 2008) showed a generally more optimistic view of the current situation and higher expectations for the future by people in the "south" rather than in the "north".[24] How "northern pessimism" and "southern enthusiasm" will shape political trajectories and whether or not this leads to intensifying the "north–south dilemma", at least as it exists in the minds of people, only time can tell. To what extent the "northerners" tend to blame the "southern migrants" for the worsening living standards in Bishkek and in what way the "southerners" can express their disappointment if their original high expectations are not met, would be the key questions on the path towards social stability.

The "south–north" opposition in Kyrgyzstan, however, may turn out to be quite illusive if we scrutinize it. It is certainly being created, manipulated and indoctrinated in the minds of common people as well as analysts, and is sometimes used by the local elite itself during election campaigns (Sjoberg 2007). The key ministerial portfolios in the government of Bakiev (such as Minister of Defence, Minister of Domestic Affairs, Minister of Extraordinary Situations, Minister of Transport and Communication, Minister of Industries and Energy Resources, Minister of Agriculture, Water and Process Industries, the Chairman of the State Committee on Taxation and others) were given to people originating from Jalalabad and Osh *oblasts*. However, a closer look at the appointments made by Bakiev reveals frequent rotation of cadres and a continuous attempt to find a better ally in any camp rather than loyalty to "Jalalabad clan", to which the President is believed to belong.

Comparative analysis of parliamentarians' biographies, nevertheless, reveals general differences in career paths of southerners and northerners. Among the southerners, the general tendency of improving one's social position and making a career by navigating a way to Bishkek is very striking. The increasing appearance of more southerners in leading positions in private business in Bishkek demonstrates the flow of active individuals from the periphery to the centre in search for better social opportunities better than any conscious or planned "clan" manifestation. Those who managed to make their way to the capital city do not demonstrate an intention to return, as is shown in internal migration trends (National Statistical Committee of the Kyrgyz Republic 2005). The appearance of people from Jalalabad *oblast* in key posts in the state and private sectors in Bishkek might have represented the manifestation of a positive social expectation by the "southerners" rather than a deliberate acquisition of power. This centrifugal tendency had developed in the Central Asian republics during Soviet times and changed very little in the minds of administrators and politicians.[25]

Once a certain level of material welfare is achieved by a southerner, an attempt is usually made to move to the north (even and usually while preserving local business). From the southerner's perspective, whose economic and political interests lie in the north, the possible division of the country is undesirable. Internal migration, therefore, guarantees a certain territorial integrity in this sense. Northerners, on the other hand, have a different perspective. For them, the accumulation of more and more southern businessmen in Bishkek who, first, still rely on their co-regionalists in the south and, second, tend to expand their network in the north, changes the everyday life in the city and creates a defensive attitude among the "old" citizens of the capital. A popular concern arose about a preferential transfer of the commercial and financial centre from Bishkek to Jalalabad[26] but came to a halt after Bakiev's removal.

At the same time, many interviewees from the south presented the belief that long years of "humiliation of the southerners by the northerners, both during the Soviet times, the Usubaliev era, and under Akaev's presidency, became a thing of the past after March 2005". In some cases even revanchist inspirations were noted. Although most people elaborated on the existence of different "southern groups" (most notably, "distinct and well-established elites in Batken, Osh, Jalalabad"[27]) and supported their arguments in favour of one group instead of another from positions of the "history of Kyrgyz tribes",[28] a concept of a collective southern identity exists in people's minds. Many analysts, especially in the south, stress the unsatisfied ambitions of southern elites thwarted by their lack of representation in the republic-level hierarchies. The slogan of the Tulip Revolution and the following presidential election was "equal division of key state positions among the non-official leaders from the south and north". As the south is a place for marginalized political movements, Bakiev undertook certain measures to secure his rule in the south by transforming the central organs there: he restored the Institution of Special Representatives of the Kyrgyz Republic in the south.

The territorial-administrative borders fixed during Soviet times are considered to be secondary to kinship and local loyalties, but still play an irrevocable role in politicians' election rhetoric. The argument in many disputes around territorial-administrative reform and delimitation of *oblasts* was based on the disproportional territorial-administrative division: for instance, it was asked "why the Talas *oblast* has such an important status within the country, if the population of only the Karasul *raion* in the Osh *oblast* considerably exceeds it in numbers?" The same reasoning was propagated during the campaign before the parliamentary elections in December 2007, often by the "southern" candidates.

It is sometimes pointed out that in the late Soviet period "socialist welfare" was about to arrive in even the most remote parts of Central Asia: as early as 1960s, construction of social houses, irrigation systems and infrastructural facilities, as well as medical and educational institutions, was started in the mountainous areas and steppe zones. However, the construction plans could not meet the increase in population in the 1970s and 1980s. After 1991 the municipal construction declined due to the lack of resources; canals and roads quickly deteriorated without maintenance (Zelichenko 2007). In the south of Kyrgyzstan, along the Tajik border, houses and land were left behind by their former Kyrgyz inhabitants, who migrated to the cities or even to the north of the country. These houses and lands are currently being bought and occupied by the Tajiks. During the "revolutionary days" in March 2005 the local activists, who were mobilizing the population for protest actions, promised land in the Chui valley and in Bishkek to the rebellious southerners. According to 2008 data, in the 48 districts around Bishkek there is illegal construction, 70 per cent of which is carried out by southern migrants (Kyrgyzstan Political Scientists' Association 2008).

An argument against the overall importance of regional identity would be whether or not successful candidates to key governmental posts preserve their previous loyalties on their way to the top. Regional affiliations and territorial identities can be cultivated by politicians streaming into the parliament. In this context, can a person get votes from a region in which he or she was not born? Study of parliamentarians' biographies shows that there are some cases in which a person born in Osh, Batken or Naryn gets elected from Chui or Bishkek. However, there are practically no cases in which a northerner moves to the south to make a fortune there. Only those originally from the south can return to their homeland from Bishkek in order to realize consolidation among their fellow southerners, to obtain additional support, or to spend some time "between jobs".

However, kinship and clan networks do not operate solely along territorial lines. A newly migrated southern family may have more motivation for permanent settlement at a new place in the north rather than in its homeland in the south. At the same time, ties with relatives, neighbours and acquaintances in the south will rarely be broken, even if there is a wish to do so. Many informants of mine complained about the impossibility of breaking with their former fellows despite their strong desire to do so. Therefore, the clan mechanism may sometimes serve as a "deconsolidating" factor, rather than a "consolidating" factor. Many "northerners" interviewed emphasized the better integrity of southern clans, while people from the south (the Osh Kyrgyz) complained about the lack of unity among their fellow people in the community, emphasizing it as the key reason for the weakness of the whole republic. Proverbs such as "to drag [a successful person who did better than others] down by the leg"[29] and "two goats' heads cannot be cooked in one pot [for a situation in which there are two competing leaders in the community]" were given as examples.

At local levels, election campaigns in particular present the first momentum for consolidation of relatives and kinship members.[30] To promote local leaders at *okrug* level, a sort of "informal consolidation pact"[31] is made. Collective gatherings at crucial family-community events, such as weddings and funerals, followed by the usual feast (*toi*), retain their consolidating social function and meaning. The unity does not necessarily happen along kinship or relative lines, for such gatherings bring together friends, neighbours and colleagues.

Power models and adaptive institutions

The Republic of Kyrgyzstan, for the whole 20 years of its history, has seen ten draft constitutions. The former President Akaev organized several referendums (in 1994, 1998, 2000 and 2002) to choose between one-chamber or two-chamber parliaments. Drafting constitutions had become a political manoeuvring tool in the hands of Akaev in order to consolidate his and his group's rule. In May 1993 the Soviet-era constitution was replaced by a new constitution, which later underwent substantial changes, and amendments were introduced to it in 1994, 1996, 1998 and 2003.

Soon after March 2005, the new president of the country, Kurmanbek Bakiev, wanted to secure his power and adopted certain measures to stay in power as long as possible. Post-revolution political instability coincided with discussions on a more suitable political system for Kyrgyzstan: whether the country should be a presidential, parliamentary or semi-presidential republic. Just in 2006 there were discussions of three separate drafts; in a period of just two months (November and December 2006) the Parliament adopted two different drafts. First, Akaev's "old majority" in the Parliament promoted their own draft in favour of a parliamentary republic, so that they had a better legal and structural basis to oppose the new President. That draft was first accepted. However, in a very short period after that another draft constitution was proposed by a faction in opposition to Akaev's former group, who had high expectations of getting more involved in decision-making processes after removing Akaev from the presidential post. This new constitution was also adopted and it gave the new President wider authority. During this "war of constitutions", as it was called by the media at the time, a number of potential competitors to Bakiev (such as the Prime Minister Felix Kulov, who had been his ally during the Tulip Revolution) were removed from power, demoted from the top political arena and marginalized. Soon after the Constitutional Court found violations in the process of adopting the constitutions, and the country re-adopted the 2003 Constitution. The President announced a referendum to be held on 21 October 2007, initiated a new draft constitution that granted him more powers over Parliament and lobbied among the parliamentarians on behalf of that draft to make sure that the new version would be adopted. As soon as the parliamentarians adopted it, however, the Parliament was dissolved by the President.

Although many political observers in Kyrgyzstan shared the opinion that Bakiev's cadres policy did not have a clear strategy,[32] the outcome of these events revealed his determined attitude for victory in the struggle for power. Interestingly enough, even before the results of the referendum were announced, political parties started preparing for their new election campaign. Some analysts would suggest that "anticipated elections" became then "a political reality in Kyrgyzstan".[33] In addition and parallel to the referendum, the new Legal Election Code was adopted to prescribe certain regulations for the coming parliamentary elections.

Local administrative reforms in Kyrgyzstan have also been instrumentalized by the central authorities to reduce the influence of the regions, by accumulating maximum revenues in the republic's budget and creating obstacles to claiming any part of it by the regional elite. Tensions between *raion* and local levels were also used by the central administration to decrease the authority of the regions. Instrumentalization of decentralisation reform was noticeable at local level as well, as local self-government bodies started interpreting the concept of the "state" for their own purposes and in their competition for power.[34] The first administrative reform in the post-Soviet era, "The Main Law on Local Administration" that was adopted in 1990–1991, remained effective without any major change until 2003. The law provided that the central government would grant more powers to those local authorities which came to power through elections. This decentralized reform concept was widely supported by the EU countries, the US, international monetary organizations and international human rights institutions (Grävingholt *et al.* 2006). The law also gave municipal authorities (city and village administrative organs) wide jurisdictions and freedom.

However, without adequate financial support from the centre and a poorly working taxation system, the law was claimed by *raion* officials to bring poor results as there was now an increase in the levels of corruption by local officials, who used illicit practices to increase their budget.[35] No real effective sanctions could be adopted against those local officials who neglected the laws of the republic. Some scholars argued that the local officials, as well as representatives of self-governing bodies, were now left alone to resolve local legal disputes and economic problems (Beyer 2007). The taxes the central government managed to collect (mainly from the large enterprises that still kept on functioning or the ones that had been privatized) were transferred to the republic's budget, while the regional, *raion*-level administrations were left with the sole option of lobbying for redistribution of the state budget expenditure for the benefit of their regions. The system of grants for special regional projects resembled the former Soviet centralized redistribution that had presupposed certain competition among the regions on the basis of their representation in the central republican governance and party organs.

Another consequence of the local administrative reform was the increase in the level of poverty and the rise of social protests. An attempt made by President Akaev in 1996 to improve the situation by cutting back on central administrative staff looked like another step on the path to decentralization and to increase the efficiency of central bureaucracy in the eyes of the Western donors sponsoring the reform, but instead it turned out to be yet another means for the President to "purge" those representatives of central and regional administration who did not satisfactorily concur with his policy.[36]

While the heads of administration in the *oblasts* and in Bishkek were appointed by the President upon the Prime Minister's nomination, and with the consent of the regional *kenesh* (local governance), the heads of *raions*, towns and villages (*ails*) were elected by local self-governing bodies, which possessed all executive power within their domains. Nevertheless, the local councils at *ail* level had to report to their *raion* officials on those duties that were delegated to them. However, the heads of the local governance could not be removed by their *raion* officials, as such decisions fell under the jurisdiction of the local council of *aksakals* (the head of kinship in the patrimonial line), the "traditional" institution re-established by Akaev in 1995.

Under President Bakiev, a clearer tendency towards centralisation was observed. The 2007 Constitution, the Legal Election Code and the parliamentary elections of December 2007 became tools for delegating more authority to the central organs of power. Earlier, the local election committees had been established by *kenesh*, but now, under the new Legal Election Code, they were to be approved by the Central Election Commission (TsIK). Although the heads of local administration were still elected by the deputies of local *kenesh* on the nomination of the head of local state administration, mayors of cities were to be elected upon the President's nomination. Nevertheless, during his campaign before the 2007 referendum, Bakiev gave signs of minor amendments. For example, while travelling in the Issyk-Kul region, he promised the heads of *ail okmotu* (primary government at *ail* level) that they would remain at their posts till the end of their term, and the new proceedings would be applicable only to their successors.[37]

During Bakiev's time in office, while the former Soviet administrative-territorial division (four levels of executive power) were preserved, there were discussions for reforming the budgetary field first and foremost. The three-level mechanism of budget redistribution (republic – *raion* – local governance) was specified, to be replaced by a two-level scheme of budget redistribution (republic – local governance). That was encroaching upon the power of *raion*-level administration (*akims* ("regional governors") and general-governors). The goal of the reform, above all, was to increase the direct budget revenues from the taxes collected locally. This two-level mechanism was condemned by the presidential administration as "too innovative" and the return to the former three-level scheme (with the simultaneous abolishing of some territorial units) was planned for the budget of 2008. The policy of preserving the three-level scheme, while aiming at a gradual implementation of a two-level scheme, was declared by officials from the Ministry of Economy and Finance (Amandykov 2007; Kozhoshev 2007). Taking into account the inconsistency of reform in Kyrgyzstan, and its dependency on the internal political struggle and international relations, the final transfer to the two-level scheme of budget redistribution, if it ever happens, would be accompanied by administrative-territorial re-division.

Towards the corporate technocratic elite?

In the changing geo-political conditions in 2005–2010, Kyrgyzstan demonstrated some tendency to adopt what can be called the "neo-liberal corporate power model" that had been also practiced in Kazakhstan and Russia. A small number of studies has appeared so far on the neo-liberal rhetoric used by the foreign and domestic actors in Central Asian countries, including Kyrgyzstan (Pelkmans 2005; Pétric 2005). The discussion on whether and how "third wave" liberalism is used and practised by the governments and local actors has not been reflected in Central Asian studies. I argue that the Kazakhstani and Russian corporate elites are the representatives of a new Eurasian neo-liberal corporate elite power model, which is characterized by big business consolidation around the utilization of natural resources as a strategic power asset, autocratic presidential rule supported by a presidential party, and the "technologization" of power, which refers to the emergence of an effective technocratic elite that protects the interests of big corporations, while its agents are viewed from a functional, but not personal perspective. In the Central Asian context, that would involve the diminishing of kinship, lineages, regional and other loyalties and the prevalence of a pure functionalist approach in recruiting the elite.[38] The privatization of Kyrgyzstan's energy sector and President Bakiev's endeavour to consolidate elite power in accessing the republic's strategic assets indicated a possible shift of power towards corporate elite structures. Bakiev's course has resulted in the consolidation of power by big business circles in the utilisation of natural resources as a strategic power asset, on the one hand, and autocratic presidential rule supported by a presidential party and "technologization of power", on the other.

In Kyrgyzstan, some attempts to reintroduce changes in gold-mining contracts were made after 2005, following the Kazakh example, in order to increase national revenues from exports. Both the Kyrgyz government and the parliament gave clear signs of limiting the rights and possibly the share of foreign companies operating in the country, particularly the Canadian-based Ceterra goldmining and exploration company, which has owned 100 per cent of the Kumtor gold mine, one of the largest operating gold deposits in Central Asia, since January 2004 (Morozova 2009: 87–89).

Water is another resource Kyrgyzstan would like to trade. Although the investment projects of constructing and exploiting hydroelectric stations Kambarata 1 and Kambarata 2 are still not completed, the inter-Kyrgyz elite rivalry for acquiring more shares in these projects is intense. Despite the existence of property rights and regulations, legal disputes (particularly on the transfer of property) are acute, as there is no clear, commonly agreed legal interpretation for property transactions. In order to build a corporate model, significant assets and amounts of strategic resource are required, which smaller and less resourceful Kyrgyzstan is unlikely to find soon.[39]

Considering the recent competition between Russia and Kazakhstan for regional leadership in Central Asia, Kyrgyz–Russian relations significantly improved under Bakiev. Consolidation of corporate elites took place at transnational level. Russia's initiative to establish an "Energy Club" within the Shanghai Cooperation Organisation was one major example in this context. Just as the interests of the late-Soviet *nomenklatura* had united the elites of the republics at the union level, the interests of the current corporate elites in Central Asian states and Russia overlap. Despite this overlap, however, close links between the national corporate elites do not help to solve various disputes and conflicts among Central Asian states such as visa regimes and border issues, as well as redistribution of water and other resources.

As was also mentioned above, strong presidential power of an autocratic character is very common among Central Asian states, including even Kyrgyzstan. President Bakiev had also been gradually consolidating his political power, by certain measures such as removing his opponents (like Kulov) and forming a new parliament. According to the constitution and Electoral Code adopted by the Referendum on 21 October 2007, the parliamentary elections in December 2007 were to be realized in accordance with the parties' election lists.

The new election regulations were used by Bakiev to form a major presidential party. According to the new constitution, the president of the country should not be a leader of any political party. Thus Bakiev remained as the chairperson of the new party, *Ak Zhol* (Bright Path) for just 24 hours: after the Ministry of Justice registered this party – amazingly rapidly – he left the post. *Ak Zhol*, however, was known to be the party that Bakiev supported and it became the favourite party in the election campaign in November-December 2007. While for the politicians, membership of *Ak Zhol* might have been just a means to obtain a seat in the parliament, the Kyrgyz President, I argue, intended to form a dominating pro-presidential party following the examples of the Russian *Edinaya Rossiya* (United Russia) and the Kazakhstani *Nur Otan* (Light of Motherland). Various politicians, even prominent opposition figures, demonstrated an instant desire to appear in *Ak Zhol*'s election list.[40]

According to the 2007 Constitution, the Kyrgyz Parliament was elected on the basis of candidate lists to be submitted by each party, which had to obtain at least 5 per cent of the overall votes. According to the Legal Election Code, special regulations to prepare these lists were also undertaken: in these lists, neither gender should number more than 70 per cent of candidates; there should be at least 15 per cent of candidates younger than 35; and no one ethnic group should field more than 15 per cent of the candidates. In addition to these regulations, there were other more specific ones. For example, for every three males, there should be a female candidate listed. Many parties registered under these conditions were known only at regional or local level, and they could hardly compete with *Ak Zhol*. Nevertheless, the above-mentioned additional measures to eliminate their influence were enacted.

However, the success of "*Ak Zhol* project" was far from being certain: the party system has always been extremely weak in Kyrgyzstan due to the lack of both clear ideological lines and alternative social programmes of the parties. The party's life turned out to be short, as Bakiev was removed from his post by riots and violence in April 2010. It is possible to observe a clear pattern of absence of social group identity among Kyrgyzstani politicians, who never demonstrated true adherence to any party programme and tended to change their loyalties, as well as parties, continuously, being driven more often by momentary and temporary benefits.

Despite the continual rapid and unsystematic rotation of cadres by Bakiev, his tendency to establish a "monopoly over economic and political patronage"[41] was becoming clearer with time. Perhaps the visibility of that technocratic scenario led to the violent removal of Bakiev from the presidency.[42] Nevertheless, the important nuance in the development of the situation under Bakiev was that this monopoly was deemed to be established not over the whole resource-redistribution mechanism (which might be difficult to realize in a country where regional powers are rather strong and tend to have an impact on the principle decisions in the political centre), but precisely over the patronage over this redistribution. Regardless of who owned these resources and who sold them, no manipulation was possible without approval of the central power. The post-2010 developments greatly jeopardized the centralization structures in the Republic of Kyrgyzstan.

Conclusion

The struggle to hold onto central power in Kyrgyzstan culminated again in spring 2010 with the regular coup d'état and widespread riots in different parts of the country, after which a new stage of the struggle for resources began. This struggle, often unseen to the general public, has been hidden behind the formation of the interim government, exploiting institutional gaps. Blurring the ongoing competition for power and resources carried on by local, trans-local, trans-regional and various trans-global actors, various media agencies and politicians portrayed the social riots and reproduced violence of summer 2010 as "ethnic" conflict. Social deprivation and inequality, and sharp competition for strategic resources remain the real factors for instability and unrest and they will continue to serve as a ground for reproducing conflict and violence in Kyrgyzstan. The more this conflict is claimed to be "ethnic", the more "ethnic" it is likely to become in the perception of its participants, and as a result, it will escalate further. The war of 2010 changed much in people's lives, and the "north–south separation" became grounded in people's perceptions and memories to the extent that it substitutes for the vision of social reality and starts to have an impact with its own logic, influencing the flow of contemporary history. The externally constructed negative image of Kyrgyzstan as a zone of continuously self-reproducing instability like the Middle East and Afghanistan is also damaging and misleading if one wants to understand the real causes of the conflict in Central Asia. In addition, the ominous image helps those involved in the struggle for Kyrgyzstani resources frame their one-sided security analyses. Understanding the patterns of local elite consolidation and their communication with the global actors present in the region is vital not only for the scholarly community, but for the wider public as well.

Notes

1 The author is grateful to Alexander von Humboldt Stiftung for providing the opportunity to conduct this research and to VolkswagenStiftung for the good chance to develop it further and expand within the framework of the project "The History of Perestroika in Central Asia".
2 On the politics of ethnicization of violence in Kyrgyzstan, see Revees (2010).
3 Based on the author's fieldwork in Osh in April 2012.
4 On the extra-legality of communist state and party institutions, see Fursov (2005).
5 For detail, see Morozova (2007, 2005a, 2005b). On the latest trend of the revision of Soviet archival material for Central Asian research, see Khalid (2006).
6 On *korenizatsia* in the Turkmen SSR, see Edgar (2004).
7 The Russian State Archive of Social-Political History (RGASPI): files of the Third Communist International; the Russian Communist Party of the Bolsheviks (RCP(b)); Central Asian Bureau of the RCP(b); the Kyrgyz Oblast Party Conference; OGPU documents in "Sovershenno sekretno", 2001, 2002, 2003.

8 The documents of the Kyrgyz *oblast* party conferences. RGASPI. F. 17. Sch. 29. D. 1, 8–9, 16, 35, 45. See also Dzhunushalieva (2006: 8).

9 The power model "supreme authority from outside – local management" has been noted by some historians working mainly on medieval and modern times; see Manz (2003: 90). The 130 years of complete Russian/Soviet control over Central Asia can be viewed within the same scheme: external supreme power versus local elites' rule. Some contributions have been made lately for interpreting Russia's model of ruling Central Asian societies within the context of post-colonialism; see Gorshenina (2007: 209–258) and Abashin (2007).

10 See, for instance, Poliakov *(*1992: 16–17).

11 Tudarkun Usubaliev was believed to be a grandchild of the poet akyn Kalygul uluu (1785–1855) and the descendent of the relatives of the khan Ormon (1791–1854) from the Sarybagysh Kyrgyz tribe, who fought for the independence of the northern Kyrgyz tribes from the Kokand khanate. This genealogy is said to be not an invented one, but real. From the conversation with Dr. Gulnara Aitpaeva.

12 Author's interviews with the functionaries of the Soviet economic sectors. Chymkent, June 2011; Bishkek, Osh, April 2012.

13 In the 1920s and 1930s, Russians and Jews constituted the overwhelming majority of the technicians and trained professionals, such as agronomists, surveyors, veterinarians and doctors; they were in direct contact with the indigenous population. RGASPI. F. 62. Sch. 4. D. 1, 13, 243. See also Martin (2001: 140–141).

14 On the specificities of academia and the educational system in the USSR Republics, see Lane (1971: 93–95) and Ilyin (1996: Chapter 8).

15 Some scholars describe how the descendants of the urban families of saints (among the Uzbek and Tajik) became recognized scientists, preserving due to that lineage some kind of intellectual if not to say spiritual authority in the eyes of the people. Abashin (2007: 223–228).

16 Representatives of the intelligentsia in Central Asia were of diverse origin. Some of them are believed to belong to the noble kinship or to be the descendants of the families of saints. The phenomenon of the socialization and integration of descendants of urban saints' families within the Soviet elite stratum was noted by very few scholars (Abashin 2005; Muminov 2011).

17 Author's interview with Roza Otunbaeva. Bishkek, July 2006.

18 Gorbachev approached the liberal intelligentsia in the Central Asian republics in search for legitimization of *perestroika*. One of the manifestations of this alliance was the Issyk-Kul Forum held in October 1986 by Chinghiz Aitmatov on Lake Issyk-Kul. The Kyrgyzstani intelligentsia propagated the idea that the writer himself initiated the organization of the event and personally invited respected figures of world cultural and intellectual life in order to set up and test *perestroika*'s "new thinking". Among the invited guests were Alexander King, Arthur Miller, James Baldwin, Peter Ustinov, Claude Simon, Alvin Toffler and others.

19 The following three sections result from research conducted in 2007–2009, so they do not offer a detailed account of the developments in 2010 and afterwards.

20 It is interesting to analyse the change in the perception of Akayev as a personality, politician and leader of the country both by the Kyrgyzstani citizens and the international community. At the beginning of the 1990s, the southern groups (particularly in Osh) supported Akayev's inauguration. This fact is sometimes attributed to Akayev's reference to the Quran on the advice of the first mufti of Kyrgyzstan, Sadyjan Kamalov (from Osh). Author's interviews, Bishkek, Osh, February 2008.

21 On discussions about liberal democracy and civil society introduced in Kyrgyzstan by Western media and NGOs, see Pétric (2005: 319–332) and Pelkmans (2005: 147–157).

22 Akayev graduated from the Leningrad Institute of Precision Mechanics and Optics in 1967 and obtained a doctorate from the Moscow Institute of Engineering and Physics in 1981.

23 Akayev was born in the ail Kyzyl-Bairak, near the town Kemen of the Chui oblast, and his wife Mayram Akayeva in the Talas oblast.
24 See, for instance, IRI (2007).
25 Interview with V.I. Maksimov, Party of the Communists of Kyrgyzstan, Osh, February 2008.
26 Author's interviews, February, August 2008.
27 Interview with a "southerner" working in the Central Election Committee in Bishkek, February 2008.
28 According to Osh Kyrgyz, their *ichkilik* group is the central group of all the Kyrgyz, since it "has been always in the south, in the centre between the right and left wings". Author's field interviews, Osh, February 2008.
29 Interview with A.A. Abdrafizova, Osh, February 2008.
30 On mobilization at local level, see, for instance, Radnitz (2005).
31 Interview with B.S. Saiev, February 2008.
32 Author's interviews, Kyrgyzstan, February 2008.
33 Author's interview, A. Evgrafov, Osh, February 2008.
34 See, for instance, Beyer (2007).
35 Author's interview with A.A. Abdrafizova, Osh, February 2008.
36 There were lots of media discussions on "purges" of the administration by Akaev. See, for instance, Mindich (2002) and Gortat (1996).
37 Author's interviews, Bishkek, February 2008.
38 For instance, in Kazakhstan, the presidential office and administration could be viewed as an example of such a technocratic elite. Representatives of the Kazakhstani elite are not supposed to have a particular Kazakh ethnic identity, while any "clan" or kinship loyalty is viewed by President Nazarbaev as a threat to the regime. Some researchers noted that the Nazarbaev's client network is based on personal loyalty. See Dave (2007: 2).
39 Similar attempts to introduce more robust centralisation schemes and find a way for a small country to join the new millennium energy boom could be seen in the Republic of Mongolia during the Presidency of Nambaryn Enkhbayar in 2005–2009.
40 This information is based on monitoring the parliamentary election campaign as it was published by Kyrgyz media sources. See, for instance, the archive of www.24.kg.
41 Such a definition is given in the recent ICG report on Kyrgyzstan (ICG 2008). Despite the fact that the author of this chapter does not accept the ICG methodology and does not concur with many conclusions of this policy-oriented report, she finds this an exact definition.
42 It is interesting to note that also in the previously mentioned case of Mongolia the transition of power did not happen smoothly, and before the parliamentary election to be held in June 2012 the former President Enkhbayar was arrested on charges of corruption.

References

Abashin, S. (2005) "Potomki svyatyn v Uzbekistane, Tadzhikistane, Kazakhstane [The descendants of the saints in Uzbekistan, Tajikistan, Kazakhstan]", in *Analitika*, June 28. Online. Available: www.analitika.org/article.php?story=20050628020303974.
Abashin, S. (2007) *Natsionalizmy v Tsentral'noi Azii. V poiskakh identichnost.* [National-isms in Central Asia. In Search of Identity], St. Petersburg: Aleteiya.
Amandykov, M. (2007) Interview, *TAZAR*, 4 April. Online. Available: www.tazar.kg/news.php?i=3848.
Amsler, S. (2007) *The Politics of Knowledge in Central Asia: Science between Marx and the Market*, London and New York: Routledge.

Beyer, J. (2007) "Imagining the State in Rural Kyrgyzstan: How Perceptions of the State Create Customary Law in the Kyrgyz Aksakal Courts", *Max Planck Institute for Social Anthropology Working Papers*, Halle/Saale.

Dave, B. (2007) "The EU and Kazakhstan: Balancing Economic Cooperation and Aiding Democratic Reforms in the Central Asian Region", *CEPS Policy Brief, No. 127*, 25 May.

Dzhunushalieva, G.D. (2006) *Evolyutsiya Kirgizskoi Gosudarstvennosti (1920–80). [Evolution of the Kyrgyz Statehood (1920–80)]*, Bishkek.

Edgar, A. (2004) *Tribal Nation: The Making of Soviet Turkmenistan*, Princeton.

Friedman, L.A. and Vidiasova, M.F. (1996) "Polozhenie SNG–Evrazii v menyayuscheisya strukture sovremennogo mira [The position of the CIS–Eurasia in the changing structure of the present world]", in *Rossiya i okruzhayuschii mir: kontury razvitiya [Russia and the surrounding world: the shapes of development]*, Moscow.

Fursov, A. (2005) "Central Eurasia: Historical Centrality, Geostrategic Condition and Power Models Legacy", in I. Morozova (ed.) *Towards Social Stability and Democratic Governance in Central Eurasia: Challenges to Regional Security*, Amsterdam: IOS Press: 23–39.

Gorshenina, S. (2007) "Is the Marginality of Russian Colonial Turkestan Perpetual, or whether Central Asia will be Included One Day into the Sphere of 'Post-Studies' ", *Ab Imperio*, 2: 209–258.

Gortat, R. (1996) *Demokratiya s gor Tyan-Shanya [Democracy from the Tianshan mountains]*, Warsaw: Centre for Social and Economic Research, December.

Grävingholt, J., Doerr, B., Meissner, K., Pletziger, S., von Rümker, J. and Weikert, J. (2006) *Strengthening Participation through Decentralization: Findings on Local Economic Development in Kyrgyzstan*, Studies 16, Bonn: Deutsches Institut für Entwicklungspolitik.

Haugen, A. (2003) *The Establishment of National Republics in Soviet Central Asia*, New York: Palgrave Macmillan.

Ilyin, V. (1996) *Gosudarstvo i sotsial'naya stratifikatsiya sovetskogo i postsovetskogo obschestv (1917–1996) [The state and social stratification of the Soviet and post-Soviet societies (1917–1996)]*, Syktyvkar: Izdatel'stvo Syktyvkarskogo Universiteta.

ICG (International Crisis Group) (2008) "Kyrgyzstan: A Deceptive Calm", *Asia Briefing*, 79, 14 August.

IRI (2007) *Kyrgyzstan National Study*, May.

Istoriya Kirgizii (1963) *[History of Kyrgyzstan]*, Vols I and II, Frunze: Kyrgyz State Publishers.

Khalid, A. (2006) "Between Empire and Revolution: New Work on Soviet Central Asia", *Kritika: Explorations in Russian and Eurasian History*, 7/4: 865–884.

Kozhoshev, A. (2007) Interview, *24.kg*, 1 January. Online. Available: www.24.kg/economics/2007/01/25/29961.html.

Kyrgyzstan Political Scientists' Association (2008) "The Lost South…?" Rosbalt News Agency, Osh, February.

Lane, D. (1971) *The End of Inequality? Stratification under State Socialism*, Penguin Books.

Luong, P.J. (2002) *Institutional Change and Political Continuity in Post-Soviet Central Asia: Power, Perceptions and Pacts*, Cambridge: Cambridge University Press.

Manz, B. (2003) "Multi-Ethnic Empires and the Formation of Identity", *Ethnic and Racial Studies*, 26/1: 70–101.

Martin, T. (2001) *The Affirmative Action Empire: Nations and Nationalism in the Soviet Union, 1923–1939*, Ithaca and London: Cornell University Press.

Mindich, D. (2002) "Neustoichivoe ravnovesie [Unstable balance]", *Profil'*, 21/291, 3 June.

Morozova, I. (2005a) "Contemporary Azerbaijani Historiography on the Problem of 'South Azerbaijan' after WWII", *Iran and the Caucasus*, 9: 85–120.

Morozova, I. (2005b) "Etnicheskii Factor v Obrazovanii Kirgizskoi Sovetskoi Sotsialisticheskoi Respubliki i Mongol'skoi Narodnoi Respubliki [The Ethnic Factor in Establishment of the Kyrgyz Soviet Socialist Republic and the Mongolian Peoples' Republic]", in G. Sevostyanov and S. Ishakov (eds) *Tragediya velikoi derzhavy: natsional'nyi vopros v raspade SSSR [The tragedy of the great power: the national question and the dissolution of the USSR]*, Moscow: Institute of Russian History, Russian Academy of Science: 227–253.

Morozova, I. (2007) "Elites, Reforms and Power Institutions in Soviet Kyrgyzstan and Mongolia in the 1920–1930s: A Comparative Historical Analysis", *Ab Imperio: The Politics of Comparison*, 2: 369–403.

Morozova, I. (2009) "External Powers' Influence upon Kyrgyz Political Elite", *Caucasian Review of International Affairs*, 3/1: 87–89.

National Statistical Committee of the Kyrgyz Republic (2005) *Demograficheskii ezhegodnik Kirgizskoi Respubliki. 2000–2004 [Demographic yearbook of the Kyrgyz Republic. 2000–2004]*, Bishkek.

Muminov, A. (2011) *Rodoslovnoe drevo Mukhtara Auezova [The Genealogical Tree of Mukhtar Auezov]*, Almaty: Zhibek Zholy.

Pelkmans, M. (2005) "On Transition and Revolution in Kyrgyzstan", *Focaal – European Journal of Anthropology*, 46: 147–157.

Pétric, B.-M. (2005) "Post-Soviet Kyrgyzstan or the Birth of a Globalized Protectorate", *Central Asian Survey*, 24/3: 319–332.

Poliakov, S.P. (1992) *Everyday Islam: Religion and Tradition in Rural Central Asia*, New York, London: M.E. Sharpe.

Poujol, C. (2005) "Islam in Post-Soviet Central Asia: Democracy Versus Justice?" in I. Morozova (ed.) *Towards Social Stability and Democratic Governance in Central Eurasia: Challenges to Regional Security*, Amsterdam: IOS Press: 50–63.

Radnitz, S. (2005) "Networks, Localism and Mobilization in Aksy, Kyrgyzstan", *Central Asian Survey*, December 24/4: 405–442.

Reeves, M. (2010) "The Ethnicisation of Violence in Southern Kyrgyzstan", *OpenDemocracy.net*, 21 June. Online. Available: www.opendemocracy.net/od-russia/madeleine-reeves/ethnicisation-of-violence-in-southern-kyrgyzstan-0.

Sjoberg, F. (2007) *Informal Networks and Politics: A Case Study of the Clan Logic in Candidate Selection and Campaigning in Kyrgyzstan*, paper presented at the European Society for Central Asian Studies Tenth Conference, METU, Ankara, 12–15 September.

"Sovershenno sekretno": Lubyanka – Stalinu o polozhenii v strane (1922–1934). (2001–2003) *["Top secret": Lubyanka to Stalin about the situation in the country (1922–1934)]*, Moscow.

Zelichenko, A. (2007) Field Report, *Rosbalt News Agency*, Bishkek, August.

2 The impact of Askar Akaev's political leadership in the process of democratization in Kyrgyzstan

Seçil Öraz

This chapter focuses on the relation between Askar Akaev's political leadership and the democratization process in Kyrgyzstan. Keeping in mind the fact that politics can be highly personalistic in Central Asia and executive power generally has a big influence in the region, political leadership seems to be an important factor in the transition of all Central Asian republics (CARs), including Kyrgyzstan. Due to the fact that the whole transition process is a very broad topic to be analysed, this chapter focuses basically on one particular aspect of transition in this country: the relation between political leadership and democratization.

Since independence in 1991, leadership patterns in each of the CARs has shown similar characteristics and played a major role in the establishment of several forms of authoritarianism: "strong presidential systems", "strongmen regimes" or "sultanates" (Ishiyama 2002: 49). In due course, Kyrgyzstan (at least initially) was a notable exception. Upon its independence, Kyrgyzstan appeared to have the highest potential to realize a real democratic transition and was viewed as a success story of economic and political reform in Central Asia.[1] However, by the mid-1990s, the initial democratic trajectory of Kyrgyzstan was reversed and it resembled more and more the other CARs. In that sense, this study analyses the role of Askar Akaev's leadership in Kyrgyzstan's initial democratic leap, its subsequent reversal from this path and its final shift to authoritarianism. These three phases in Kyrgyzstan's political transition seemed to be parallel to the three stages of Akaev's leadership. Therefore, it seems important to understand the relation between Askar Akaev's political leadership and Kyrgyzstan's overall transition process. Did President Akaev contribute to the process of democratic transition in Kyrgyzstan or not? Which aspects of democratic transition did Akaev affect? Were there any differences in the presidency of Akaev in pre-independence and post-independence periods? Was Akaev basically an authoritarian leader or was he merely adopting a democratic discourse initially to gain legitimacy?

As was mentioned above, Askar Akaev initially posed a somewhat different profile relative to his other Central Asian colleagues. Even at the beginning of the transition period, he had already gained the reputation of being the most liberal leader among the Central Asian presidents in the international community. Indeed,

Akaev deserved this reputation to a certain degree. He succeeded in carrying out a series of reforms, which was also confirmed and appreciated by the outside world, as Akaev seemed to be willing to transform his country into a democratically governed one by initiating democratization via the formation of democratic institutions, and introducing political pluralism, rule of law and civil society. Simultaneously, Akaev was also committed to realizing radical economic reforms such as leaving the rouble zone, adopting a new national currency, implementing land reform and privatization policies, and having the country become a member of various international organizations such as the United Nations (UN), the Organization for Security and Co-operation in Europe (OSCE), the International Monetary Fund (IMF), the European Bank for Reconstruction and Development (EBRD) and the World Trade Organization (WTO). Kyrgyzstan would become the first of the former USSR countries to complete the accession negotiations with WTO and become a full member of the organization. These steps helped Akaev to develop a very positive image in the eyes of the Western world. Consequently, in a very short period of time, Kyrgyzstan became the major foreign aid recipient as compared to any other member of the Commonwealth of Independent States (CIS) and was labeled as "the island of democracy" in the "sea" of autocracies (Anderson 1998). This perception resulted in the emergence of an optimistic expectation of Akaev in the West, especially in terms of his future success in realizing what he had promised about democratic reforms (Huskey 2002: 74–78; Tolipov 2006: 67).[2]

All these factors made the issue of leadership even more important in the democratic transition of Kyrgyzstan as compared to the other Central Asian countries. In general, it can be argued that the difference displayed by the leaders' attitudes and policies toward transition determined the level of improvement in the transition processes of each Central Asian regime. As Boris Rumer suggests, in Central Asia, regimes with varying degrees of authoritarianism were established behind a pseudo-democratic façade. These regimes varied from relatively moderate ones, such as that in Kyrgyzstan, to full-blown despotisms, as in Turkmenistan (Rumer 2005: 3). Rumer's classification is in harmony with Sally N. Cumming's, who also describes Akaev's government in Kyrgyzstan as mildly authoritarian, Nazarbaev's government in Kazakhstan as authoritarian with limited liberalization, Karimov's government in Uzbekistan as located between sultanism and authoritarianism, Rahmonov's government in Tajikistan as oligarchic and Niyazov's government in Turkmenistan as the closest to sultanism (Cummings 2002: 8).

This chapter begins with a brief theoretical framework for the concept of political leadership. Then, Akaev's political career is analysed in three stages, which also corresponded to and considerably affected the process of post-Soviet transition to democracy in Kyrgyzstan. The first stage (1990–1995) included Akaev's rise to power in the last days of the USSR and his emergence as the first president of the newly independent Kyrgyzstan. The second stage (1991–1995) corresponded to Akaev's adaptation of liberal policies in political and economic spheres, and the third stage (1995–2005) witnessed a setback in his democratic reforms and a shift towards an authoritarian mode of leadership (Spector 2003: 2). In due course, the policies Akaev implemented, the constitutions he adopted, the relations he was engaged with the rest of the state bureaucracy, political elites, various sections of the society, the outside world, and the social, political and economic circumstances all seemed to be indicating such a shift. Thus, the main methods of the study are discourse analysis and policy analysis. For discourse analysis, principal sources used are press analysis, published official documents, biographies of Akaev and his books. For policy analysis, the main sources are legal documents such as the Kyrgyz constitutions, and related laws and decrees. In addition to certain statistical data on Kyrgyzstan published by certain institutions such as OSCE, Freedom House and International Crisis Group (ICG), the works of prominent scholars are also utilized.

Concept of political leadership

As Blondel (1987: 1) once put it,

> If one reduces politics to its bare bones, to what is most visible to most citizens, it is the national political leaders, both at home and abroad, that remain once everything else has been erased; they are the most universal, the most recognized, the most talked about elements of political life.

Analysis of the impact of political leadership on politics can be considered as a relatively new phenomenon as the literature on this topic started to develop only after the mid-1970s, when the functions of states expanded and started to dominate social and economic lives of countries. The developments of the contemporary world thus underlined the centrality of political leaders in order to facilitate social progress to shape state policies. Thus, the argument followed that: "political leadership often makes a crucial difference in the lives of states and other human communities" (Tucker 1995: xi).

In very simple terms, political leadership is defined as the "reciprocal process of mobilizing various economic, political, and other resources, in a context of competition and conflict, in order to realize goals independently or mutually held by both leaders and followers" (Burns 1978: 425). As Carl Friedrich mentioned, the most common element used in the definition of political leadership, however, is "power" because "any theory of political leadership is grounded in a theory of political power" (Friedrich 1970: 17). However, it is a fact that although power is the most common element of political leadership, it is not the only one. Political leadership is very complex in terms of its elements, which makes it difficult to build a general theory about political leadership among political scientists. As James MacGregor Burns (1978: 2) suggests, "Leadership is one of the most observed and least understood phenomena on earth."

Nevertheless, this least understood phenomenon can be classified by several factors such as (1) the character of the leader, (2) the followers with whom the leader interacts, (3) the organizational or societal context in which the leadership interaction occurs, (4) the agenda of problems or tasks which confront the leader, (5) the techniques which the leader uses to mobilize support and (6) the effects of leadership (Peele 2005: 192). In that sense, political leadership is conceptualized as "an umbrella concept, which can be understood only if one examines all the ingredients and their combination" (Hermann 1986: 187). As such, in classifying political leadership, some scholars focus on differences intrinsic to the leadership process, whereas others look at the differences in the outcomes of that process or differences in sources of power (Kellerman 1986: 193). For the purposes of this chapter, classifications made by Weber, Burns and Linz and Stepan will be used in order to analyse Akaev's political leadership.

Max Weber's classification is considered one of the oldest and most familiar methods of classifying leadership. He preferred to categorize leadership by reference to its source of authority. In that sense, Weber suggested that there were three types of legitimate authority for political leadership: *legal-rational, traditional* and *charismatic* (Weber 1947, 1958: 77–128, 1986: 232–244). In the case of legal-rational authority, obedience belongs to the legally established and impersonalized office. In traditional authority, the person or persons who enjoy authority are designated according to the traditionally transmitted rules and thus become the object of peoples' obedience. As for charismatic authority, it is related to "specific sanctity, heroism, or exemplary character of an individual person" (Weber 1947: 328) and, therefore, it is "lodged neither in office nor in status but derives from the capacity of a particular person to arouse and maintain belief in himself/herself as the source of legitimacy" (Willner 1986: 246).

Another method of classifying leaders was illustrated by James MacGregor Burns, whose main emphasis was on the relationship between the leaders and the led. Burns (1986: 295) wrote that

> Leadership, unlike naked power-wielding, is thus inseparable from followers' needs and goals. The essence of the leader-follower relation is the interaction of persons with different levels of motivations and of power potential, including skill, in pursuit of a common or at least joint purpose.[3]

Burns suggested that this interaction could take the forms of transactional leadership and transformational leadership. In this sense, in transactional leadership the relationship between the leader and follower is functional, as the leaders provide certain goods, values or services in exchange for votes, money or support. On the other hand, transformational leadership "ultimately becomes moral and it raises the level of human conduct and ethical aspiration of both leader and led, and thus it has a transforming effect on both" (Burns 1978: 20).

Finally, for the purposes of this chapter, Linz and Stepan's table, which illustrates the leadership characteristics of specific different regime types, is very useful (see Table 2.1). In their table, Linz and Stepan (1996: 40) defined four types of nondemocratic regimes, *totalitarianism, post-totalitarianism, authoritarianism* and *sultanism* with four dimensions, *pluralism, mobilization, ideology* and *leadership* (Linz 1964: 291–342).

Table 2.1 Leadership characteristics according to regime types

Regime types	Leadership characteristics
Democracy	Elected by free elections, exercised within constitutional limitations and state of law. Subjected to free elections periodically.
Authoritarianism	Exercised power within formally ill-defined but predictable norms. Effort to co-opt old elites. Had autonomy in state careers and military.
Totalitarianism	Ruled with undefined limits and unpredictability without laws and procedures. Often charismatic. Recruitment by party organization.
Post-totalitarianism	Ruled with unspecified but reasonably predictable limits. More bureaucratic and state technocratic than charismatic.
Sultanism	Personalistic and arbitrary. No legal constraints. Compliance to leader based on fear or reward. Strongly dynastic.

Source: Linz and Stepan 1996: 45.

Emergence of Askar Akaev and his first term of office (1990–1995)

Akaev's political life started in October 1990, when he was elected by the Kyrgyz parliament as the first president of the Kyrgyz Soviet Socialist Republic (SSR).[4] At the time he was elected, he was head of the Kyrgyz Academy of Sciences as a physics professor. Unlike other Central Asian presidents, he was not originally a member of the Communist Party of Kyrgyzstan (CPK). What convinced parliamentarians to vote for Akaev in the October 1990 presidential elections was mainly Akaev's own stance. Known as a liberal figure with no close ties to the CPK, Akaev

> presented himself as a strong, technocratic leader, who had no ideological commitment to the CPK and who had a clear idea of where to lead his country in a time of economic turmoil, emphasizing the establishment of a democratic, pluralist society and of a liberal democratic, multiparty, political system.
>
> (Abazov 2003: 45–46)

That image as a promoter of political and economic reforms brought him both the support of the major opposition group, the Democratic Movement of Kyrgyzstan, and the votes of the reform-minded deputies in the parliament. In that sense, the election of Akaev instead of his rival Masaliev, who was the First Secretary of CPK, was rather unusual. As a part of the Soviet legacy, in the other CARs, the first secretaries of communist parties automatically resumed power to rule the new republics.

Shortly after his election as president by the Kyrgyz parliament, Akaev strengthened his charisma and public support, as he succeeded in restoring peace in the Osh region and declaring, first, national sovereignty and then independence of Kyrgyzstan in 1991. Akaev was also able to cope successfully with the protests of non-titular nations against the new land law adopted by the Kyrgyz parliament in May 1991, which described the land and natural resources of Kyrgyzstan as the wealth of ethnic Kyrgyz. He further increased his popularity with the way he dealt with the August coup attempt against Gorbachev. Unlike the majority of Soviet leaders, Akaev opposed the coup right from the beginning and took measures in that regard. As a result, although he was a totally new name for Kyrgyz citizens at the time he was elected as the president by the parliament on 12 October 1991, he was re-elected by popular vote. Following his re-election, he succeeded in strengthening his image as a promoter of political and economic reforms, creating further public support.

One important development took place in 1993 when the new constitution of the Kyrgyz Republic was adopted. The 1993 Constitution, in basic terms, "provided a legislative framework for further democratic transition" (Abazov 2003: 46). Being proud of the constitution adopted by the parliament, Akaev described it as Kyrgyzstan's first free, sovereign and basically individual-oriented constitution. He also suggested that the new constitution accepted the superiority of "person" over "the state" (Akaev 1995: 25–26). According to Akaev (1995: 27):

> In the Constitution of the Kyrgyz Republic, we managed to fully and accurately identify the wonderful ideas of democracy, like priority of human rights and liberties over all the values, firm guarantees of private interests, private property, private life, national reconstruction of the Kyrgyz, protection and development of all the ethnic minorities constituting together with the people of Kyrgyzstan.

This new constitution indeed embraced the constitutional ideas of liberal democracies by strengthening the separation of powers between the executive, legislative and judicial branches, by guaranteeing protection of human rights and freedoms, and by providing legal grounds for the creation of a civil society. In fact, although the new constitution did not create strong parliamentarianism, it did not intend to create a strong presidential rule either. The constitution gave substantial powers to the president but also provided the parliament with a mechanism to balance presidential power. In that sense, even if it had certain shortcomings, the 1993 constitution at least provided a basic framework for the establishment of a democratic system by defining Kyrgyzstan as a democratic, law-governed, secular state based on principles of freedom and independence (Huskey 2002: 77; Kovalskii 2001: 235).

Therefore, in contrast to the other Central Asian states, a multi-party system, NGOs and a civil society were largely allowed to develop in a freer atmosphere in Kyrgyzstan. The Law on Social Organizations was signed by Akaev and it provided a tolerant environment for the formation and functioning of opposition parties; they could now be established without state interference, participate in elections and freely organize their activities (Fuller 1992: 28). In a parallel fashion, Akaev was supportive of the foundation of civil society in Kyrgyzstan and a progressive legislation for NGOs was passed. Additionally, there were improvements regarding the establishment of a relatively more independent media (Akaev 1995: 115).[5]

As a result, in the early years of the post-Soviet era, Kyrgyzstan was viewed as one of the leading reformist countries in Central Asia. It was suggested by some international observers and scholars that Kyrgyzstan was actually "an island of democracy" (Anderson 1998; Abazov 2003) in a region where autocratic regimes seemed to be the norm. According to one expert, during this era:

> The president adhere[d] to the constitution in domestic and foreign policy, the multiparty parliament discusse[d] and adopte[d] laws freely, the government publicly advance[d] economic and political programmes and regularly reporte[d] to the parliament. The opposition ha[d] its own press, and often criticize[d] the government's actions.
>
> (Kovalskii 2001: 236)

Kyrgyzstan looked promising indeed as compared to the "authoritarian rule in Kazakhstan and Uzbekistan, the civil war that continued for five years in Tajikistan and the Stalinesque personality cult that President Niyazov developed in Turkmenistan (ICG 2001: 1).

However, in time, especially after 1994, an authoritarian tendency was observed in Akaev's leadership. The first sign was the disappearance of the initial harmony between Akaev and the parliament, *Jogorku Kenesh*, mostly due to the economic problems of the country and the corruption scandals in the government. As a result, the parliament now wanted more control over the executive branch. Subsequently, Akaev held a referendum in January 1994 to ask the citizens whether they supported his economic and political policies and wanted him to continue his constitutional tenure until 1996. In this referendum, Akaev succeeded in receiving the approval of citizens both for his policies and the continuation of his presidency. In spite of the public confidence, however, the *Jogorku Kenesh* still refused to support Akaev and the government. This negative attitude considerably slowed down the reform process, which resulted in the resignation of the government and the dissolution of the parliament by Akaev in September 1994 and announcement of new parliamentary elections to be held in February 1995 (Kovalskii 2001: 239). This event was perceived as a "quiet revolution" (Gleason 1997: 99), engineered by Akaev. Furthermore, before the elections, Akaev announced another referendum for October 1994, which eventually limited parliamentary powers by allowing the constitution to be amended by referendums and creating a new bicameral parliament. Hence, the separation of powers principle was also damaged (Kort 2004: 160). Akaev's usage of referendum as a tool for policy making without the involvement of the parliament was now strongly criticized by his opponents who claimed that "Akaev behaved not as the head of executive branch but a kind of republican monarch who served as the guarantor of the constitution operating at the pinnacle of state power" (Handrahan 2001: 468). Akaev now resembled more a republican monarch rather than the head of the executive in a democratic state. As such, it was pointed out that he was reverting to the commonly seen method of rule in Central Asia by practising "a thin democratic rhetoric but more authoritarian forms of rule" (Anderson 1998: 55).

In that regard, it has been argued that Akaev's leadership between 1991 and 1995 encouraged the base for a *delegative democracy* (O'Donnell 1994: 67),[6] in the sense that once elected by popular vote, the leader believes that he/she can govern the country as he/she sees fit. As such, after being elected as the president Akaev was authorized to govern the country as he saw fit and he was delegated to exercise full authority. In this framework, he utilized referendums for making constitutional changes, forced governments to resign and dissolved the parliament.

Akaev's second and third terms of office (1995–2000, 2000–2005)

> I would like to also mention about my personal position on democratic development. I want to say that there are a number of various myths on this subject. Some of them go as far as to depict me as transforming from a democrat into an autocrat. I say openly if it had not been for my democratic conventions and principles with regard to opposition.... Kyrgyzstan would have just a part of the current opposition political parties and media that we currently have. The many opposition leaders who exhibited great zeal in aggravating libellous considerations would have been in a different place. In terms of democratization, among the post-Soviet countries, the Kyrgyz Republic is one of the leading countries. And I do not want to minimize my personal role in this process.
>
> (Akaev 2002)

Contrary to what Akaev said back in 2002 about his contribution to the democratization of Kyrgyzstan, the trajectory of his leadership obviously turned towards a more authoritarian path since mid-1995. On 23 December 1995, Akaev began his second term of office by receiving 71.9 per cent of the votes against Masaliev and Sherimkulov in the presidential election (Abazov 2003: 47). During this time, Akaev began to lose his liberal reputation. Although in rhetoric he continued to underline his loyalty to the principles of democratic development, the regime in Kyrgyzstan became increasingly authoritarian. Through 1995 and after, Akaev obviously employed certain methods that are normally associated with authoritarian leaders, such as abolishing some of the democratic principles of the 1993 Constitution via referendums, increasing intolerance against opposition groups and parties, and electoral frauds. In this general framework, the most frequently utilized instruments were the referendums held in February 1996, October 1998 and September 2002. As a result of these referendums (each of which was approved by overwhelming margins), constitutional amendments were accepted which codified a strong presidential rule and a weak parliament with a ceremonial post of prime minister. Those new powers allowed Akaev to dominate and manipulate all three branches of state (legislature, executive and judiciary) in order to pave way for the creation of a powerful central executive. Akaev gradually reduced the powers of the parliament in favour of the executive to such an extent that the parliamentarians thought that *Jogorku Kenesh* turned into a "working cabinet" for the president (ICG 2001: 8). Likewise, the judiciary was also manipulated and put under the control of the president. In that sense, courts were frequently used to silence political opponents by issuing verdicts, by manipulating the election results and by repressing the media, once the freest in Central Asia (Azizian 2003: 3). The more Akaev expanded his powers, the more he moved to pressure the opposition forces. In that sense, independent newspapers were frequently closed down, or sentenced to pay heavy fines which led them to bankruptcy. Journalists were under the pressure of losing their jobs or being charged with heavy fines, so a big majority practiced self-censorship. Furthermore, human rights activists were harassed, and elections were manipulated (Freedom House 2003).

In a similar fashion, Akaev also did not seem to respect one of the very basic tenets of democracy: a constitutionally limited term of office. According to the constitution, running a third time for the presidency was not allowed. Thus Akaev, who would be completing his second term in 2000, could not participate in the new presidential elections to be held on 29 October 2000. However, the Constitutional Court ruled that Akaev had the right to run for a third term, although it was constitutionally not allowed. The court concluded that the constitution changed the scope and structure of the powers of the president in 1993, and Askar Akaev had been elected for the first time in 1995 (Connery 2000: 6). Thus, he had the right to stand for presidential election once more. However, as Huskey (2002: 86) argued, "the Constitutional Court decision represented a prelude to a presidential election campaign in 2000 that shattered any remaining illusions about Kyrgyzstan's claim to be an oasis of democracy in Central Asia." Simply put, Akaev succeeded in staying in office for a third time (2000–2005).[7] According to the results of the 2000 Kyrgyz presidential elections, Akaev was re-elected by taking 74.4 per cent of the votes (OSCE/ODIHR 2001: 14), so it seemed as if he got what he wanted: to win the election in the first round by an overwhelming majority in order to prove that he expressed the will of the nation and that he could govern Kyrgyzstan effectively. As was put by one observer, Akaev believed that "in a winner-take-all presidential election, he needed more than a minimum winning majority" (Huskey 2002: 89). Nevertheless, because of all the irregularities concerning the election, neither the international observers nor the Kyrgyz people believed that Akaev represented the will of nation.

From this point of view, in spite of the initial optimism toward him, Akaev started to move away from his path toward democracy and Kyrgyzstan deviated from its initial liberal trajectory. There emerged public resentment and impatience against Akaev and his policies which grew on an almost day-to-day basis. In that sense, it can be argued that the public unrest had already emerged since the late 1990s. The Aksy events,[8] a couple of spontaneous demonstrations in Bishkek, Narin and Osh during 2001–2002 and the eventual establishment of the reform movement, "For the Resignation of Akaev and Reform for the People", in 2002, were the indicators of a growing public opposition and unrest in this period (*Kyrgyzstan: A Political Overview*). These events proved that Akaev's increasingly authoritarian rule would become even more intolerable from the perspective of the Kyrgyz people, especially when combined with the quickly deteriorating economic conditions and corruption claims about Akaev and his family.

Shortly after the March 2005 parliamentary elections, these sporadic opposition movements gradually turned into a major mass protest, the Tulip Revolution. On 24 March opposition politicians agreed to organize a major rally in Bishkek, gathering supporters from the various regions of the country as well as the capital city of Bishkek. In the morning, several thousand people gathered in the capital and headed in the direction of the presidential building, the White House. According to one of the ICG Reports (2005: 8)

> The protestors were very diverse: Bakiev, Usen Sydykov and Beknazarov brought their supporters; Roza Otunbaeva helped transport activists from the south; Jeenbekov brought people from Talas and Japarov from Kochkor, while supporters of Atambaev and Melis Eshimkanov came from their villages near the capital. Workers at bazaars, many of them from the south, joined in. There were also young people from different organizations.

The demonstrators gathered on the square close to the White House. With the arrival of the several hundred protestors from Osh, the crowd marched straight to the White House, and soon afterward, a fight broke out between these protesters and the police outside the building. Despite the attempts of the police to prevent them, the protestors were able to enter the building within minutes, throwing papers and chairs out of the windows. At that point, the opposition leaders tried to take control of the situation in order to stop looting. However, they failed to do so and the protests resulted in the eventual resignation of Akaev on 4 April 2005.[9]

The 15-year-long rule of Akaev thus came to an end dramatically and quite suddenly, despite the fact that Akaev had declared that he would not seek re-election after the expiration of his term of office in October 2005, respecting the decision of the Constitutional Court. If he had stepped down earlier voluntarily, he would have been the first president in a Central Asian republic to leave office on his own. Instead, he became the first president in a Central Asian republic ousted from office by a popular uprising.

When we look into the post-Soviet political developments in Kyrgyzstan from the perspective of leadership style and democratic transition, we can argue that the regime in Kyrgyzstan was not very stable and evolved from a delegative democracy to authoritarianism between 1995 and 2005. This shift was mostly due to Akaev's presidency, which provided the basis for a delegative democracy, just as it did during his previous term. He would use a mixture of selected democratic norms of majoritarian rule and authoritarian practices. During Akaev's three terms of office, especially after the late 1990s, however, the democratic norms of majoritarian rule, such as elections and tolerance toward the opposition, were not seen in Kyrgyzstan, as Akaev's presidency turned out to be strongly authoritarian. His choice of authoritarianism became much more visible by the amendments to the constitution, electoral frauds and repression of various potential opponent forces within the political arena, such as the media, political parties, courts and the parliament. These practices helped Akaev to establish strong executive control over policy making by transferring powers of the legislative branch, either to the chief executive (the president) or to those bodies that were dependent on the executive. Later, with other measures, the parliament's size, structure and power, as well as the immunity of parliamentarians were reduced.[10] Furthermore, the parliament's approval required for the appointment of the cabinet members, the director of the National Bank and the Attorney General and parliament's right to initiate in domestic and foreign policy was no longer required. In addition, although Akaev did not choose referendums over competitive elections as Nazarbaev, Karimov or Niyazov did, instead he limited the competitiveness of the elections by using legal sanctions in an illegitimate way. This attitude further increased his tendency toward authoritarianism.

The reasons lying behind the change in Akaev's leadership have been widely discussed since then. Although to examine this issue in detail is beyond the scope of this chapter, a brief analysis is nevertheless necessary. In that sense, Luong analysed the situation in a power-based manner, which underlined an inverse relationship between the president's perception of power and the level of political openness, which meant that the greater the perception of power the lesser the desire for political openness. Luong (2002: 28) argued that Akaev liberalized the political system in order to include smaller parties in the political process because he was "bargaining from a position of weakness relative to other established elites". This, in turn implied that he "withdrew his support for democracy later in transition because he perceived that the balance of power had shifted in his favour" (Luong 2002: 29). Collins, on the other hand, put the role of clans and clan politics in Kyrgyzstan as the main reason behind Akaev's divergence from his liberal reforms. Collins further stated that clan pacts carried Akaev to the presidency and led him to implement a democratic-oriented programme due to the high levels of trust within his clan. However, at the same time these clan loyalties have required Akaev to distribute political power and economic resources among his own clan members, leading to an over-reliance on his group to the exclusion of others. This has resulted in even more authoritarian policies.[11]

Another opinion came from McGlinchey, who argued the issue from the point of "determinants of regime outcomes" and evaluated leaders' access to economic sources of rule as the most important determinant (quoted in Spector 2003: 26).[12] In that sense, McGlinchey argued that Akaev's authoritarian attitude can be explained as behaviour motivated by his reluctance for losing his free access to power and wealth, which became especially apparent during his last term of office. Huskey (1995: 829), on the other hand, proposed that Akaev had became disillusioned with the classical democratic road and looked for an alternative path of proto-democracy as he thought that the Kyrgyz were "not yet mature enough for genuine democracy". This change in Akaev's leadership style was also viewed as a new tactic to overcome opposition and guarantee a measure of social and political stability. As such Akaev's more authoritarian policies were seen as politically necessary concessions to conservative forces in central and local bureaucracies (Huskey 1995: 830). In that sense, Akçalı also focused on Akaev's priority of political stability, which limited and even prevented democratic tendencies and attempts. She wrote that "the basic priority given to political stability resulted in a process in which democratic formations and movements [were] repressed for the sake of realizing the long-term goal of democratic consolidation" (Akçalı 2005: 56). To put it differently, "democratic demands and movements, which [were] perceived to be potential threats to political stability, [were] repressed during the transition period" (ibid.).

The strong influence of traditional tribes and tribal loyalties, lack of a strong civil society as well as powerful opposition parties, and economic problems all contributed to the Kyrgyz political system turning out to be vulnerable and fragile, resulting in Akaev's path shifting toward a less democratic way of governing. The state structures became more and more centralized while at the same time the parliamentary mechanism became less and less effective.

Whatever the reasons were, one fact remains obvious: Kyrgyzstan failed in its democratic transition by the end of Akaev's era and this deficiency caused the Kyrgyz experience to be understood as incomplete. The transition process in the country carries the properties of "pseudo" (Rumer 2005), "delegative" (O'Donnell 1994: 55), "obstructed" or "defective democracies" (Merkel 1999: 361 quoted in Geiss 2006: 23). As such, Kyrgyzstan is considered to be a "backslider" (Fish 2001: 56),[13] or a country of soft authoritarian regime. Therefore, although Kyrgyzstan was perceived as a promising candidate in the so-called "fourth wave of democratization" (McFaul 2002: 212–244) at the beginning of its independence, in time it turned out to be the case that it was not radically different from the other CARs.

Conclusion

Kyrgyzstan's post-Soviet developments under the rule of Akaev seem to support the main argument of this paper: political leadership matters and it often makes a crucial difference in the destinies of countries, especially during unpredictable processes such as democratic transition from an authoritarian rule (Imanaliev 1998: 15). In that sense, the relation between political leadership and the democratic transition process can be clearly observed in the case of Askar Akaev and post-independence Kyrgyzstan. Basically, transformation in Askar Akaev's leadership style during his 15-year-long presidency matches with the transformation of Kyrgyzstan from its initial liberal path to an authoritarian one. The shift in Akaev's trajectory also changed the framework within which his political leadership style is discussed.

In that sense, it can be argued that Akaev's authority was closer to a *legal-rational* one during 1990–1995 according to its source of power in the Weberian sense. Since Akaev neither had any ties with the Communist Party hierarchy nor any personal history as the leader of the Kyrgyz Republic, unlike the other four Central Asian presidents, his election was rather a rational choice for the voters, who believed in him for realizing the future development of Kyrgyzstan. However, these characteristics of Akaev's leadership could not be sustained. In relation with the changes in his policies, his source of power became very much *traditional* rather than *legal-rational* after the mid-1990s onward, because soon after he started to lose public support around him, his source of power gradually shifted towards traditional clan ties. However, this reliance on clan support constituted an irony in itself as he had both publicly called for discarding clan norms and adopting democratic ones on the one hand, and used Kyrgyz tribalism to become part of the political system on the other (Collins 2004: 248; Handrahan 2001: 472). It must, however, also be argued that Akaev's leadership had some nuances of a *charismatic* type of authority, especially in his first years in office. His charisma, however, eroded over the years mostly due to his gradual reversion to authoritarianism that ended up in his removal from office.

According to the relation between the leaders and the led, as James MacGregor Burns illustrated, Akaev's leadership style could be named as *transactional* between 1990 and 1995, since in that era Akaev was engaged in various reforms on behalf of Kyrgyz citizens, and in return he gained the trust of the voters. Nevertheless, after 1995, as his authoritarian tendency started to evolve, Akaev limited the number of people around him and legitimized his power upon a small group composed of *akims* and *tribal leaders*, whose support seemed to be enough to keep him in power.[14] In due course, his policies aimed to satisfy the members of this group rather than the nation as a whole. This attitude made Akaev's relation with his "led" to change, which made him more of a *transformational* leader, just like the other Central Asian presidents.

According to Linz and Stepan's table, Akaev's rule fits to a large extent with Linz and Stepan's definition for democratic leadership, which includes being elected by and subject to periodic free elections, as well as staying within the constitutional framework and respecting rule of law during his first years in office (Linz and Stepan 1996: 3–7). However, later on, as Akaev started to disregard the constitution by running for the presidency for the third time, and by preparing a solid basis for almost unlimited power with new constitutional amendments, he turned out to be an *authoritarian* leader according to the same classification.

The transition of Akaev's leadership from being a transactional-democratic leader depending on a legal-charismatic base of authority to a transformational-authoritarian one depending on traditional authority weakened the democratic development in Kyrgyzstan after the mid-1990s. Consequently, although it started out on its path of democratic transition as a parliamentary republic under the democratic norms and principles of the 1993 Constitution, Kyrgyzstan slowly became an authoritarian presidential republic. This may be problematic in the future, as presidential rule may actually increase the probability of the emergence of non-democratic regimes during transitional periods (Cummings 2002: 8–12; Dukanbaev and Hansen 2003: 32; Fish 2001: 50–51). This argument may be especially valid in a region like Central Asia, where there was no prior democratic experience and where political leaders act in somewhat arbitrary and personal spheres in which they can operate independently. According to Farkhod Tolipov (2006: 63)

> the first leaders of the post-Soviet and newly independent Central Asian states are very interesting phenomena in terms of their roles, images, status and personality. Their accession to and retaining of power, their ruling of respective countries and their soon-to-be ending presidencies play a crucial role in shaping the political systems of these young states.

In that sense, the case of Askar Akaev and Kyrgyzstan is an explanatory one in order to get a better understanding of the democratization attempts in this region. Although a full explanation of the failed democratic experiences in Central Asia must address many other variables, such as the Soviet legacy, economic problems and socio-cultural structure of the region, the political leadership issue is certainly a help in achieving this aim.

Notes

1 For further information on this see Chotaeva (1998: 56) and Kyrgyz Republic (2001).
2 Although an optimism emerged in the West around Akaev and his democratic and liberal image in his first years in office, the fact is that his democratic image would not last during his further behaviour. As Merry states, Akaev turned out to be a "great disappointment to many in the West who naively saw him as a Jeffersonian democrat in the heart of Asia. Sadly, a better parallel is Zimbabwe's Robert Mugabe, who also won many admirers in his early years before his agenda narrowed to maintaining personal power" (Merry 2004: 38).
3 Burns described the difference between "power wielder" and "leader". He described power wielders as those who exercise influence by mobilizing their power base in destructive ways through establishing direct physical control over others, as in a war or conquest. Leaders, on the other hand, exercise power when people with certain motives and purposes are mobilized, in competition or conflict with others, institutional, political, psychological, and other resources so as to arouse, engage, and satisfy the motives of followers. For further information, see Burns (1986: 287–299).
4 On 23 October 1990, the Supreme Soviet of Kyrgyzstan held an extraordinary session. Election of the next leader of Kyrgyzstan was the most important discussion topic of the session. There were three candidates for the post of presidency: Absamat Masaliev, the First Secretary of the Communist Party of Kyrgyzstan (CPK); Apas Dzhumagulov, the Chairman of the Council of Ministers of the Kyrgyz SSR; and Jumgalbek Amanbaev, the First Secretary of Issyk-Kul Regional Committee of the CPK. However, neither Masaliev nor the other two candidates succeed in gaining the required number of votes, or the absolute majority, in the first round. The second round of voting also failed to produce the necessary majority. Such a situation

required the elimination of all candidates and identification of new ones according to the newly adopted republican law on presidential election (Gleason 1997: 60). The opposition group among the parliamentarians proposed Askar Akaev, who was not a deputy at that time, and the parliament elected Askar Akaev as the first president of Kyrgyzstan on 30 October 1990.

5 For further information on these developments, see Altinay Kuchukeeva and John O'Loughlin (2003), Anne Garbutt (2004), M. Holt Ruffin and Daniel Waugh (1999) and Zairash Galieva (1998).

6 For further discussions about the applicability of delegative democracy in Central Asia and Kyrgyzstan, see also Bruce Parrott (1997: 1–39) and Eugene Huskey (1997: 242–276).

7 In this period, Akaev took a number of measures against his rivals by sponsoring new forms of coercion. Arrest of the three most prominent candidates for the presidency by the criminal prosecution was the most important one. Feliks Kulov, Daniyar Ussenov and Topchubek Turgunaliev, whose immunities were removed with the October 1998 referendum, were sentenced to prison after they indicated their intention to participate in the election. Akaev also created another obstacle to restrict the participation of alternative presidential candidates in the elections by issuing a new language law that required the president to be fluent in Kyrgyz. In line with the new law, a Kyrgyz language exam was to be organized by a linguistic commission. After the exam eight candidates were eliminated, while Akaev had the highest score (Akçalı 2005: 43). It was also stated that Akaev offered ambassadorial and executive posts to potential opponents and manipulated all forms of the media; newspapers, radio and television broadcasts. For more information on these developments regarding the elections, see Dyryldaev.

8 The Aksy events occurred in March 2002 and resulted in five people being shot dead and several injured by the police during a demonstration held for the release of an oppositionist, Azimbek Beknazarov, who was a popular deputy from Jalalabad. The international community and the oppositionists labelled the events as a clear example of human rights violation. Furthermore, with the Aksy events, Akaev was confronted with criticism of using state security organs against the population. After these events, Akaev fired the key ministers involved in the decision to open fire, which resulted in the eventual resignation of the entire government. The events also made the opposition groups to cooperate more closely in order to force Akaev to resign. For further information, see Akçalı (2005) and Judith Beyer (2006: 23–24).

9 For a closer look at the period before and after the Tulip Revolution, the reasons lying behind it and its consequences, see Kynev (2005) and Akaev (2010).

10 The proposal introduced and accepted in the 1998 referendum included an increase in the number of deputies in the Legislative Assembly (upper house) from 35 to 60, and a decrease in the number of representatives in the People's Assembly (lower house) from 70 to 45. Unlike the 1993 constitution,

> the new proposal would have the Legislative Assembly elected based on proportional representation (48 of the seats) and on party lists (15 of the seats). On the other hand, the People's Assembly would be indirectly elected by the local *keneshes* (local legislators) with six seats going to each *oblast* – there are six regions in Kyrgyzstan – and six to the city of Bishkek.
>
> (Connery 2000: 7)

In that sense, according to the personal interview of Joyce Connery with Galina Sergunina, who is from International Foundation for Election Systems, conducted on 10 June 1998, local observers criticized the proposal as a "presidential effort to create a pocket parliament" (ibid.). This was due to the fact that the *keneshes* were influenced strongly by the *akims* (regional governors) who, in turn, were appointed by the president. So this meant that 42 members of the parliament would be under the direct control of Akaev, which led to the weakening of the parliament. It was argued that, in doing so, Akaev forged a de facto ruling alliance with *akims* of six regions, who were now linked to the president as leaders of local government. Under this new system, power was highly centralized in the hands of the president, as the president would appoint the *akims*, who in turn would appoint the officials in towns and villages. Actually this system aimed to establish the "institution of akimiaty", which was perceived as the backbone of authoritarian rule (Huskey 1997: 258–259).

11 For details, see Collins (1999, 2004: 224–261, 2006).
12 For details, see Eric McGlinchey (2003).
13 "Backslider" is a term in Fish's classification of the post-communist countries in transition with regard to the ratings received by Freedom House in 1999–2000. Although it requires an update, it still provides concrete data in the comparison. Fish's classification includes four categories of countries: "democracies", "democratizers", "backsliders" and "autocracies". In this regard, "democracies" consist of countries that received freedom scores of 1 or 1.5 in recent Freedom House surveys, while "democratizers" received scores ranging between 2 and 4, and "backsliders" scored better than 5 but had previously scored better. "Autocracies" never scored better than 5 and were evaluated as the countries which moved directly to new forms of authoritarianism without undergoing democratization. According to the classification, Czech Republic, Estonia, Hungary, Latvia, Poland, Slovakia, Slovenia are placed in the first category; Georgia, Macedonia, Moldova, Mongolia and Romania in the second category; Albania, Armenia, Belarus, Bulgaria, Crotia, Kazakhstan, Kyrgyzstan, Russia and Ukraine in the third category; Azerbaijan, Bosnia, Tajikistan, Turkmenistan and Uzbekistan in the last category (Fish 2001: 56–58).
14 The relation between Akaev and regional *akims* was reciprocal. Akaev made certain compromises with them and in return they remained loyal to him. For more information, see Huskey (1997: 250–255) and Interfax (1994: 46).

References

Akaev A. (1995) *Kyrgyzstan on the Way to Progress and Democracy*, Bishkek: International Department/Presidency of Kyrgyz Republic.

Akaev A. (2002) *The Future of Kyrgyzstan*, Washington D.C.: Center for Strategic and International Studies.

Akaev A. (2010) "Po Pyat' Kopeek: 'S Kotla Sorvalo Kryshku' [Five Kopecks: 'The Lid was thrown off the Pan']", *Moskovskii Komsomolets-Kyrgyzstan*, April.

Abazov, R. (2003) *The Political Culture of Central Asia: The Case of Kyrgyzstan*, Conflict Studies Research Center.

Akçalı, P. (2005) "Democracy and Political Stability in Kyrgyzstan", in B.N. Schlyter (ed.) *Prospects for Democracy in Central Asia*, Stockholm: Swedish Research Institute in Istanbul: 41–58.

Anderson, J. (1998) *Kyrgyzstan: Central Asia's Island of Democracy*, Amsterdam: Harwood Academic Publishers.

Azizian, R. (2003) *Democratization in Central Asia: The Asian Way?* Asia-Pacific Center for Security Studies, Hawaii. Online. Available: www.aprc.jp/kokusai/2003/33.pdf (accessed 25 January 2009).

Beyer, J. (2006) "Rhetoric of 'Transformation': The Case of the Kyrgyz Constitutional Reform", in A. Berg and A. Kreikmeyer (eds) *Realities of Transformation: Democratization Policies in Central Asia Revisited*, Baden-Baden: Nomos: 43–62.

Blondel, J. (1987) *Political Leadership: Towards a General Analysis*, London: Sage.

Burns, J.M. (1978) *Leadership*, New York: Harper and Row.

Burns, J.M. (1986) "Power Wielders and Leaders", in B. Kellerman (ed.) *Political Leadership: A Source Book*, Pittsburgh: University of Pittsburgh Press: 287–299.

Chotaeva, C.D. (1998) "Modeli Razvitiya Kirgizstana i Mezhdunarodnii Opyt [The Kyrgyz Model of Development and International Experience]", in *Demokraticheskie Processy v Tsentralnoi Azii: Opyt i Perspektivy* [Democratization Process in Central Asia: Experiences and Perspectives], Bishkek: Mezhdunarodnii Universitet Kirgizstana (International University of Kyrgyzstan), Institut Tsentralnoi Azii (Institution of Central Asia): 55–58.

Collins, K. (1999) "Clans, Pacts, and Politics: Understanding Regime Transition in Central Asia", unpublished doctoral dissertation, Stanford University.

Collins, K. (2004) "The Logic of Clan Politics: Evidence from the Central Asian Trajectories", *World Politics*, 56/2: 224–261.

Collins, K. (2006) *Clan Politics and Regime Transition in Central Asia*, Cambridge: Cambridge University Press.

Connery, J. (2000) "Caught between a Dictatorship and a Democracy: Civil Society, Religion and Development in Kyrgyzstan", *Fletcher Journal of Development Studies*, 16: 1–18.

Cummings, S.N. (2002) *Power and Change in Central Asia*, London: Routledge.

Dukanbaev, A. and Hansen, W.W. (2003) "Understanding Politics in Kyrgyzstan", DEMSTAR Research Report No. 16. Online. Available: www.demstar.dk/papers/UPKyrgyzstan.pdf (accessed on 16 April 2007).

Dyryldaev, R. "Ten Years of Akaev's Presidency". Online. Available: www.eurasianet.org/departments/election/kyrgyzstan/kew110100.shtml (accessed on 15 April 2007).

Fish, S.M. (2001) "The Dynamics of Democratic Erosion", in R.D. Anderson, Jr., M.S. Fish, S.E. Hanson and P.G. Roeder (eds) *Postcommunism and the Theory of Democracy*, Princeton: Princeton University Press: 54–95.

Freedom House (2003) *Annual Report.* Online. Available: www.freedomhouse.org/uploads/special_report/20.pdf (accessed 30 April 2007).

Freedom House (2006) *Country Report: Kyrgyzstan. Countries at the Crossroads.* Online. Available: www.freedomhouse.org/modules/publications/ccr/modPrintVersion.cfm?edition=7&ccrpage=31&ccrcountry=122 (accessed 30 April 2007).

Friedrich, C.J. (1970) "The Theory of Political Leadership and the Issue of Totalitarianism", in B.R. Farrell (ed.) *Political Leadership in Eastern Europe and the Soviet Union*, Chicago: Adline Publishing Company: 17–27.

Fuller, G.E. (1992) *Central Asia: The New Geopolitics*, Santa Monica: Rand.

Galieva, Z. (1998) "Civil Society in the Kyrgyz Republic in Transition", *Central Asian Monitor*, 5: 7–10.

Garbutt, A. (2004) "Donor Trends and Civil Society Development in Central Asia", *ONTRAC: The Newsletter of the International NGO Training and Research Center*, No. 26, January.

Geiss, P.G. (2006) "State and Regime Change in Central Asia", in A. Berg and A. Kreikemeyer (eds) *Realities of Transformation: Democratization Policies in Central Asia Revisited*, Nomos: 23–42.

Gleason, G. (1997) *The Central Asian States Discovering Independence*, Boulder: Westview Press.

Handrahan, L.M. (2001) "Gender and Ethnicity in the Transitional Democracy of Kyrgyzstan", *Central Asian Survey*, 20/4: 467–496.

Hermann, M.G. (1986) "Ingredients of Leadership", in M.G. Hermann (ed.) *Political Psychology: Contemporary Problems and Issues*, London: Jossey-Bass: 179–192.

Huskey, E. (1995) "The Rise of Contested Politics in Central Asia: Elections in Kyrgyzstan, 1989–90", *Europe–Asia Studies*, 47/5: 813–833.

Huskey, E. (1997) "Kyrgyzstan: The Fate of Political Liberalization", in K. Dawisha and B. Parrott (eds) *Conflict, Cleavage and Change in Central Asia and the Caucasus*, Cambridge: Cambridge University Press: 242–276.

Huskey, E. (2002) "Kyrgyzstan: An Economy of Authoritarianism?" in S.N. Cummings (ed.) *Power and Change in Central Asia*, New York: Routledge: 74–96.

Imanaliev M. (1998) "Demokratishesckie Processy v Postkomunisticheskom Obschestve [Democratization Processes in Post-communist Societies]", in *Demokraticheskiye Processy v Tsentralnoi Azii: Opyt i Perspektivy* [Democratization Processes in Central Asia: Experiences and Perspectives], Mezhdunarodnyi Universitet Kirgizstana [International University of Kyrgyzstan], Institut Tsentralnoi Azii [Central Asia Institute], Bishkek: 13–19.

ICG (International Crisis Group) (2001) "Kyrgyzstan at Ten: Trouble in the 'Island of Democracy'", Report No. 22, 28 August.

ICG (International Crisis Group) (2005) "Kyrgyzstan: After the Revolution", Asia Report No. 97, 4 May.

Interfax (1994) "Akaev Fears 'Shouters, Politicians' in New Parliaments", *Daily Report: Central Eurasia*, in English, 23 November.

Ishiyama, J. (2002) "The Prospects for Democratization", in S.N. Cummings (ed.) *Power and Change in Central Asia*, London: Routledge: 42–58.

Kellerman, B. (1986) *Political Leadership: A Source Book*, Pittsburgh: University of Pittsburgh Press.

Kort, M. (2004) *Central Asian Republics*, New York: Facts on File.

Kovalskii, V.F. (2001) "Democratic Declarations and Political Realities", in A. Vassiliev (ed.) *Central Asia: Political and Economic Challenges in the Post-Soviet era*, London: Saqi Books: 235–251.

Kuchukeeva, A. and O'Loughlin, J. (2003) "Civic Engagement and Democratic Consolidation in Kyrgyzstan", *Eurasian Geography and Economics*, 44/8: 557–587.

Kynev, A. (2005) *Kirgizstan do i posle Tulpanovoi Revolutsii* [Kyrgyzstan before and after the Tulip Revolution]. Online. Available: www.igpi.ru/info/people/kynev/1128082583.html (accessed on 14 February 2011).

Kyrgyz Republic (2001) *Kirgizskaya Respublika: Novyye Perspektivy, Kompleksnaya Osnova Razvitiya Kyrgyzskoi Respubliki do 2010 goda* [Kyrgyz Republic: New Perspectives, Complex Framework for the Development of Kyrgyz Republic till 2010], Bishkek.

Kyrgyzstan: A Political Overview. Online. Available: www.ukdf.org.uk/regional/RS26E.doc (accessed on 15 February 2009).

Linz, J.J. (1964) "An Authoritarian Regime: The Case of Spain", in E. Allardt and Y. Litunen (eds) *Cleavages, Ideologies and Party Systems*, Helsinki: Transactions of the Westermack Society: 291–342.

Linz, J.J. and Stepan, A. (1996) *Problems of Democratic Transition and Consolidation: Southern Europe, South America, and Post-Communist Europe*, Baltimore: John Hopkins University Press.

Luong, P.J. (2002) *Institutional Change and Political Continuity in Post-Soviet Central Asia*, Cambridge: Cambridge University Press.

McFaul, M. (2002) "The Fourth Wave of Democracy and Dictatorship: Noncooperative Transitions in Postcommunist World", *World Politics*, 54/2: 212–244.

McGlinchey, E. (2003) "Paying for Patronage: Regime Change in Post-Soviet Central Asia", unpublished doctoral dissertation, Princeton University.

Merkel, W. (1999) "Defekte Demokratie", in A. Busch (ed.) *Demokratie in Ost und West*, Frankfurt: Suhrkamp.

Merry, W.E. (2004) "The Politics of Central Asia: National in Form Soviet in Content", in D.L. Burghart and T. Sabonis-Helf (eds) *In the Tracks of Tamerlane: Central Asia's Path to the 21st Century*, Washington: Center for Technology and National Security Policy: 25–42.

O'Donnell, G. (1994) "Delegative Democracy", *Journal of Democracy*, 5/1: 56–69.

OSCE/ODIHR (Organization for Cooperation and Security in Europe) (2001) "Kyrgyz Republic Presidential Elections", *Final Report*, Warsaw, January. Online. Available: www.osce.org/documents/html/pdftohtml/1384_en.pdf.html (accessed on 20 April 2007).

Parrott, B. (1997) "Perspectives on Postcommunist Democratization", in K. Dawisha and B. Parrott (eds) *Conflict, Cleavage and Change in Central Asia and Caucasus*, Cambridge: Cambridge University Press: 1–39.

Peele, G. (2005) "Leadership and Politics: A Case for a Closer Relationship?" *Leadership*, 1/2: 187–204.

Ruffin, M.H. and Waugh, D. (1999) *Civil Society in Central Asia*, Washington: University of Washington Press.

Rumer, B. (2005) "Central Asia at the End of the Transition", in B. Rumer (ed.) *Central Asia at the End of the Transition*, New York: M.E. Sharpe: 3–70.

Spector, R.A. (2003) "The Transformation of Askar Akaev, President of Kyrgyzstan", Berkeley Programme in Soviet and Post-Soviet Studies Working Paper Series. Online. Available: http://istsocrates.berkeley.edu/~bsp/publications/2004_02-spec.pdf (accessed on 20 February 2009).

Tolipov, F. (2006) "Power, Nation-Building, and Legacy: A Comparative Analysis of Central Asian Leadership", in A. Berg and A. Kreikmeyer (eds) *Realities of Transformation: Democratization Policies in Central Asia Revisited*, Baden-Baden: Nomos: 63–80.

Tucker, R.C. (1995) *Politics as Leadership*, revised edition, London: University of Missouri Press.

Weber, M. (1947) "The Types of Authority and Imperative Co-ordination", in A.M. Henderson and T. Parsons (trans.), T. Parsons (ed.) *The Theory of Social and Economic Organization*, New York: The Free Press.

Weber, M. (1958) "Politics as a Vocation", in H.H. Gerth and C.W. Mills (trans., eds) *From Max Weber: Essays in Sociology*, New York: Oxford University Press: 77–128.

Weber, M. (1986) "Types of Authority", in B. Kellerman (ed.) *Political Leadership: A Source Book*, Pittsburgh: University of Pittsburgh Press: 232–244.

Willner, A.R. (1986) "Charismatic Leadership", in B. Kellerman (ed.) *Political Leadership: A Source Book*, Pittsburgh: University of Pittsburgh Press: 245–249.

3 Colour revolutions and constitutionalism

The case of Kyrgyzstan

Anita Sengupta

This chapter is an attempt at examining the complex process of constitutionalism in Kyrgyzstan. It looks into debates surrounding the adaptation of the constitution in post-independence Kyrgyzstan and the amendments that it went through since its adoption. The chapter seeks to examine these changes in the background of political events and developments particularly since the "Tulip Revolution". The course of transition in the post-Soviet phase has occasioned the emergence of new actors in Kyrgyzstani politics and in a number of cases these new actors have been instrumental in defining changes. The chapter also examines whether they have also been crucial factors in reinforcing regional cleavages based on regional affiliations. The first section looks into developments in the process of constitution making; the second moves on to an analysis of recent developments within the political process, culminating in the ethnic tensions in southern Kyrgyzstan and the subsequent change in the Kyrgyz political system, the most significant of which is of course the introduction of the June 2010 Constitution with its intention to limit presidential powers and introduce a novel system of proportional representation.

It has been eight years since the "Tulip Revolution" and questions about what the "revolution" achieved in terms of constitutional, as well as real political reforms have once again assumed significance. The debate in Kyrgyzstan today is centred on whether anything actually changed after the events of March 2005. Was the "Tulip Revolution" truly a revolution or was it merely a revolt against the old order? Can the events of April 2010 be identified as a second "revolution"? The answers are varied, with different shades of public and political opinion reflected in them. Opinion is divided among those who consider the significance of the events in terms of a change of regime and constitutional reform through a national referendum, and others who want to see the continuation of the revolution until a number of issues including that of corruption are resolved. It is argued, for example, that the constitution calls for greater representation from women who now constitute about one-third of the deputies. Yet, it is also true that the economic situation has not improved considerably and many migrate to Russia, Kazakhstan and Europe for work. The energy situation is another likely cause of concern, and the rising price of fuel triggered the events of April 2010. Hydro-electric resources remain undeveloped. The gap between what is specified in the constitution and how it is actually realized is also significant.

It has been suggested that a large part of the debate surrounding the Tulip Revolution can be summarized under three broad groupings (Cummings and Ryabkov 2008). The first examines the degree to which the events preceding the revolution were made possible by the democratization efforts of the Akaev era. This involves a discussion of the nature of the democratization process and the degree to which efforts at democratization can create expectations that then require implementation and response. The second examines how the process of building formal institutions has coexisted with informal institutions. This is done in the context of recent discussions of state–society relations that see these spheres as intertwined rather than separate, and particularly intertwined through informal networks. Here a large part of the discussion is focused on the north–south divide within the country and the extent to which the geographical distribution of political support for the regime and its institutions became crucial in the determination of the way the events unfolded (see Ryabkov 2008).[1] This once again assumed relevance after the recent ethnic clashes between the Kyrgyz and the Uzbeks in southern Kyrgyzstan during the summer of 2010. And, third, there is focus on mobilization and how informal and formal institutions as well as domestic and international actors were energized into action in the crucial run-up to these events. Here, various institutions like those based on traditional solidarity, pre-existing organizations and institutions like the *aksakals* (elders), *kurultai* (assembly) and *palvan* (wrestler) have been highlighted (Temirkulov 2008). Through all of these there has been an attempt to examine the democratic impulse that motivated the actions and whether the developments following the revolution justified the description of these events in terms of "democratic change". A significant part of the conclusion to these issues stresses that the significance of the events needs to be analysed in terms of a complex dynamics of local politics where popular discontent, particularly at the rural level, was mobilized by local elites in the course of a highly competitive electoral process (Lewis 2008). A common thread connecting all the three strands of the debate is the success or the failure of constitutionalism in Kyrgyzstan.

Constitutions differ according to traditions, physical, economic and social conditions, worldviews, cultures and historical experiences of people. Despite such diversity of constitutions, a universally valid concept of constitutionalism as a set of ideas and principles which form the common basis of the constitutions is generally accepted. According to the most commonplace understanding, constitutionalism embraces essentially the idea of limited government (Preuss 1995). Constitutionalism also means that the authority of the government is not wielded according to the will and arbitrariness of people, but according to legal rules or rule of law. Thus, a constitution is not merely a manifesto or a political programme, or merely a factual description of the state of a polity, or the pure political will of the sovereign or of the ruling elites, but the embodiment of a legally enforceable normative programme, which generates legal obligations both for the rulers and the ruled. The character of this normative programme varies considerably according to the specific historical experience, tradition and hopes of the people of a country. Constitutionalism also implies that constitutions are laid down in written documents and embody the unequivocal certainty of the supreme legal principles in one single and coherent text; that they are the supreme law of the land and hence obligate not only the executive branch of the government but the legislature as well; that they contain a bill of rights; and finally that they define the scope of admissible ends, means and strategies of individuals and groups pursuing their interests and realizing their values. However, none of these is an indispensable element of the idea of constitutionalism.

The most basic and original function of constitutionalism has been the limitation of power. Under certain circumstances this function has been extended into a device for power sharing between social forces, none of which has the strength to assert a monopoly of authority. Choosing social contracts over power sharing points to another function of constitutions, that of legitimizing the political authority. The power of the modern state requires a secular justification, which the constitution provides. Closely related to this is the integrative function of modern constitutions. Not all constitutions simultaneously perform all of these functions and neither do they always harmonize. In general it has been argued that constitutions that are very concerned with the problem of social integration tend to weaken their legitimizing function (Preuss 1995). Here, the situation of post-communist countries is particularly significant. These states have had to accomplish processes of nation building, constitution building and marketization of the economy simultaneously, while these processes have often been contradictory. Many of the states are also either internally heterogeneous, in that their populations contain representatives of several peoples, or externally heterogeneous, with the dominant part of the population being representatives of a people who also live in adjacent countries, and whose existence as a nation state is contested. Very often in these countries the constitution is an essential part of the simultaneous processes of nation building, of generating a market sphere, of establishing legality and the rule of law and of creating the main features of democratic rule. The existence of various alternatives clearly indicates that the quest for constitutionalism is a complex process. In post-Soviet Central Asia, including Kyrgyzstan, the process was further complicated by the fact that rules, institutions, social practices and cultural patterns had to be devised and anticipated in a written text. The aim was to simultaneously create the constitution itself and its most important prerequisites.

The framing of the constitution

Debate on the form that the constitution would assume is not new to Kyrgyzstan. A short summary of developments surrounding the adoption of Kyrgyzstan's first post-independence constitution, given below, reflects some of the major debates. During the immediate post-independence period one of the key points of contention was whether the parliament should remain unicameral or become bicameral. Another intensely debated issue was whether the electoral system required change.[2] Another concern of constitutional reform in the Kyrgyz Republic was its possible impact on the north–south divide within the country.[3] A new form of government together with a new electoral system could dramatically change the equation for political parties by providing them with seats in the parliament and redefining the way the country would be governed. The Constitutional Commission in the Parliament completed a draft constitution in October 1992. Here, the relations between executive and legislative agencies, along with some other issues like property rights, were subjects of heated discussion. President Akaev maintained that the balance of power had already been in favour of the legislature. He pointed out that if parliament approved the Constitutional Commission's draft, the government of the Republic would be turned into a puppet government ("Kyrgyz President criticizes…", in Gonenc 2002: 199). This version of the Constitution was rejected as a result of the disagreement between Akaev and the Kyrgyz Parliament. A new version of the draft was discussed in the December 1992 session of the Parliament, now renamed the *Jogorku Kenesh.*

After the adaptation of the constitution, debates centred on the relations between the executive and the legislature, language policies and privatization, particularly that of land (Gleason 2003). The draft version of the constitution that was favoured by Akaev provided for a presidential system with strong executive powers. The Parliament preferred the earlier draft of the constitution that had been in favour of a stronger legislature. Akaev argued that a parliamentary system would spell disaster for the country since it would encourage regional and clan divisions. As the economic situation deteriorated and the debate on the new constitution continued in the first half of 1993, Akaev asked the Parliament and the government to cooperate in completing the new constitution and turn to the economic problems being faced by the country (Brown 1993, in Gonenc 2002: 199).

Consequently, the Parliament completed the draft constitution. On 15 April 1993, in the course of a second reading of the draft, the Supreme Soviet stripped the President of some of the powers which had been approved in the first reading. As a result, Akaev threatened either to create a Constituent Assembly, or to call early presidential and parliamentary elections. The proposal to create a Constituent Assembly appealed to the liberal democratic opposition, which had been critical of the approval of the constitution by a parliament elected during the communist period. During the discussions, the opposition forces also criticized the draft on the ground that it granted too much power to the President and weakened the legislature. On the other hand, ethnic Russians articulated their demands concerning dual citizenship and granting Russian the same status as Kyrgyz. However, Kyrgyz was accepted as the state language and in the draft constitution there was no reference to Russian as an official language or language of inter-ethnic communication.[4] However, Akaev was able to persuade the Parliament to review its decision and recognize Russian as a language of inter-ethnic communication. The Supreme Soviet approved the draft constitution on 5

May 1993. This approval was the outcome of a compromise between the President and the Parliament. The new constitution came into effect on 5 May 1993, and established a presidential-parliamentary form of government where the head of the state and the highest legislative body both had fairly wide powers. The *Jogorku Kenesh* played an important role in forming the government and its structures and also identified the main trends in the country's domestic and foreign policies. The Parliament and the President had the right to submit the most important issues for referendum. The constitution created legal conditions in which the legislative and the executive branches could function independently (Gonenc 2002: 98–201, section on Kyrgyzstan).

It has been argued that at the beginning of the process of bargaining for a new constitution, three sets of actors dominated the negotiations. The first was President Akaev and his core advisors, the second were leaders from the Chui oblast (representing the northern oblasts) and third were the leaders from the Osh oblast (representing the southern oblasts) (Luong 2002: 156–188, section on Kyrgyzstan). However, attempts at liberalizing the political and economic system in Kyrgyzstan during the first years following independence created small openings for the inclusion of actors outside the set of established actors. Newly formed political parties were able to participate in politics to a far greater extent than before. However, the predominance of regional political cleavages continued to determine the formulation of institutional preferences. The central issue at stake was the existing balance of power both among the regions and between the regional and central governments. At the regional level, the concerns were about where the locus of political authority would lie. From the perspective of central leaders, the intensification of interregional political competition held the threat of leading to political instability. There was initially support for an electoral system that would elevate the status of political parties vis-à-vis regional leaders in nominating candidates, determining seats and supervising the electoral process. At the same time, party leaders were aware of their dependence on strong regional bases of popular support (Luong 2002).

At the time, there was contestation on four basic issues: the nomination of candidates, the selection and jurisdiction of the central- and district-level electoral commissions, the determination of seats and the structure of the parliament (Luong 2002). It has been argued that in its final form the electoral law primarily reflected the regional leaders' preferences – particularly those of the southern ones. While the central leaders did achieve some of their goals, their success came only with significant adjusting or complete abandonment of their preferred version of the electoral law to accommodate the northern and/or southern leaders. First of all, due to the strength of the opposition coming from the south, central leaders revoked their support for an electoral system based on proportional representation and even the use of party lists for a system where seats are determined according to population. Second, for both the nomination of candidates and the composition and jurisdiction of the Central Electoral Commission (CEC) and District Electoral Commission (DEC), central leaders and party leaders had to accept a much lesser role than they preferred because of the objections from northern and southern regional leaders. Finally, although central leaders ultimately succeeded in winning sufficient support for a bicameral parliament, even this was not achieved without garnering the support of the north and conceding to the south (Luong 2002). The process of negotiation that dominated the making of the constitution has been reflected through the entire process of changes that the constitution subsequently underwent. That the process was an ongoing one is reflected in the number of amendments through which the constitution has now attained its current form.

In December 1993, there was a crisis within the cabinet and in September 1994 the legislature dissolved itself. This allowed the President to suspend the constitution and in October 1994, Akaev announced a referendum to amend the constitution in order to establish a bicameral parliament. A bicameral parliament was elected in February 1995. In the course of the referendum, the Kyrgyz people approved 50 amendments to the 97 articles of the 1993 Constitution. The new version of the constitution granted more powers to the executive and tipped the balance of power in favour of the President. In December 1995, the nation went to the polls to elect the next President, in which Akaev won by an overwhelming majority. The post-election context proved to be different from the pre-election context and the new realignment of political forces led to another series of constitutional amendments. A national referendum on 10 February 1996 amended the constitution once again and expanded the powers of the President at the expense of the legislature (Pannier 1996a and 1996b, in Gonenc 2002: 201).

Amendments were again made to the Kyrgyz constitution in 1998 through a nation-wide referendum. These amendments were proposed by Akaev and they provided for the legislation of private land ownership, modification of the structure of the Parliament and the restriction of the Parliament's role in the legislative process, including drafting the budget. The deputies in the Kyrgyz Parliament rejected most of the President's proposals. The opposition and the bulk of the population particularly criticized the draft amendment introducing private land ownership and called for cancellation of the referendum. In return, Akaev defended the referendum, noting that farmers should feel that they are the masters of the land. The Kyrgyz people once again went to polls on 17 October 1998 to decide on the amendments proposed by the President. Of the 96.26 per cent of the voters who participated in the voting, 90.92 per cent of them voted in favour of the amendments. With the referendum the following changes were made: (1) private ownership of land was introduced, (2) approval of the government was required before Parliament's discussion of budget spending and (3) the number of deputies in the Legislative Assembly was changed from 35 to 67 and in the People's Assembly from 70 to 38. Apart from these changes, several regulations concerning the immunity of the deputies and their freedom of speech were introduced (Gonenc 2002).

Parliamentary elections were scheduled for February 2000. By this time, uneven social and economic developments created tensions in the state (Elebaeva and Pukhova 2007). In the interim, the party system within the state had also undergone transformations. The number of parties increased from 8 in early 1994 to 27 in late 1999, which called for amendments in the electoral system. The previously disunited opposition also showed signs of unification and in October 2000 about ten parties came together and formed the *People's Patriotic Movement*, which insisted on redistribution of powers in favour of the Parliament. To normalize the situation, the government agreed to grant certain concessions. In September 2002, a constitutional conference was convened to discuss a new version of the constitution. After the referendum of 2 February 2003, the Law on the New Version of the Constitution of the Kyrgyz Republic was adopted in February 2003 (Elebaeva and Pukhova 2007). In 2003, the number of political parties reached 43, yet all of them were small and lacked a broad social basis. Under the new version of the constitution the President retained his political domination (Elebaeva and Pukhova 2007).

Despite the ongoing process of negotiation that characterized the process of constitutionalism, regional discontent in the country continued. In spring 2002, thousands of people took to the streets in the south to protest against a controversial border pact with China and the jailing of an opposition parliamentarian, Azimbek Beknazarov. Clashes in the Aksy region and the public outcry that followed forced Prime Minister Kurmanbek Bakiev's government to resign in May 2002. It also brought to an end the efforts of the regime to unite the two regions under one authority. The resignation of the Prime Minister Bakiev, the symbolic representative of the south, in the aftermath of the event intensified the regional division leading up to the parliamentary elections in 2005. The largest protests in the early days of the post-election unrest in 2005 took place in the south. In March 2005, protests in Bishkek led to the resignation of the Prime Minister, while the President left the country, in the co-called "Tulip Revolution".

The politics of united fronts

In the post-Tulip Revolution period the quest for constitutionalism continued and eventually the 2007 Constitution was adopted. In January 2006, the opposition moved towards greater unity with a newly established *People's Coalition of Democratic Forces*, composed of 18 parties and movements. The new opposition insisted on further amendments to the constitution. In March 2006, President Kurmanbek Bakiev established a constitutional working group under Parliamentary Deputy Beknazarov (Elebaeva and Pukhova 2007). The working group drafted three new constitutions. However, the constitutional reform process was criticized as lacking transparency. There was also much critical discussion about insufficient public information on the complicated issue of the form of government. All constitutional amendments were mainly concerned with the redistribution of power between the two publicly elected bodies of presidency and parliament with regard to forming and dismissing the government and exercising legislative powers. The proposed constitution curtailed some of the powers of the President. It also stated that the *Jogorku Kenesh* would now have 90 members (a change from the earlier 75) who would be elected for five years. In a change from the previous constitution where all the members were elected in single member constituencies, half of the present parliamentarians were now to be elected on a proportional system and the other half on a single-member constituency basis. While proposing the draft bill on "changes and additions" to the constitution, it was suggested by the official representative of the constitutional working group that the new proposals aimed to create a mixed presidential-parliamentary form of government. Under the amended constitution the legislature would have greater powers, including the right to appoint the Prime Minister. It would also restrict the President's ability to dissolve the Parliament.

In the constitution, executive power is vested in the government and the Prime Minister is the head of the government. Unlike previous constitutions, the 2007 Constitution deprived the President of the right to preside over meetings of the government. However, it did allow the President to assign goals and objectives to the government. In other words, the President could at his discretion interfere with the work of the government. The authority of the government was vested in the Prime Minister; however, he depended on the President. The President could also suspend any government regulation, which was the case in the 2003 Constitution. Whereas the 1993 Constitution defined the authority of the Prime Minister in great detail, the 2003 and 2007 Constitutions do not mention the authority of the Prime Minister separately. The effective functioning of the state depends on the government and therefore it is important to know who dismisses the government. The main issue under debate focused on who would appoint the cabinet members and dismiss them from office. It is still not clear whether the government is responsible to the President or the Parliament. This is a potentially conflictual issue (Iskakova 2007a).

Gulnara Iskakova argued that in the 2007 Constitution, the President is the ultimate approval authority for dismissing the government. According to her, the constitution introduced a shift from a semi-presidential form, as was the case in 1993, to a presidential-parliamentary one in 2007 (Iskakova 2007a). She elaborated that in the 1993 Constitution the government was dependent on the confidence of the *Jogorku Kenesh*. While the President could dismiss some members of the government, it was the Parliament that had the power to dismiss the entire government. In the 2003 and 2007 Constitutions, however, the President could discharge the government provided that he accepted a petition for resignation submitted by the Prime Minister, or the *Jogorku Kenesh* adopted a vote of no confidence against the government. The President would then concur if the *Jogorku Kenesh* passed another vote of no confidence against the government within three months, in which case the President had the discretion either to dismiss the government or to dissolve the Parliament. Iskakova further noted that the 1993 and 2007 Constitutions also differ with regard to forming the government. Some drawbacks of the 2003 Constitution were removed from the 2007 Constitution. For example, according to the 2003 Constitution a juridical entity to form the government was a political party. According to the 2007 Constitution, it is the members of the Parliament who have the power to form the government.

According to this Constitution, the President appoints the Prime Minister, who is proposed by the members of Parliament who belong to a political party that has over 50 per cent seats in *Jogorku Kenesh*. If there is no such party, or if the members of parliament fail to propose a candidate for the position of Prime Minister, or if the Prime Minister fails to propose the structure of the government, then the President has the power to assign this power to other members of Parliament from other political parties. Failing this, the President also has the power to dissolve the *Jogorku Kenesh*.

Compared to the 1993 Constitution, the 2003 and 2007 Constitutions gave the President wider powers in the appointment and dismissal of governmental bodies and officials like the Chamber of Control, the Chamber of Accounts, the Central Electoral and Referendum Commission, the Constitutional Court, the Supreme Court and the Arbitration Court. Executive power is vested in the government headed by the Prime Minister, while legislative power is vested in the Parliament. However, different branches wield authority for the purpose of checks and balances (Iskakova 2007a).[5] Thus, the President may enjoy some legislative powers as well. All previous constitutions conferred the following power on the President: the right to initiate legislation, the right to adopt edicts and the right not to sign a draft law adopted by *Jogorku Kenesh* and send it back with objections. If the *Jogorku Kenesh* disagrees with the President, it has to adopt it with two-thirds vote. In addition, the President has the power to schedule a referendum on any issue, except making amendments to the constitution, in which case he needs the consent of 60 per cent of the members of the Parliament. It must also be pointed out that overriding the presidential veto is difficult and decisions on budgetary issues, normally considered to be within the realm of legislatures, are vested in the government rather than the Parliament. However, now the President does not have wide authority for dissolving Parliament and he cannot adopt edicts having the power of law. Also, the Parliament no longer delegates its legislative authority to the President.[6] Thus, it has been argued that while the constitution does offer prospects for more accountable government, the political situation within the state may undermine the reform. The constitution was signed into law by President Bakiev on 9 November 2006. As the constitution was a compromise between the authorities and the opposition forces, it appeared as a peaceful alternative for the resolution of conflictual issues. The *Jogorku Kenesh*, however, did not approve the new constitution and the Kyrgyz government resigned on 19 December 2006. Felix Kulov argued that the resignation was realized to accelerate the holding of parliamentary elections made necessary by changes to the structure of Parliament. On 30 December 2006, the parliament changed the constitution once again, returning previous powers to the President. In January 2007, the Parliament denied Kulov the position of Prime Minister and President Bakiev chose Azim Isabekov to head the new government. The new cabinet that was formed under Prime Minister Azim Isabekov existed for less than a month. Azim Isabekov was chosen as he was close to Bakiev, ignoring the claims of Felix Kulov. It is suggested that this was also a tactic for splitting the opposition and keeping power with the President. A number of opposition members joined Isabekov's cabinet. However, the negotiations between the President and the opposition forces influenced the realignment of these forces (IPP 2009).

While these are only some of the formal changes proposed in the constitution, it is also significant to take into account certain political developments that followed these changes. Here, the politics of united fronts played an important role. For example, Felix Kulov's united front *For a Decent Future of Kyrgyzstan* attempted to organize a transfer of power by putting pressure on President Bakiev and forcing him to hold early presidential elections. However, the situation was complicated by the fact that Kulov was rejected as the Prime Minister twice. The creation of the united front *For a Decent Future of Kyrgyzstan* restructured the political process. Another movement, *For Reforms*, which had organized the opposition rallies, split up and a group of politicians decided to quit the movement because they were both unwilling to support Felix Kulov and were opposed to his views on forcing President Bakiev to resign before his term expired. The movement insisted on constitutional reforms and not just another change of regime. This group, led by Almaz Atabaev, Azimbek Beknazarov, Roza Otunbaeva and Edil Baisalov, set up a new movement called *For United Kyrgyzstan.* However, there was very little unity on various issues among the politicians who joined this new front and many of them were not willing to see Felix Kulov as the head of the coalition government (IPP 2007).

A number of opposition politicians were invited to join the new cabinet by President Bakiev who had begun negotiations with the moderate opposition in the middle of March 2007 after the *For United Kyrgyzstan* and the *For Reforms* movement had set dates for rallies. In the meantime two trends had developed within these two fronts. Both were geared towards putting pressure on the President by the threat of mass rallies. However, part of the opposition thought that it was necessary to enter into a negotiation process to press President Bakiev into making possible concessions. These included changes to the constitution, which would restore provisions in the November 2007 Constitution, forming a new cabinet involving the opposition and transforming the national TV Corporation into a public network. Another opposition faction refused to take part in negotiations with the President and insisted on advancing early presidential elections as its principle demand. It was expected that the new President would make the rest of the changes. Besides the shifts in cabinet and the creation of new opposition movements the issue of Kyrgyz entry into the Heavily Indebted Poor Countries (HIPC) Initiative also aggravated political tension in the country and a discussion involving all the political forces unfolded around the HIPC issue. Being a mechanism for international debt relief providing assistance to the world's poorest countries, the HICP Initiative had been launched at the G7 Summit in Paris in 1996, following a proposal from the World Bank and the IMF. A broad political dialogue between the President and the members of the opposition, primarily Almaz Atambaev, became another important process. The negotiations influenced the alignment of political forces in Kyrgyzstan. Talks between a part of the opposition and the authorities highlighted the split in the opposition's attitude towards President Bakiev and the role of the President as the main political force. In November 2007, *For Reforms* organized a demonstration to bring changes to the constitution that had been ignored by the Bakiev government since the Tulip revolution. It has been argued that, in the course of the week-long protests that followed, the government's inability to deal with mass demonstration became clearly evident (Marat 2008).

It has been suggested that the main trend for the immediate future of Kyrgyzstan was a change in the layout of the political arena where new political centres were being created (IPP 2007). Three such groups can be identified. The first was a politically transformed parliament where a new structure of influence formed by party factions would be created. This put the issue of forming a new parliament from party lists on the agenda. The possible outcome of the process would be self-dissolution of the Parliament with subsequent parliamentary elections according to new rules in autumn of 2007 or spring of 2008. The second was a bloc of politicians in the executive who were independent of the President. Their position and desire to change current cabinet relations with the President would intensify the conflict between the President and the cabinet. A third group was the non-governmental organizations and local civil society groups which remained vibrant in Kyrgyzstan.

A further dimension has recently been added to the debate with the proposal of the former Kyrgyz Prime Minister and opposition leader Felix Kulov for Russia and Kyrgyzstan to enter into a confederation (Blagov 2007). Kulov has suggested in the opposition *Agym* newspaper that a confederation with Russia would offer Kyrgyzstan a way out of two persistent problems: friction between the northern and southern parts of the country and economic malaise. Kulov warned that Kyrgyzstan faces the possibility of sectional breakup if it continues on its present political course, though he also added as a caveat that the union would only function on condition that Kyrgyzstan retained its national sovereignty and statehood. Russian experts and politicians have reacted to the proposal with muted scepticism. However, it has also been noted that such a union could bring Moscow certain strategic benefits.

On 14 September 2007, Kyrgyzstan's Constitutional Court annulled the constitutional reforms endorsed by the Parliament in November and December 2006. The Court recognized only the constitutional changes made in February 2003 as a result of a national referendum. According to the Court, by endorsing both the November and December Constitutions, the Parliament exceeded its capacities because constitutional changes can only be made as a result of a referendum. Accordingly, President Bakiev held a referendum on 21 October 2007 on the constitutional amendments. A change in electoral law was also proposed from the first-past-the-post system to party-list voting. There were two separate questions asked in the referendum. One asked for approval of the new constitution and the other asked for approval of the new electoral law. About 75 per cent of the voters approved the changes, with an official turnout of 80 per cent. Following the referendum, President Bakiev called for early elections in December 2007 (Marat 2007).

The 16 December 2007 elections were held under a new election system, including new provisions for translating votes into seats. This required voters to pass two separate thresholds determined as percentages of all registered voters nationwide. It was perceived that the system could defeat the objective of proportional representation and might lead to an endless cycle of elections despite assertions that it aimed to stabilize the country. The *Ak Zhol Eldik Party* of President Bakiev won 71 of the 90 seats with 46.99 per cent of votes. The *Social Democratic Party of Kyrgyzstan* won 11 seats and the *Party of Communists of Kyrgyzstan* won eight seats. The new members of the Kyrgyz cabinet took the oath of office on 10 January 2008 and the President emphasized the fact that the newly elected leaders should now concentrate on measures to stimulate economic growth ("Kyrgyz President Addresses..." 2008).

The elections, however, elicited criticism from the opposition and were termed as a "serious retreat from democracy", as described by the former Foreign Minister Roza Otunbaeva. The main reason for the lingering discontent was that the *Ata Meken Party*, the largest opposition force in the country, could not be represented in the Parliament, even though it had 8.3 per cent of the votes nationwide. Election authorities justified the exclusion on the fact that the *Ata Meken Party* did not clear an electoral threshold in the southern Osh region. The potential problems of keeping the main opposition party unrepresented in the Parliament have also been brought to the forefront. In the aftermath of the elections, a new opposition bloc, *For Justice Movement* created an "alternative parliament" that included the *Ata Meken Party* and the *Ar-Namys Party*. A number of other civil groups also joined this new movement. The "alternative parliament" convened in February 2008 and empowered itself to discuss and propose alternative viewpoints on the most important issues relating to the country's public, political and economic life. The present split with the upcoming presidential elections has been characterized as a "civilizational" one, with "traditional" society calling for a powerful authority while "civil" society strives for democratization ("Mars Sariev..." 2009). The opposition selected Almazbek Atambaev of the *Social Democratic Party* as its candidate. President Bakiev won the elections with 78 per cent of the votes going in his favour.

However, during the winter of 2009–2010, Kyrgyzstan regularly suffered from blackouts and electricity cut-offs while energy prices rose. There were sporadic protests over the rising prices of fuel but also over issues like the continuing US presence in the country. In April 2010 Russia imposed duties on energy exports to Kyrgyzstan claiming that a customs union between Russia, Belarus and Kazakhstan had compelled it to do so. This influenced fuel and transport prices and led to massive protests in Talas on 6 April. Two prominent opposition leaders, Omurbek Tekebayev and Almazbek Atambayev, were arrested by Kyrgyz authorities. This was followed by protests in Bishkek where hundreds of protesters gathered in the *Ala Too* Square and then surrounded the White House. On 7 April demonstrators took over the parliament building and opposition leaders announced the formation of a new government. Soon thereafter, there were reports that President Bakiev had left Bishkek for Osh. In addition to Bishkek and Talas, rallies and protests were held in Naryn, Tokmok and Issyk-Kul.

The interim government headed by Roza Otunbaeva announced that it would hold on to power for six months. However, Bakiev refused to resign and tension mounted in the country. On 20 April, the Belarusian President offered Bakiev and three members of his family asylum and Bakiev departed from southern Kyrgyzstan with some members of his family. However, he continued to insist that as the elected President he still held constitutional power in Kyrgyzstan. Unfortunately, Bakiev's departure from southern Kyrgyzstan was the signal for the beginning of ethnic tension in the region. Clashes between Kyrgyz and Uzbeks in Osh and Jalalabad brought into question not just the tradition of ethnic co-existence in the various regions of Kyrgyzstan but also the validity of the constitutional process and systems of governance in the country.

The immediate cause of the events of April 2010 was without doubt a worsening of the economic situation and subsequent price rises in the country. However, they were also influenced by a lack of confidence in the government, fuelled by allegations of corruption against members of the President's family and his close associates. These allegations included the fact that the violence in Osh was motivated and financed by a desire to delay the referendum process on the new constitution that would seek to institutionalize a system of proportional representation and reduce the powers of the President. Much of the attention therefore reverted to the constitutional process in the country with the expectation that the new constitution would put the country on a firm footing and end the violence in the south.[7] The interim government conducted discussions on the new constitution, which would limit the power of the President. The constitution was an attempt to balance the legislative and executive powers by creating two strong positions, that of the Prime Minister and of the President and leaving the balance between the two to be worked out in practice. The President still enjoys veto power except in matters related to budget and fiscal policy. The new constitution also broadens the base of power sharing by increasing Parliamentary seats from 90 to 120. However, a novelty was introduced by limiting the maximum number of seats that a party can hold to 65. In theory this ceiling still allows a single party to hold a majority. However, given the fact that defection among the deputies is frequent, in reality it would mean that coalitions become necessary.

The new constitution also does away with a constitutional court, so that all disputes over the interpretation of the constitution will be handled by the Supreme Court. This is different from most parliamentary systems where there is clear separation of powers between the legislature, executive and judiciary. Part of this was of course necessitated by the fact that the Constitutional Court had not played an active role in Kyrgyzstan and allowed the President to consolidate his power. Other key provisions of the constitution follow standard practice and are in agreement with the recommendations of the Venice Commission.[8] Following the outbreak of violence in the south, several parties that had initially been positive about the referendum altered their stance and called for the postponement of the referendum or achieving legitimacy through other means. These parties included the Party of Communists of Kyrgyzstan, *Akyikat* (Justice) and *Zamandash* (Contemporary). The government, however, was keen on an electoral mandate in the face of ethnic unrest and political turmoil. The referendum became necessary not just to legitimize the government within the state, but also within an increasingly critical international community. This also meant that the participation of the Uzbeks in the referendum was seen as essential. As a result, virtually all of those who had fled to Uzbekistan were encouraged to return in time for the voting. The nationwide referendum on 27 June 2010 approved the new constitution and also the name of Roza Otunbaeva as the interim President by 90 per cent, with about 72 per cent of the population participating in the referendum.[9]

In October 2010, parliamentary elections were organized according to the new constitution. According to the system of proportional distribution the five winning parties that received more than 5 per cent of the votes divided the shares of the 22 parties that failed to cross the 5 per cent mark. The Kyrgyz nationalist opposition party, *Ata Zhurt*, which has strong support in the South, led with about 9 per cent of the votes and 28 seats. The pro-government *Social Democratic Party* was in second place with just over 8 per cent of the votes and 26 seats. In the third place was the pro-Russian *Ar-Namys Party* headed by the former Prime Minister Felix Kulov with 25 seats. *Respublika* had about 7 per cent of the votes and 23 seats. *Ata Meken* had 18 seats. Although the *Ata Zhurt Party* was the clear winner, it formed a coalition with the *Ar-Namys Party* and remained in opposition. Both the parties expressed scepticism about the constitutional changes and expressed the opinion that power should remain with the President. The government was formed by the *Social Democrats*, *Ata Meken* and *Respublika*, who have 67 seats in the Parliament. Almazbek Atambayev has been the Prime Minister since December 2010.[10]

Conclusion

The accelerated pace of regime change in the post-Soviet space between 2003 and 2005 redefined notions about political transformation in the Soviet successor states. It also brought to the forefront a phenomenon starting with the dissatisfaction of a large number of citizens with the electoral process and their government's interference in the process, leading to mass rallies and ending with the opposition leaders coming to power (Tastenov 2007).[11] In March 2005, in the course of a series of events that echoed this pattern, President Askar Akaev and his government were overthrown after widespread accusations about mismanagement of parliamentary elections in February and March 2005. Kurmanbek Bakiev was appointed as interim President. Akaev formally resigned as President on 4 April 2005 and in the subsequent presidential election in July 2005 Bakiev was elected as the new President of the country. In its early stages, this development had been variously referred to as the "Pink", "Lemon", "Silk", "Daffodil" or "Sandpaper" revolution by various opposition groups and commentators. But it was the "Tulip Revolution", a term used by Akaev himself that became the most commonly used term. The terminology of the revolution evoked similarities with the "Rose Revolution" in Georgia and the "Orange Revolution" in Ukraine in 2004. The political and constitutional crises in Kyrgyzstan revealed a clear need for constitutional reform.

It has been argued that the real challenge before Kyrgyzstan is to develop institutions and practices that would uphold the values of the constitution. In any case, reservations have already been expressed about the functioning of a parliamentary system in the post-Soviet space. Therefore, one of the major issues debated during and after the revolution was the question of constitutional change and this has remained at the forefront of political discourse in the Kyrgyz Republic, particularly following the events of April and June 2010. The country's leadership has been locked in the old and familiar debate on dividing power between the President, Government and Parliament and has concentrated on finding a balance between central state institutions via amendments to the constitution. This remains a complicated process, particularly since the quest for constitutionalism presents numerous alternatives. The new 2010 Constitution attempts to resolve some of these issues by putting into place a system where executive power is balanced by legislative responsibilities.

This chapter has been an attempt to examine the events surrounding March 2005 or the "Tulip Revolution" in terms of the constitutional changes that either followed the events or fell short of the mark, culminating in the constitution of June 2010. Here, of course, a number of institutional and local factors played certain roles that have been documented and debated in a series of writings after the revolution.[12] It has been generally concluded that the aims which motivated the events of March 2005 were complex and varied and are still in the process of being resolved. One of the most significant motives, of course, was related to representation and power sharing. The Kyrgyz election just prior to the March 2005 events is generally identified as the casue of the events of March 2005. Therefore, the significance of arriving at a better understanding of constitutional processes cannot be overemphasized. As was suggested earlier, constitutionalism essentially suggests the idea of a limited government by establishing a balance between individual powers. The chapter emphasized that the various changes that the Kyrgyz constitution underwent were attempts at finding the best form of this balance within the political system. It is reasonable to assume that this will be an ongoing process, particularly since the party that won the largest share of votes is actually opposed to a change in the nature of the political system and has become a part of the opposition. The Venice Commission reflected this in its concluding remarks when it noted that the draft of the constitution "reflects the intention of the drafters to arrive at a better balance between the powers of the main state organs, strengthening both Parliament and the Government and the rule of law and human rights" (ECDTL 2005).

Notes

1 See for instance Ryabkov (2008). Ryabkov, however, rejects the hypothesis that the north tends to support the opposition and the south supports the President, arguing

instead that the north is more pessimistic in general about state and non-state institutions.

2 These two points remain significant even today after six amendments to the constitution. However, there is also acceptance of the fact that constitutions by themselves cannot ensure compliance by all branches of the government. It is the functioning of the political system that provides guarantees that the government will respect the constitution.

3 The Kyrgyz are divided between the rich north and the poorer south. Politically the most influential groups came from the Chu Valley and the Naryn region in the north. In the later Soviet period Usubaliev, a Sarybagysh from the Sary-Bagysh kin grouping inhabiting the Chu valley, headed the Kyrgyz SSR for nearly two decades. During *perestroika* Masaliev from the southern town Osh replaced him, ignoring the opposition from the Sarybagysh. Masaliev was replaced with Akaev who enjoyed the support of the Sarybagysh group. This division of political influence requires a permanent search for compromises. Akaev was a northerner and the opposition to his leadership came from the south.

4 The current Kyrgyz Constitution accepts Russian as an official language.

5 See a number of comments and opinions on the 2007 Kyrgyz constitution in the European Commission for Democracy through Law (Venice Commission) (ECDTL 2007). See also Gulnara Iskakova (2007).

6 See Constitution of Kyrgyz Republic: New Wordings as Approved by Referendum on October 21, 2007 www.venice.coe.int/does/2007/CDL(2007)124-e.asp.

7 However, doubts have been expressed over the success of the constitutional process having an effect on the stability of the state. See, for instance, Shermatova (2011).

8 The final text of the Constitution was published on 20 May. For the full text, see "Novaya Konstitustiya..." (2010).

9 For details see "Novosti..." (2010).

10 The coalition government and particularly the members of the newly constituted Cabinet have already been criticized as not inspiring confidence. See, for instance, Ageeva (2010).

11 For a detailed study of the causes of the colour revolutions see Tastenov (2007).

12 The *Central Asian Survey* devoted an entire special issue to this in 2008.

References

Ageeva, E. (2010) "Kirgizstan: Chto za KADRom? Deputaty 'slepili' Kabinet Ministrov [Kyrgyzstan: What's behind the Camera? Deputies 'Sculpting' Cabinet Ministers]", *Fergana.ru*, 21 December.

Blagov, S. (2007) "Moscow Gives Cool reception to Kyrgyz Russian Confederation Proposal", *Eurasia Insight*, 11 June.

Brown, B. (1993) "Akaev Appeals for Cooperation between Legislature and Government", *OMRI Daily Digest*, 17 February.

Cummings, S.N. and Ryabkov, M. (2008) "Situating the 'Tulip' Revolution", *Central Asian Survey*, 27/3–4: 241–252.

Elebaeva, A. and Pukhova, M. (2007) "Political Transformations in Kyrgyzstan 1991–2006", *Central Asia and the Caucasus*, 2/44: 67–78.

ECDTL (European Commission for Democracy through Law) (2005) Opinion No. 342/2005, *Interim Opinion on Constitutional Reform in the Kyrgyz Republic*, 64th Plenary Session, Venice, 21–22 October, on the basis of comments by Mr Kestutis Lapinskas and Mr Anders Fogelklou.

ECDTL (European Commission for Democracy through Law) (2007) Comments and opinions on Kyrgyz Constitution. Online. Available: www.venice.coe.int/does/2007/CDL(2007)124-e.asp (accessed 15 July 2007).

Gleason, G. (2003) *Markets and Politics in Central Asia: Structural Reform and Political Change*, London and New York: Routledge.

Gonenc, L. (2002) *Prospects for Constitutionalism in Post-Communist Countries*, Leiden: Martinus Nijhoff.

Iskakova, G. (2007) "Constitutional Reform and Powers of the Highest Government Bodies in Kyrgyzstan: A New Balance", *Kyrgyzstan Brief*, No. 8, January/February.

Iskakova, G. (2007a) "Constitutional Reform in Kyrgyzstan: How Can a Hastily Adopted Constitution Affect the Development of the Country?" *Public Speaker Series*, Social Science Research Centre, American University of Central Asia, Bishkek, 31 January. Online. Available: www.src.auca.kg.

IPP (Institute for Public Policy) (2007) *Analysis of Political Events in Kyrgyzstan for January–April*, Bishkek.

IPP (Institute for Public Policy) (2009) *Analysis of Political Events in Kyrgyzstan, January–April*, 7 May. Online. Available: www.ipp.kg/en/analysis/390.

"Kyrgyz President Addresses First Session of New Parliament", Kyrgyz Daily Digest, *Eurasianet* (11 January 2008). Online. Available: http://digest@eurasianet.org.

"Kyrgyz President Criticises Republic's New Draft Constitution", *SWB*, SU/1548 B/9–10, 26 November 1992.

Lewis, D. (2008) "The Dynamics of Regime Change: Domestic and International Factors in the 'Tulip' Revolution", *Central Asian Survey*, 27/3–4: 265–277.

Luong, P.J. (2002) *Institutional Change and Political Continuity in Post-Soviet Central Asia: Power, Perceptions and Pacts*, Cambridge: Cambridge University Press.

Marat, E. (2007) "Parties Mobilize for Parliamentary Elections in Kyrgyzstan", *Eurasia Daily Monitor*, 4/179, 27 September.

Marat, E. (2008) "March and After: What has Changed? What has Stayed the Same?", *Central Asian Survey*, 27/3–4: 229–240.

"Mars Sariev: Civilization Split Comes on against Presidential Election", *Bishkek News Agency 24.kg*, 19 March 2009. Online. Available: http://eng.24.kg/politics/2009/03/19/7442.html (accessed 19 March 2009).

"Novaya Konstitutsiya Kirgizstana Zhdet Svoevo Referenduma [New Constitution of Kyrgyzstan Waiting to be put to Referendum]", *Fergana.ru*, 21 May 2010.

"Novosti Tsentralnoi Azii, Kirgizstan [News from Central Asia: Kyrgyzstan]", *Fergana.ru*, 2 July 2010.

Pannier, B. (1996a) "Referendum Called for Amendments to Constitution in Kyrgyzstan", *OMRI Daily Digest*, 4 January.

Pannier, B. (1996b) "Kyrgyzstan Set for Referendum on Akaev's Powers", *OMRI Daily Digest*, 9 February.

Preuss, U.K. (1995) "Patterns of Constitutional Evolution and Change in Eastern Europe", in J.J. Hesse and N. Johnson (eds) *Constitutional Policy and Change in Europe*, London: Oxford University Press.

Ryabkov, M. (2008) "The North-South Cleavage and Political Support in Kyrgyzstan", *Central Asian Survey*, 27/3–4: 301–316.

Shermatova, S. (2011) "Razdvoeniye Kirgizii [Division of Kyrgyzstan into Two]", *Fergana.ru*, 8 February.

Tastenov, A. (2007) "The Color Revolution Phenomenon: From Classical Theory to Unpredictable Practices", *Central Asia and the Caucasus*. Online. Available: www.ca-c.org/online/2007/journal-eng/cac-01/04/taseng.shtml (accessed 20 March 2007).

Temirkulov, A. (2008) "Informal Actors and Institutions in Mobilization: The Periphery in the Tulip Revolution", *Central Asian Survey*, 27/3–4: 317–335.

Part II
Identity

4 "Circle of trust"

Functions and mechanisms of patron–client relations in the private farm

Aksana Ismailbekova

Introduction

With the disintegration of the Soviet Union in 1991, Kyrgyzstan has pursued a programme of economic reform designed to transform the centrally planned economy to one based on market principles. A successful transition to a market economy in Kyrgyzstan would depend in large part on the implementation of reforms in the agricultural sector and in rural areas. Despite considerable progress with land reform and farm restructuring since 1991, the achievements fall short of original expectations of the international donors. In other words, although collective farms were dismantled and land was privatized "agricultural transformation has not produced a quick increase in production because most land remains in collective ownership; most peasants prefer to remain in the safety of large cooperatives" (Csaki and Lerman 1997: 428). Despite the reorganization of collective farms into small cooperatives, most of the villagers still do not know how to use land in a sustainable and effective way and they lack knowledge on how to exist in a market economy producing for national and international markets. People in rural areas remain poor and young people continue to migrate to urban areas or Russia in search of better opportunities. Furthermore, as local services are inefficient, people make contact with local entrepreneurs in order to make ends meet. This chapter specifically focuses on the unique "*kolkhoz*" case that is reshaped after the destruction of collective farms and their reorganization into small entities.

In this chapter, the internal dynamics of the new private farm and its significance for local people in Kyrgyzstan are analysed with a specific focus on the question of why the new workers are seen by those outside of the farm as suspicious, untrustworthy and strange. Is it merely an expression of the conflict surrounding the dissolution of the former *kolkhoz* and the emergence of the new private farm? Or are local people correct in their perception that the new farm management is disorganized and fraught with internal competition? I shall argue that the management of the new private farm constitutes a kind of "space" which seems to be disorganized, insofar as it does not conform to conventional notions of business administration, but which has its own internal logic and, thus, is accessible to ethnographic description. I unravel the basis of the patron's authority, the manipulative strategies that he employs, and the struggles of clients, as they attempt to pursue their own ends, while maintaining or augmenting their favourable position in the eyes of the patron. In doing this, I concentrate on what probably will prove to be an ephemeral moment in the history of the region, a moment characterized by patron–client relations that are inherently neither forced nor voluntary, but intersubjectively constructed.

I further explore the conditions under which patron–client relations are generated and sustained, first, by showing how the *kolkhoz* was transformed into a private enterprise and, second, by looking at the conditions and interpersonal relations within the new enterprise, specifically at the dynamics of patron–client relations as they emerge and continue to transform. Such conditions and relations correspond to idealized models neither of collective farms nor of private agricultural enterprises; rather, in the uneven transformation from one system to another, makeshift organizational forms have emerged, which are in some ways continuous with earlier Soviet experiences. The new enterprise becomes a setting in which cooperative action results from informal relations among actors with various aims and intentions.[1] Despite the diversity and complexity of social relations, the common interests that bind clients are the resources in which they are all interested and over which they all compete.[2] I argue that the actors pursue their own ends by developing certain strategies that are suitable under the harsh conditions of a situation in which their options and expectations are limited. They also accept the flexible and ambiguous rules of the farm, manipulate "kinship" ties as well as information about their background and qualifications, and engage in "exchange", which they employ as a kind of "starting mechanism". Thus emerge the very ambiguous and diffuse characteristics of patron–client relations, which combine moral and instrumentally manipulative action, allowing actors to accommodate to a wide range of situations. However, conflicts are likely to occur when "shared" resources are selectively distributed among a few clients. In such a competitive situation, actors' strategies for access to resources include disguised processes of exclusion and inclusion; for example, denouncing others for their shortcomings and aligning oneself with those who do not contradict one's own interests. However, patronage itself is not static or unchanging; rather, it is an ongoing process which demands the creative engagement of actors who constantly reconstruct or reorganize their social relations, once their aims are achieved. As I shall show in the following parts, the patron–client system emerges under particular conditions and takes different forms.

The setting

Before turning to the private farms and their internal power relations, it is necessary to provide background information about the field site. Orlovka, a small village in Kara-Balta *raion*, is located in the northern part of Kyrgyzstan. It is a semi-rural area, approximately 28 kilometres away from the capital, Bishkek. According to the local village administration documents, a "population of 4,510 to 6,000 people has arisen around Orlovka (1993–2004) and 60 per cent of the population consists of Kyrgyz ethnic groups, 40 per cent consists of representatives of other ethnic groups." This village was ethnically German during the Soviet era; however, many residents emigrated to Germany after the collapse of the Soviet Union. There are two adjacent villages to Orlovka, Bistrovka and Rot-Front. Orlovka is linked to the town of Kemin, one of the large-scale industrial centres of Chui valley, with the largest cement-tile factory, a sugar refinery and a brewery company. Moreover, due to the mass out-migration of Germans, many opportunities were opened up for people from remoter regions [*priezzhie*] (such as cheap houses with basic facilities, gas, electricity and water, as well as access to main or important roads and markets). As a result, the village became a heterogeneous place with complex social relations and life styles. In spite of its relatively small size, the village is a dynamic place with several stores, a small cafe, retail kiosks, a school and a hotel. The majority of the residents are employed at the local factories in Kemin, and these factories export cement, slate and beverage products (beer, lemonade and wine) to neighbouring countries. Thus, one can conclude that this village is neither peripheral nor central; rather, periphery and centre intersect in this semi-rural area where there are diverse opportunities from business to cattle breeding. The soil is fertile and supplied with water. The temperate climate and favourable conditions yield harvests in abundance (*Chuy Encyclopedia* 1998).

Reorganization of the collective farm

It is important to keep in mind that a *kolkhoz* during the Soviet time was a social microhabitat based on self-management, collectivism and subordination; in other words, a *kolkhoz* was a "total social factor" (Verdery 1996). However, collectivization led to tens of thousands of Kyrgyz moving to western China in the 1930s. The *kolkhozes*, headed by a political officer (usually a Slav) had to comply with the demands of crop rotation imposed by the mechanism of central planning. Members of a *kolkhoz* were subject to strict regulations, norms and principles. A considerable number of these rules and regulations concerned *kolkhoz* workers, their position in a family, behaviour in public places, and rights and duties in relation to children and men. This social microhabitat in the *kolkhoz* was one of the most basic institutions which had reproduced Soviet ideology (Humphrey 1998). However, the emergence of the *kolkhoz* in Kyrgyzstan was a result of the complex processes of collectivization between 1927 and 1932, destruction of herds and famine. Thus, as a result of a long history and attachment of people to their *kolkhoz*, the villagers decided to stay together and cosmetically reorganize the collective farm into a joint agriculture enterprise (*kooperativnoe khozyaistvo*; the change in name also being a slight one, from *kollektivnoe khozyaistvo*, "collective enterprise"). The previous name of the *kolkhoz* "Trud" (meaning "labour" in Russian) has been changed into "*Emgek*" (meaning "labour" in Kyrgyz), but other than this change, the unit itself remained as a collective farm until 2006. However, individuals who wanted to leave the farm had a right to withdraw from the farmland and property[3] (including livestock). However, during my field research I was told that none of the *kolkhoz* workers had withdrawn their land shares from the farm. In other words, the farm's land is divided on paper into individual shares (about one hectare), but in reality people kept their lands within the general administration of the farm. The private farm has maintained the Soviet type of organization, as everywhere else in the other post-Soviet countries (Nikulin 2003; Zanca 2000) in terms of its internal structure, policy and language.[4]

Emergence of the privately owned enterprise

Right after the privatization policies were put into effect in 1993, the administrators of the village Orlovka had to slaughter and sell 200–300 cattle due to high prices for lubricants, spare parts, seeds, material and electricity in order to keep the *kolkhoz* economy alive and to survive. The high costs of maintaining a kindergarten, bakery and a cultural house were also prohibitive. Since 1994, this *kolkhoz* had a huge debt of one million *som* (€1 is 50 *som*) and was suffering from massive losses,[5] so the distribution of common property was not possible. Finally, due to limited options, the only possible way was to sell the *kolkhoz* for the sake of those who were able to remain there. The difficult task was to find a purchaser who would buy the *kolkhoz* in spite of the complicated bureaucratic procedures. The former *kolkhoz* chairman had to find a purchaser and sell the *kolkhoz*. When the chairman finally found a prospective purchaser in 2005, he also had to convince him to buy the *kolkhoz* by demonstrating its prospects and opportunities. As the chairman said, he had provided many options in case the client wanted to increase his status and authority in the village because of his ambitious plans in the future to be a deputy of the Kyrgyz Republic. If not, then the purchaser would not lose a "cent" from buying the *kolkhoz*, since it could easily justify his expenditure if he decided to sell it in the future. However, it is important to mention here that the purchaser would buy only the non-land assets, such as buildings (house of culture, garages, gas storage, water supply, repair shops, barns), machinery (tractors, lorries, combine-harvester), fuel and livestock (cows and horses). In order to buy the farm, the purchaser had to pay money for the property share of the farm because workers and pensioners of the collective farm have the right to a share of the non-land assets (property share) of the enterprise. According to the law, the size of each recipient's property share is determined by the length and the nature of his or her service on the farm, such that higher salaried and longer-working recipients receive larger shares.[6] But the former chairman decided to sell the property without taking into consideration the length and nature of the workers' service on the farm. This way, he wanted to sell the shares of non-land assets for the workers (including himself) who worked at the farm between 1994 and 2004 (during this time he actively worked) and thereby to get the money from the farm property into their pockets. Moreover, due to massive out-migration of Germans, many opportunities were created for people from more remote provinces, such as cheap houses with basic facilities of gas, electricity and water, as well as access to main or important roads and markets. As a result, the village became a heterogeneous place with complex social relations and lifestyles. In this process, the chairman convinced younger workers to take his side and promised them a reasonable offer. For him, it was crucial to increase the number of his supporters. When it was time to divide the *kolkhoz* and distribute shares in cash, disputes emerged among three groups: local workers with many years of experience, the farm workers who came after the Germans and the administrators of the *kolkhoz*. The reason why this last group was interested in the disintegration of the *kolkhoz* was because of their expectation of personal benefit from this property. Since many of the *kolkhoz* workers were Germans, their shares made up the greater part of the total share (63 per cent). To that end, the ex-chairman of the *kolkhoz* wanted to divide it among the people by hiding the total shares that had been allocated to the Germans, claiming that these shares were taken by the state fund. In this situation, people would get less, without even recognizing that they were deceived. The *kolkhoz* headman and other state officials wanted to assert private claims over the *kolkhoz* properties under their control from which they would seek to obtain personal profit through the illegal transfer of rights over it. However, the local workers and pensioners demanded that the farm property shares be distributed according to the law (length and nature of service) and they decided to involve the legal authorities to solve their problem. Only with the involvement of legal authorities was it accepted that the *kolkhoz* was to be divided according to the working experience of each person, that is, each individual would be entitled to a specific amount according to their length of service and salary over the last years. Those who had worked in the *kolkhoz* for 25 years got the highest part of the shares in money; however others, whose working experience was limited to five years or less, got a small amount of money.[7]

In 2006, a leading young businessman, Rahim Muratov, bought the "*kolkhoz*", which was now a private farm, despite its bankruptcy and low productivity.[8] For many villagers, it was still hard to believe that the "*kolkhoz*" did not belong to them anymore. They were also still angry at the former *kolkhoz* chairman for his inability to manage the "*kolkhoz*" properly and his attempt to take the property money. Some blamed themselves for voting in favour of the sale when the question was raised whether to sell the farm or not. As of 2008, the confusion still remained unsolved in the village. Meanwhile, other newcomers from the neighbouring village of Vostok started to move to Orlovka, to work at Rahim's private farm.

"Private farm" workers: outsiders of the village[9]

Rahim Muratov, who became president of the fund known as Enterprise and Credit of the Kyrgyz Republic (*Fond predprinimatelstva i kreditirovaniya v Kirgizskoi Respubliki*) had earlier worked as a manager of the fund for one and half years and contributed 3.4 million *som* to the state budget (*Aalam* 2007). He was born and raised in the village of Vostok, which is located 45 kilometers from Orlovka village. According to an election brochure dated 28 January 2005, he graduated from the Academy of Medicine in Bishkek with distinction in 1998. Later in 2002 he was enrolled to study law at Lomonosov Moscow State University. He leads one of the biggest construction companies in Kyrgyzstan called "Bi-Stroi". In addition to this, he has a milk exporting business in the Chui valley. In 2006, he bought the bankrupt *kolkhoz* from local villagers of Orlovka and turned it into a private enterprise. According to the workers of the farm, his mother is Kazakh and his Kazakh relatives have high positions in Kazakhstan. They also help him to export milk to Kazakh companies.[10]

Immediate changes took place in the private farm, which was now in "new hands". Rahim's first task was to dismiss local *kolkhoz* workers from their positions after distributing their shares in cash. His second task was to replace these dismissed workers with his "own co-villagers" from Vostok, with whom he had a special relationship based on asymmetrical ties with unequal power and resources, and exchange of tangible and intangible assets and services. In this specific case, new director, Rahim, decided to bring his own people from his village in order to avoid a plethora of social relationships with the *kolkhoz*. In other words, there was a symbiotic relationship between the farm and the village that involved interrelated and interdependent interaction between the agrarian enterprises and the rural community (Nikulin 2003: 147).

Although Rahim made a significant contribution to the village life by providing financial support for the school, hospital and kindergarten, there were some cases in which conflicts would emerge. An elderly *kolkhoz* worker told me that at one time one of his colleagues stole a few bags of fodder to feed private livestock. The individual was caught by new farm guards and was immediately dismissed. The new owners had explained to him that the *kolkhoz* was not like it was before; one could not easily enter the *kolkhoz* and "steal" a few bags of fodder or oats, since now it is a private property. As Humphrey states (1998: 5), "a kolkhoznik [*kolkhoz* worker] until recent times held rights over property, and rights of other kinds, by virtue of a politically defined status, and one, furthermore, which was virtually non-negotiable." In other words, taking what you need from the *kolkhoz* was now stealing and not a way of supplementing one's income, as was the common understanding integrated into the old system. As a result, for the former workers, "stealing" from the *kolkhoz* was easily legitimized and justified since they were entitled to rights over the *kolkhoz* property which was typical in many post Soviet countries (Firlit and Chlopecki 1992; Anderson 1996; Verdery 1996).

The private farm owned by Rahim specializes in dairy production and canned meat (*konserva*). Although the main goal is to export the products of the farm to Kazakhstan, they failed to expand their production beyond the village market, mostly due to lack of modernized machines. As the farm is undergoing a period of new transition, many workers nevertheless seemed to have a clear and positive idea about the future of the farm and opted for getting positions there. In my interview with the head of the private farm, for example, I was told that they were going to bring new machines from Europe, develop production of meat and increase the capacity of milk to supply the local dairy companies.

The current condition of the private farm is still disorganized, especially regarding the process of dividing the stock. Some parts of the *kolkhoz*, such as the bakery, the bathhouse and the mill were given to local people, but the boundaries of the properties have not been defined yet.[11] The overall condition of the buildings such as barns, house of culture and garages are not good: they have old roofs, broken windows and doors, and now they are all undergoing reconstruction. Cars, broken-down tractors, old lorries and big red grain harvesters are taken elsewhere for repair. The current conditions of the new workers are also very difficult because they sleep in cattle sheds and work for more than the regular hours per day. But the new owner of the farm was confident that soon the farm would be different and prosperous.

Operation of kinship system: access to the private farm

In this section, I examine both the operation of the kinship system in order to see the process through which potential workers gain access to the private farm and their respective strategies. Before examining kinship, it is important to know that lineage affiliations and patron–client relations interact and reinforce each other. I will illustrate lineage affiliations of private farm workers, managers and experts and examine to what extent Rahim and his workers are close to one another.

The relationships between Rahim and some private farm workers had already been established prior to the emergence of the private farm. Most of the elder generations had built their bonds with Rahim during the first parliamentary elections in 2005, whereas the younger generation became closer to him only before the elections in 2007. During my research, I met with several young people who were trying to establish patron–client ties with Rahim.

In this general context, it is important to have an idea about how patron–client relations are established. First, potential workers approach Rahim's closest relatives and establish contact with them in his village, Vostok. From time to time they share their concerns with them, ask them to pass on a message to Rahim, and write down the potential workers' problems. When Rahim comes to the village, he collects all these cards and gets into contact with the people who wrote them, if he deems them to be an interesting case. However, before he does that, he gets background information on these potential workers from his relatives. His close relatives, therefore, become mediators between the patron (Rahim) and his prospective clients.

Another method was to find Rahim's close acquaintances, who are considered to be his "trusted" workers. The "trusted" workers frequently play a big role in appointing positions in a private farm because they are the ones who manage the farm. In this way, the "trusted" workers of the farm draw their "own people" or establish prospective workers on their side. Many people come to Rahim's house to greet and meet him face to face, and he listens to each one and takes into consideration their concerns. The most important thing is that the villagers greet Rahim first, mentioning his deceased father and emphasizing how they were close friends and brothers. They also mention his childhood and his leadership abilities. Sometimes, if people belong to his lineage, *Ak-Zhol*, and other related village lineages, they just mention their father's name and then their own names. If people come from neighbouring villages or from different regions, they specify their district name and point out that they are distant relatives (*tuugan*). On several occasions that I witnessed, men approached the "trusted" workers in order to get positions in the private farm. They did not stress the name of the village.[12] In other words, people draw on alternative survival strategies based on extended families, distant kinship members and lineage relations. For example, a man named Chopa who lives very close to a patron's grandmother's house borrowed a combine harvester (*kombain*) from Rahim. He was cleaning the patron's garden or watering his cattle. Chopa says that they are "close relatives", but when we drew the genealogical chart it was seen that their grandfathers joined only in ninth generation. However, the correctness of the lineage information for Chopa was not very important and he was not very much bothered with it. As Guenther Schlee (2009: 9) argues "the importance of hiding the fact that identification (or the 'price' or 'value' of that information) is 'fake' is linked to contractuality". The case of Chopa is also related to the contractual element, which makes the relationship between patron and client (himself) negotiable and sustainable, although his *uruu* [lineage] belonged to the younger segment, whereas the patron's lineage belongs to an elder segment. But both actors share common ancestors, and trace their ancestry for seven generations in the male line as a proof of identity.

When the state is unable to provide support, patrons are perceived as source of support; thus, the people now reorganize their actions in a different manner within the framework of new socio-economic circumstances. The Soviet-era practice of collective shared labour, once performed for the benefit of the state, is now performed for the benefit of selected individuals. These selected individuals become patrons because local client loyalty is assured through a combination of economic security and solidarity which is integrated into the overarching kinship ideology (*tuuganchylyk*). This serves to justify and legitimize both the system as such and how it operates. Kinship ideology, consisting of hierarchy and interdependent obligation, and kinship solidarity in times of need present and function quite well as moral justifications (Asad 1970). The traditional Kyrgyz family organization gives patron–client relations cultural legitimacy in three additional ways: first, hierarchical structures which demand obedience on the part of clients; second, ideological kinship ties and extended kinship terminologies; third, cultural values such as loyalty, deference and solidarity. It is possible to argue that "kinship", whether it is true or fake, functions as a strategy to enter the farm and get benefit of support of the patron, and it is seen as an important starting mechanism to establish patron–client ties.

"Private farm": individual benefits and cooperative action

In order to understand the workers' positions and their functions within the private farm, it is necessary to take a closer look at its organization and administration. Table 4.1 illustrates the position of each worker within the private farm

Table 4.1 Organization and administration in a private farm, Orlovka 2007

Specialization	Name	Age	Residence	Background (lineage or ethnic group added by the author)
Chairman	Rahim	34	Vostok	Belongs to lineage Ak-Zhol
Administration				
1 Main engineer	Kalybek	34	Vostok	Belongs to lineage Ak-Zhol
2 Chief accountant	Maria	47	Vostok	Belongs to lineage Ak-Zhol
3 Economist	Dooronbek	52	Bishkek	Belongs to lineage Sarybagysh
4 Supplies manager	Alimjan	40	Tokmok	Tatar
5 Personnel Department	Farida	55	Orlovka	Turkish
Milk Production Unit (MTF: Molochnaya tovarnaya ferma), *agriculture and livestock*				
Animal technician	Narynbek	52	Vostok	Belongs to lineage Ak-Zhol
Livestock expert	Zakir	46	Vostok	Belongs to lineage Karatukum
Agronomy expert	Almaz	47	Orlovka	Kyrgyz, belongs to lineage Tata
Veterinarian (surgeon)	Efim	50	Tokmok	Russian
Mechanization expert	Burulbek	45	Vostok	Belongs to lineage Ak-Zhol
Milk supplier	Oroz	46	Vostok	Belongs to lineage Ak-Zhol
Machine-operators:				
1 Tractor-driver – 1	Muras	40	Vostok	Belongs to lineage Karatukum
2 Combine-driver – 1	Edil	43	Vostok	Belongs to lineage Ak-Zhol
1 Tractor-driver – 2	Chopo	44	Vostok	Belongs to lineage Ak-Zhol
2 Combine driver-2	Salamat	39	Vostok	Belong to lineage Kochokbai
Unskilled workers service				
Builder	Sanovich	57	Bishkek	Ukrainian
Cattle breeder	Nadyr	34	Vostok	Belongs to lineage Kochokbai
Calf rearer	Altyn	27	Vostok	Belongs to lineage Karasakal
Cattle breeder	Chynar	33	Vostok	Belongs to lineage Ak-Zhol
Cattle breeder	Marat	36	Orlovka	Belongs to Tata lineage
Livestock herder	Asyl	26	Vostok	Belongs to Tata lineage
Driver	Alim	38	Bishkek	Dungan
Dairymaid	Jyldyz	30	Orlovka	Belongs to Tata lineage
Dairymaid	Munara	40	Orlovka	Belongs to Karatai lineage
Dairymaid	Venera	24	Orlovka	Belongs to Kenjebai lineage
Kolkhoz guards	Omurbek	22	Vostok	Belongs to lineage Ak-Zhol
Kolkhoz guards	Marat	44	Vostok	Belongs to lineage Karatukum
Kolkhoz guards	Chubak	25	Vostok	Belongs to lineage Karatukum
Kolkhoz guards	Ilich	29	Vostok	Belongs to lineage Sagyndyk

structure, specifically their "specialization" (qualifications obtained during the Soviet era), name, age, residence and lineage. The majority of workers are from the village of Vostok and they belong to the patron's lineage, *Ak Zhol* (the other four main lineages are *Karatukum, Kochokbai, Shaibek Sagyndyk*). There are also representatives of other nationalities, mainly Turkish, Dungan, Tatar, Russian and Ukrainian. Out of 28 workers on the farm, only three dairy maids and one Kyrgyz man is from Orlovka village, which has four main lineages: *Tata, Karatai, Kenjebai, Suurdu.*

As can be observed from the table, the private farm is organized in a hierarchical model where the highest authority belongs to the chairman of the farm, followed by the chief specialists, and the unskilled workers who are at the bottom of the ladder. The structure of the farm is divided into certain sectors following the Soviet model: unit and brigade. There are three sections within the farm: governing committee, production sector (livestock, milk) and unskilled workers service. The farm consists of only one brigade that is responsible for milk production and livestock, although it specifically concentrates on milk production.

The governing committee of the farm consists of the chairman, main engineer, chief accountant, economist and supplies manager, all of whom have responsibility for managing, supplying, budgeting, reporting and making presentations during meetings to the main director. On the second level are the chief specialists responsible for sectional production (milk production, hay-making and cattle breeding), each in charge of sections according to their specialization, such as mechanization expert, veterinarian, animal technician, agronomist and machine-operator, although from time to time some are engaged in other tasks as well. On the third level are the unskilled workers, set up for tasks of guarding, milking, building and repairs. The majority of the private farm workers got their qualifications during the Soviet era. As Humphrey points out (1998), due to wage discrimination during Soviet times, people were motivated to get their training as specialized workers. These workers had been actively engaged in their *kolkhoz* before the disintegration of the Soviet Union. Since independence, their qualifications were not as valued as was the case in Soviet times. Many private farm workers have subsidiary plots and several cattle, but what they do is not considered as "work" (*jumush*) because they do not get salaries from the state. Instead, the majority of young people move to Russia in search of better opportunities.[13] Due to the emergence of the current private farm, many of the workers got new positions that were equivalent to those in their previous *kolkhoz.* They continued to work as before, but this time they took up voluntary work with different intentions and expectations so as to secure their social well-being (education, medical treatment and bureaucratic support in times of need). However, the experiences of the Soviet trained specialists, and the usage of Soviet terminologies such as order (*prikaz*), decision (*reshenie*), directions (*razporyazhenie*) and general plan (*orgplan*), in association with the management and regulations of the farm members, clearly indicates the continuity of the Soviet experience.

Among the farm workers women are in a minority: there are only four full-paid workers, whereas there are 24 men including seasonal workers. Private farm workers can be classified into two categories: in the first category are those who are more experienced and who had acquired their qualification during the Soviet era, now aged between 40 and 55; in the second category are young men aged between 25 and 35, who have low service positions and constitute the majority. Dairymaids are mostly from the local village, since the Vostok village women cannot come to the *kolkhoz*, due to tasks and responsibilities at home. However, local dairymaids are considered experienced workers, who have worked in the *kolkhoz* since the Soviet era. They come at particular times and then return to their homes. They work all year round, compared to the unskilled workers whose work is based on split shifts on a temporary basis.

Each worker is expected first to concentrate on his or her specific job, and then take other responsibilities related to construction or repair. During my visits to the farm, I noticed that a tractor driver was cleaning the calf-house one day; the next he was building a toilet and fixing the windows. I expected, however, that a specialized worker should engage in his or her specific task. But it turned out that this private farm did not have strict regulations and responsibilities for each worker and thus tasks and liabilities are blurred. Workers spent more time cleaning, fixing and setting up new doors, gates and windows in the farm. This kind of arrangement was explained by one of the chairman, Narinbek, as follows:

> We need a smaller number of specialized labour on the farm which has a different economy now as compared to the Soviet times, when the *kolkhoz* had to create a lot of opportunities for its workers for various small tasks.

Nevertheless, the management requires that workers take on several tasks at once. For example, they have to clean, reorganize, renovate, and repair huge farm buildings by fixing doors, windows and gates and by constructing new buildings on the one hand, and to concentrate on grain production, cattle breeding and milk production on the other. The strategic plan of the farm is twofold, albeit ill defined. First, the workers get hazy and unclear orders to finish everything within a given time. Second, the workers have not yet carried out any profit maximizing business.

The different sectors of the farm have their own locations; administration is located at the main office of the farm, which is in the centre of the village about 15 minutes by foot. However, the farm itself is situated at the end of the village near the agricultural fields. Usually, administrators come to the farm on Fridays for general checks, but farm workers rarely go to the main office. The garage, mill and store barns are located between the main administration and the farm. In addition, agricultural machinery, big lorries, dairy equipment, and other tools are also kept there. I could not obtain more information on the actual numbers of agricultural machines, because I was not allowed to enter the property of the private farm.[14] The farm has around 120 horses, 150 cows, 16 pigs, 35 calves and some sheep. It still breeds livestock seasonally; in winter, cattle are kept on the farm, but in summer they are moved to the open pasture (*jailoo*). A livestock herder, Asil, took only horses and some sheep the previous year. This year, 150 cows remained on the farm since the younger ones were designated for milking, and the older ones for slaughtering to produce beef. Asil has a special responsibility, on Rahim's behalf, for herding sheep. He had been working with his family for Rahim for five years, and their relations are based on mutual support and deference.

Beyond the "salary"

Another basic issue that needs to be focused on is related to the salaries of private farm workers that are neither guaranteed nor specified, as they do not sign a contract in advance. The wage is defined according to experience, specialization and other criteria. The wage of administrators is about 2,000–3,000 *som* per month (€40–60), chief specialists 1,000–2,000 *som* (€20–40) and unskilled service personnel 1,000 *som* (€20). The total amount that workers receive is not enough for a single family to survive on in the village, since it does not cover food, clothing and housing costs. The wages would probably only cover their transportation and lunch. The salaries of those who have higher-level qualifications are almost equal to those who have middle-level qualifications, such as a tractor-driver. A non-trained watchman of the farm has the same salary as a combine-driver or veterinarian. Thus, the wages of the farm workers, that is, the clients, are almost equal taking into account the fact that the highly qualified workers spend their own money on copying, developing and scanning documents of the farm on a voluntary basis. Moreover, the patron is aware that his highly qualified workers spend their salaries for the prosperity of the farm. Therefore, by spending their own money, workers increase their status in the eyes of patron. In this case, it is crucial to analyse their decision to work, that is, what influences their decision to work with a low salary rather than not to work at all.

"Salary" is a symbolic term that demonstrates the position of the "worker" on the "private farm" which can be used as a justification. Yet, the real salary is absent or invisible. The salary is not talked about or widely discussed inside or outside the private farm. Once, the salaries of the workers had been withheld up to five months due to the elections, but they did not complain about this. Instead, they had continued to work as if they had received an adequate salary, while at the same time they had been financially contributing to life-cycle events and travelling from one village to another. Probably, alternative sources of income helped to sustain them. In this situation, people justified the absence of a decent salary as if they were helping their "brother" in times of need. On one occasion when they received free sugar and flour, I thought it was probably given in place of their salaries, since the cost of sugar and flour was almost equal to their actual wage. But the workers assured me that these products were not considered as the "real" payment for their work. It was likely that their loyalty and devotion were not equal to sugar and flour; instead they seemed to expect more than that.

The workers also talked about the future opportunities Rahim, the patron, would offer them. Moreover, the private farm still remained the only place for survival and offered a stable life and certainty in an environment of instability. Although local workers were interested in working on a private farm for various reasons, with diverse aims and expectations, they all seemed to be interested in something "beyond the salary". In the eyes of the villagers, the workers had a reputation of working in the *kolkhoz* that they wanted to maintain, on the one hand, and they benefit from additional support from Rahim in times of need, on the other. Moreover, their responsibilities have fashionable names, such as "work" and "specializations", although only in symbolic terms. The legitimization of their relationship with Rahim as compared to others justifies their condition as "employed". The *kolkhoz* has lost its former significance as a milieu of collective action with the arrival of "newcomers", without a specific common aim and plan. The ideology of the "collective farm" (Humphrey 1998) does not correspond to the reality of the *kolkhoz* structure due to the low salary, lack of social benefits, and absence of collective responsibility afforded to the workers. Using the "formal structure" of the farm as ideological justification, workers disguise their patron–client relationships under the umbrella of "employer-employee relationships". This "employee and employer" relation provides access to the institutional support of the village (those who work in the farm) because the workers have access to transportation in the private farm. Such support is shown, for example, when the workers are invited as guests for a meal. The reason behind this is to provide the villagers with access to farm equipment such as combine harvester, tractors and lorries. Rahim controls and permits machines to be used in the village, but driving and operating agricultural machines are carried out by the workers because the spare parts for the machines, extra fertilizers and fuel are controlled by the drivers. In particular, the villagers are heavily burdened at harvest time in the autumn and sowing in spring due to lack of machines, and the farm workers know that they can negotiate the price for the combine harvester. As a result, working on the farm gives them confidence that they will at least have access to the machines in times of need.

Many people still consider the "work" to be related to making money, whereas "help" is related to the obligation. In this situation, the farm workers face a dilemma: on the one hand, they work for low salaries; on the other hand, they are attached to the patron as if they are "brothers" and obliged to "help" him. So the workers combine the provided options: to benefit from the low salary by working very hard to help their "brother". In this case, the clients neither violate the rules, imposed obligations and norms of the community, nor complain about the bad conditions, low salary and poor food. Rather, they work in the farm to enter the "circle of trust" of the patron and rely on him in times of need. In addition, their devotion goes beyond immediate material needs, as what they want is to get support in an uncertain future, cattle in life-cycle events, valuable material for housing, a network for medical treatment, and bureaucratic support at times of need, in short, further advancement in their lives. The "low salary" is not an obstacle; instead, it is an invisible but quite justifiable tactic.

Thus, the farm is full of ambiguous relations, vague attitudes and suspicious gazes from other workers, yet at the same time this is a demonstrative place in which people can display their loyalty to their patron by working hard, checking others and contributing to its development. The workers, therefore, are actively involved in diffuse and particularistic relations. They enter the farm, as they want to benefit from the various support mechanisms provided by the patron.

However, in some few cases, there are families which do not get any salary at all. Instead, shelter and food are provided to them. In the next sections, two such families will be described: the family of Marat who belongs to the lineage of Orlovka, and the family of San Sanovich who is from a different ethnic background. Both families live permanently in the farm (whereas the other workers live and work in the farm for five days, then spend two days at home), work more than others, but do not receive any wages. The members of both families neither belong to the lineage of the patron nor do they have their own established extended families. Instead, as will be elaborated later, they are "dependant clients" whose relations with the patron are neither forced nor voluntary.

The Maratov family

This is the young family of Maratov, who is in his thirties and has five children. Marat has been working in the *kolkhoz* since his childhood; these days he works as a cattle-breeder in the calf-house. Although his wife works as a dairymaid, due to her maternity leave she was assigned as a watchwoman of the farm. According to Marat, to rent a room in the village costs 1,000 som (€20), excluding electricity and water. As a result, it is beneficial for the family to live on the premises (the *kolkhoz* as he always calls it) in a small house (*sarai*) consisting basically of two rooms, where electricity and water are free of charge.

When the *kolkhoz* was sold, Marat talked to the new headman and asked him if he could stay at the private farm[15] as his children were young and he did not have a house. In exchange, he offered to work there. Marat was told at that time that Rahim needed a local person who knew the farm very well; therefore, the headman had agreed to take him as a cattle breeder. His responsibilities include clearing out the cattle sheds of 300 metres, preparing fodder and carting away the dung every day. Marat, apart from fulfilling the responsibilities that come with his own position, repairs empty farm-sheds by fixing a new floor, doors, gates and windows. Additionally, he is also in charge of calf-rearing and collecting milk from the private farm starting at 3:00 a.m.

Rahim brought a cow for Marat's children to milk and provided the family with a piece of land near their house for private production. Sometimes Marat would be allowed to earn extra money outside the farm. At the beginning, he was also very enthusiastic about the fact that Rahim had promised to help him build his own house, and he would even receive some building materials. After some time, however, Marat complained that he did not have sugar, flour and tea at home. Furthermore, he had not received his salary for almost five months, even though he had been working like a "slave" doing everything that Rahim asked him; on occasions, he had even repaired the houses of Rahim's close friends and relatives. During the interview, when he learned that Rahim was on his way to the farm, however, he got very excited and asked his wife to clean the yard. When he was talking to me a minute previously, he had expressed his anger about his patron's colleagues, but a visit from the patron himself seemed enough to change his mind immediately.

The house (with free electricity and water) and the cow are the main incentives to work at the farm for Murat; otherwise "job" is just a word, with no real content. He stated that he did not have any choice because nobody could help him outside the farm and he had no idea where else to go and where to work. He was ostracized by his close friends and his extended family had their own problems. Therefore, he was all alone with his family and his own problems. Instead, it was better for him to be at the private farm and do what his patron's workers asked him to do. He was aware that a few words to the patron from the workers would result in being dismissed from the farm. One early morning, for example, Marat had accidentally spilt five litres of milk, but he was accused by one of the farm chairmen, Narinbek, of losing 50 litres. Nevertheless, he could not protest against this accusation and prove that it was only five litres. As Marat said, the farm workers could easily accuse him of stealing things from the farm, drinking vodka, or refusing to work. In order to justify his position in the farm, he should always listen to the farm administrators, and do what they ask him to do: even when, for example, "his children were sick, and the administrators might order him to slaughter large number of cattle during the night". He was sometimes asked by the chairman to repair the roof of his private house and he had to work there for free for another week. Marat had to negotiate and deal with the administration very well and to get along with other *kolkhoz* workers as his position in the farm continues to remain uncertain.

The family of San Sanovich

San Sanovich is a 56-year-old farm worker who has been living on the private farm since 2006. He is originally from Ukraine. He came to Kyrgyzstan to complete a big construction project. While he was working in the previous boss's yard, several police officers had approached him and demanded to see his passport. When he showed his passport, which was not registered, it was taken away by the police. He could not get his passport back, as he had no money at the time to pay the fine. His boss rudely refused to give him a cash advance and did not pay his salary on time. San was then forced to leave his boss in search for another job so as to get some cash to pay the fine, get his passport back, and buy a ticket back to Ukraine. San applied for the position of construction worker at the farm of Rahim and was accepted. Rahim also helped him get his salary back from his previous boss. Then San started to build the patron's guesthouse project and successfully completed it within three months. According to San, Rahim had shown interest in him by not giving the agreed salary for the project and keeping the promised passport. Instead, Rahim organized a small wedding party for San and his Russian bride, a lady in her early thirties. This was an opportunity for the patron which completely erased the question on salary. Marriage would be one of the reasons that San decided to take patron's offer to stay.

San was also in crisis because he did not have a house, money or passport; so when Rahim offered him a place on his farm, he agreed to move there. San is frequently called upon to provide assistance and services at any time they are required, including tasks outside the private farm, such as fixing electricity in Rahim's guesthouse, renovating a shower and toilet in Rahim's grandmother's place, or fixing the heating system in Rahim's brother's house. However, his job in the farm is twofold: he takes care of the 16 pigs of the farm and he is responsible for reconstructing the old farm buildings. He does not get a salary unlike other workers but makes extra money from buying and selling pigs to cover his living expenses. Furthermore, whenever Rahim comes to the farm, he visits San and brings food, clothes and extra money. He was allowed to stay in Kyrgyzstan because he can manage many responsibilities at the same time: a pig tender, a builder, a turner, an electrician, a fitter, a welder, and an assistant for others in terms of mechanization and construction. In my interview with him, San told me that Rahim once politely asked him: "Father (*Batya*) please, help me to complete the farm project, after that I will help you with the housing and passport."

Once I went to San's house, which was located at the left corner of the farm. Next to his, an additional cattle-shed is situated where Dungan, the driver, lives. San invited me to enter his house which was a dark single room with a big TV. His wife was watching TV. San started to complain to me that one day, when he was outside, Marat's wife stole some of his jars. He also mentioned that a while ago Marat had borrowed money from him and since then he had not returned to the farm.

Internal dynamics of the private farm

In this section, I will elaborate on the internal dynamics of the private farm in further detail by focusing on the nature of the patron–client relations and the basic variations these relations take by analysing the resource base of patronage and clientage, as well as the balance between affective and instrumental ties on the one hand, and voluntarism and coercion on the other. The nature and variations of the complex patron–client ties reveal a pattern in which cooperative action coexists with individual interest seeking.

The nature of patron–client ties

The above cases revealed that workers in the farm depend on patron–client relations that are characterized by unequal status, wealth, influence, power, and interpersonal and face-to-face relations that are vertically dyadic. The distinctiveness of the patron–client relations is based on the ability to incorporate contradictory features (voluntary and compulsory, instrumental and affective). Despite a power imbalance, both actors are interdependent and are involved in reciprocal exchange of services and goods. This relation's ability to advance diffuse interests gives it flexibility and resilience (Eisenstadt and Roniger 1980; Foster 1963; Gellner 1977; Gouldner 1960; Powell 1977; Scott 1977; Silverman 1977). These elements are the core factors in patron–client relations, and substantially differ from other power relations.

The relationship between patron and client in the private farm case is multi-dimensional (Mayer 1977) and covers a wide range of situations. The farm workers provide subsidiary services which can be very different in nature: to build a mosque, to campaign for the boss in the elections and promote his reputation, and to help organize the life-cycle events of the patron by serving guests and preparing food. Clients orient themselves strategically and act in response to the "particulars of the situation" because of the unpredictable expectations on the part of the patron. Thus, patron–client relations are fluid and diffuse and both sides accommodate each other's needs in a fuzzy division of labour.

The face-to-face dyadic relationship between the patron and his clients can be schematically represented as shown in Figure 4.1.

In the private farm context, clients can be categorized into two groups: "local clients" and "dependant clients". There is no possibility of "local clients" being "dependant clients" and vice versa because this is an ascriptive categorization. The "local clients" belong to the lineage of the patron while "dependant clients" belong to another ethnic group or a different lineage. The "dependant clients" belong to the category of unskilled workers. The "local clients" belong to the category of administration and skilled workers. Nevertheless, as Lemarchand (1972) has pointed out, patron–client relationships can be complementary and cross-cutting across ethnic, class or other lineage cleavages. In this respect, the clients themselves differentiate and distinguish those who belong to the categories of "local client" and "dependant client" groups.

As Powell (1977: 157) points out, "enforcement, compliance, and performance are bound up in, and limited to, the face-to-face relationship between the client and patron." It is nonetheless possible to say that each worker is tied to Rahim in diverse ways and for diverse reasons. In other words, each client has his or her own diverse intentions and purposes, and their duties, rights and actions are not clearly defined. The dyadic contract between patron and client is highly personalized in content, by word of mouth and informal agreement. Clients' implicit relationships with the patron, which is disguised under the kinship terminologies, reveal mutual interpersonal relationships. Mutual expectation is backed by the community values (they are from the same village) or kinship terminologies *batya-synok* (father and son) and *aga-ini* (younger brother and elder brother).

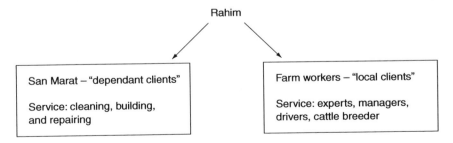

Figure 4.1 Patron-client network pyramid.

In such a framework, exchange becomes one of the main binding principles of patron–client relations. According to this principle, the patron possesses access to political, economic and cultural resources that are important for his client's basic needs. In exchange, clients provide goods, political loyalty, labour and other services. Patron–client contracts, therefore, fit into a different power position (Foster 1961:1281) and occur between two different individuals with unequal resources, status and power. Scott (1977) points out that reciprocity involves basic needs and resources of patron and client, however, the balance of exchange is related to maintaining the relationships. A crucial point in patron–client relationship is dependence that is perceived by the client as "legitimate". In other words, for clients, the exchange balance makes the relationships legitimate. Any change in the "balance" can lead to a change in the legitimacy of the exchange network.

Eisenstadt and Roniger (1980: 52) adopt the term "generalized exchange" from Mauss, and then try to connect it with specific exchange, attempting to explain the crucial analytical characteristics of patron–client relationships. They claim that the importance of generalized exchange is that it creates the connection between "instrumental relations" and "power relations" on the one hand and "solidarity" and "expressiveness" on the other hand. However, generalized exchange is structured in many ways and it can be best applied to kin group members with their own rules and obligations. Moreover, it contains strong elements of power and hierarchy. Within the context of patron–client relations, they state that "the paradoxical combination of features of the patron–client nexus is a specific type of social relations because it regulates the exchange or flow of resources between social actors and constitutes a special combination of *specific exchange with generalized exchange* (Eisenstadt and Roniger, 1980: 55). Gouldner (1960: 35) analysed a generalized norm of reciprocity in which "certain actions and obligations [are seen] as repayments for benefits received on the basis of past behaviour". Thus, Gouldner's "generalized form of reciprocity" can be best applied in the context of the private farm: mutual reciprocity as an "exchange" pattern maintained and regulated between a patron and his clients serves to arrange the exchange of goods and services across time and space.

As noted above, the farm has two types of workers: the older trained specialists and younger non-trained workers. The experienced workers received support from Rahim in times of need such as medical emergencies, helping children to enrol in university, getting money and cattle for life-cycle events and building houses, and receiving bureaucratic support in the form of informal connections when they need official documents such as passports or drivers' licenses. When in the future, these individuals need to educate their children, marry them, find them appropriate jobs [*baldardy butuna turguzuu*] and help them settle in, they need the help of patron again. As such, a patron's support in the past results in a client's repayment in the present time. In other words, a client feels obliged to work for a patron for little money and feels indebted.

In comparison with the older generation, the younger men are in the process of building their families and constructing their own private houses. Their future and plans are uncertain, but they are aware of the fact their options are limited as they lack educational and professional qualifications. Therefore, they consider working in the farm as the best option, since their future plans and the stability of their current position depend on it. Their devotion goes beyond the immediate material needs and the wages they may receive. Instead, they look towards the future with expectation. For example, in case of marriage young workers can approach a patron and ask him to sponsor their wedding expenses in terms of paying dowry, slaughtering cattle, and organizing the wedding party. In other cases, they can get help in transportation facilities, building materials, medical treatment, and further advancement in their lives. For example: Oroz first initiated his relations with Rahim by giving the patron's grandmother a bag of sugar and one of his fattest sheep because at that time (2005) he needed a stable job.

There are also seasonal workers on the farm. These are tractor-drivers and harvester-operators who are called upon during sowing and harvesting times. They are also responsible for irrigating, manuring, and hay cutting in spring. Apart from their actual tasks on the farm, they live in the village of Vostok where they usually help the patron's grandmother to breed her cattle, to cultivate a small piece of plot, to make hay and to water livestock. Their wives usually come to clean her house, prepare food, and actively involve themselves in taking care of her.

It is important to highlight exchange elements between the older and younger workers. The former are obliged to work for the patron due to their previous interaction and exchange of goods and services obtained in the past. They are involved in a set of duties and obligations because they developed customary relationships with the patron which were internalized through repayment in the form of farm-labour. However, the younger generation without many qualifications still joins the farm and plays the role of good and honest workers in order to strengthen their position within the farm in anticipation of support in return. The younger workers establish exchange relationships with their "elder brothers", which would provide them additional support. Thus, the multifaceted meaning of helping "one's brother" leaves room for reinterpretation and a strengthening of a client's relationship with the potential patron. They use the strategy of "starting mechanism" (Gouldner 1977) of norm reciprocity meaning that those who first initiate their social interaction with the patron in the early phase of their lives will continue to protect their interests in the future.

However, the "norm of reciprocity" (Gouldner 1977: 38) also produces a shadow of indebtedness that is extended over time periods, and a "balancing mechanism" develops in which each side repays their dues. Apart from the regular duties, there is symbolic "equivalence" in the relations between the patron and his clients which imposes on each the duty to repay the other on an "equal basis". Thus, patrons also benefit from their clients' support, although reciprocity cannot be quantified since the exchanged goods and services are dispersed across time and space.

As noted above, whether young or middle-aged, qualified or unqualified, clients have particular experiences and skills with which they can expect to reinforce their positions vis-à-vis the patron, since the condition under which patron–client relations emerge rests on mutual benefit and support. In reality, the actions and strategies of the elder and younger generations coincide because they have to make ends meet, apply their existing experience in the hazy division of labour, and get their low wages.

Variations of patron–client relations

Although many variations on patron–client relations have been made, for this chapter, I use the analysis of Scott (1977: 129) who described patron–client relations in terms of the resource base of patronage, resource base of clientage, balance of affective and instrumental ties, and balance of voluntarism and coercion. Scott (1977) argues that it is mainly the resources that hold patron–client cluster together. Here, in the specific case of the private farm, however, there are also social actors who decisively choose a combination of different resources at the same time. In order to elaborate my argument further, the resource base of the patron and his clients need to be looked at.

The resource base of patronage and clientage

Rahim could bring together several clients in his farm due to his ability not only to assist them but also to support their families in times of need. For his own purposes, he needed labour power to construct and transform the "old *kolkhoz*" into the bigger private farm. Today, Rahim provides housing and jobs for his clients and employs them to work in his private business sector. For example, he has several shops, a security agency, land, private farm, restaurants, and a business in the milk industry. By controlling scarce resources, the patron is capable of enhancing the material well-being of his workers, their health, and resolve any issues related to the state bureaucracy. Besides providing housing and jobs for his clients, the patron is as highly valued as a skillful, knowledgeable doctor.

What the patron receives from his clients (free labour), however, is of greater value. For a patron this bond is more likely to be beneficial because dependant clients such as San are talented masters, exceptional in dealing with electricity, cattle breeding, constructing buildings and repairing machines. Local clients also have their own specializations as farmers and suppliers of various services. Furthermore, everyone in the farm is responsible for providing extra services for the patron in his personal and professional needs inside and outside the farm.

In short, what we see is a system of mutual benefits: the clients know that in addition to certain benefits such as salary and/or benefits provided to them as workers in the farm, they may also get the support of the patron in providing them cattle and money, especially in life-cycle events. As for the patron, he not only benefits from the professional skills of his clients as technicians and experts on the farm, but also utilizes their free labour for his own personal goals in a flexible manner.

Balance of affective and instrumental ties

In a patron–client dyadic relation, both affective and instrumental ties play major roles. As Boissevain (1966: 18) points out, patron–client relations are based on "a self-perpetuating system of belief and action grounded in the society's value system". In the case of the "local clients", they stress their shared lineage with the patron (by being distant relatives or from the same village) and manipulate it for diverse purposes, and their readiness to help is justified through kinship ideology, which allows them to expect from the patron houses, cars, cattle, medical treatment, or payment of dowry. As for the "dependant clients" who are not attached to their patron through "kinship", we see cross-cutting ties based on intra-ethnic relations and intra-lineage relations. They are not invited to the patron's feasts or involved in other more serious tasks; they cannot even vote since they do not have the right documents. The dependant clients are limited only to "kinship" terminologies father/son [*batya/synok*] or younger brother and elder brother [*ini/aga*]. Apart from this, they express their loyalty through very hard work and their solidarity through being honest. As a result, the options available to them and their background affiliations bring very different expectations.

The more kinship legitimacy patron–client ties have with more freedom of movement, the more likely affective bonds of "local client" would be nominal; whereas the less kinship legitimacy patron–client ties have with less freedom of movement, the more likely affective bonds of "dependant clients" would be maximal. The "local clients" have more options than the "dependant clients" and they obtain more material benefits. Therefore, under different conditions they are more likely to leave their patron in search for another promising one. As for the dependant clients, they tend to remain, since their options are much more limited and they have greater degree of gratitude emanating from close affective bonds or emotional attachments that they have for their patrons. The degree of dependence on material interests can also be measured by whom they are distributed to and who fight for them in the private farm.

Balance of voluntarism and coercion

There is also a difference in the degree of coercion and voluntarism in patron–client ties. In the case of "dependant clients", they voluntarily enter into the patron–client relationships due to their limited options (no house, no passport) and legitimize their relations through kinship terminologies. The patron requires them to participate in various tasks without any wages and he limits their freedom of movement. There is a "balance exchange" (Scott 1977) between the patron and his clients which makes the relationship legitimate. Any change in this "balance" can lead to a change in the legitimacy of the exchange network. In patron–client relations, the "balance" is a mechanism which helps asymmetrical relationships to be legitimate on the one hand, and disguise the "exploitative" relations on the other.

Clients try to find a "balance" between choice and voluntarism as well as stability and uncertainty. Thus they opt to take the side on which they receive highest security and stability in terms of basic needs for subsistence living (clothes, food and housing), in addition to a small piece of plot for private production. For clients, the patron–client bond fulfils their basic needs for subsistence, even though unpaid labour is also involved in the relationship. Thus, forced or voluntary, the legitimacy of their relations comes through an exchange balanced by their limited options. As Scott (1977: 30) claims, "a relationship of dependence that supplies these minimal guarantees will retain a core of legitimacy." Compared to the "dependant clients", the "local clients" have more freedom and are dependent on the patron only for their jobs, future assistance with state administration, or transportation.

It must, however, also be stressed that the exchange relationships are also subject to change, as tensions may emerge and intensify between a patron and his clients. In asymmetrical relations the interests of actors do not intersect (Scott 1977) because a patron's main interest is in intangible assets (power, prestige, honour) whereas clients are more interested in tangible assets (money, cattle, work).[16] At times of uncertainty, change and economic crisis, clients do work hard to gain their patron's trust and to have access to resources, so that they will be able to be independent to buy a private house or cattle. It is nonetheless possible to say that after a certain point, when the actors reach the point where they deserve independence and acceptance, the patron attempts to retain and enhance his power by not giving his clients further opportunities, and restricting their lives. For example, San works very hard to go home, but Rahim always finds ways to keep him at his farm, such as providing him certain options in the farm, preventing him from contacting other patrons and limiting his freedom of movement. To put it differently, as soon as clients try to move up the ladder and try to pursue their own interests, their patron takes the initiative to keep them in the private farm. Since the clients' actions are bound by permission, imposed obligations and several restrictions, the patron may still control their actions outside the farm. So, although the workers work in the farm without any clearly defined set of responsibilities and although their tasks change across time and space, they cannot leave the farm. Therefore, this results in a situation in which earlier promises and kinship terminologies emerge as tools for a patron to act strategically and to improve his own benefit. As such, the patron balances strongly opposing elements, such as "forced" and "voluntary" labour, and enhances his position and power vis-à-vis his clients by keeping them dependent on him.

Cooperative action versus individual contribution

As mentioned above, a patron benefits from his clients in diverse ways. The foremost benefit in this case is having trained specialists and qualified experts with long-term experience in the farm who work for low pay. Thus, it is more likely that these workers are capable of rebuilding the farm within a short period of time. The common factor that keeps these clients together therefore is the "patron" with his tangible and intangible resources. In choosing strategies for increasing his benefit, the patron tries to manage his clients in such a way that the chosen strategy does not lead to conflict but instead promotes a self-regulating system in which actors are in situational alliances, although they may have different interests.

Thus, there is an interesting constellation: on the one hand, individuals pursue their own interests in the farm; on the other hand, these individuals are involved in cooperative action. In other words, they find ways of seeking their own interests and being involved in cooperative action by balancing their choices. As Coleman (1986: 25) has pointed out, "so long as an actor can exchange power over actions which have little or no effects on his interests, in return for power over actions which interest him, this is the best means of gaining his interests." Despite the existence of individual interests, undefined tasks and vague management, these individuals are involved in cooperative action; they breed cattle, renovate the farm,and produce crops as a group. But at the same time, individuals attempt to increase their influence on other actors and thereby satisfy their own interests. To put it differently, instrumentally oriented individuals always seek to satisfy both their needs and the expectations of their patron. Thus, in theory the interests of patron and clients do not intersect; if they do, then the patron always finds ways to solve the problem in his own "creative" way. However, the interests of clients usually intersect with each others' because they have to share the same resources, resulting in misunderstandings and distrust of each other. In order to understand individual interests within the context of cooperative action in more depth, one has to look at trust between patron and client, which is based on exchange, as well as distrust between clients, which leads to competition.

Conclusion

The agricultural sector in Kyrgyzstan including the collective farms has undergone extensive reform in the post-Soviet era. Despite the legal changes in its name, people still consider the farm a *kolkhoz* and use this term in their daily conversations and activities. The chapter focused on how people responded to the post-Soviet changes, which introduced new internal power dynamics and resulted in the emergence of new interest groups with their peculiar strategies and conflicts around the resources in the farm. In this context, it showed how a private farm becomes a place for the emergence of different kinds of patron–client clusters by using an overarching ideology of kinship which becomes a matter of survival for the clients. They act differently in times of need by manipulating "kinship" as a tool for acceptance and justification. Clients emphasize the importance of being "*kolkhoz* workers" and acknowledge that there is "security" beyond the salary. Since the formal structure of the Soviet-era *kolkhoz* does not fit into present day reality, the *kolkhoz* lives in the minds of people through nostalgic attachment. This nostalgic memory leaves room for possible manipulative strategies used by clients to justify and legitimize their positions, their dependency and subordination in their relations with the patron.

As a result, clients neither violate the existing norms nor change them; instead they use them for their own benefit in order to satisfy their instrumental needs.

The main characteristics of patron–client relations are based on mutual support, asymmetrical power and exchange, and face-to-face relations. In each patron–client cluster or pyramid (a single patron with several clients), the degree of instrumentality and effectiveness of bonds play a major role. "Local clients" as compared to "dependant clients" are more likely to have material interests because of their firm requirements and immediate expectations, whereas "dependant clients" are limited to just housing and job services as an expression of their gratitude. The relationships between a patron and his clients are based on a dichotomous configuration that is neither forced nor voluntary. There is ambivalence in these relations: on the one hand, the patron accepts his clients, provides them with support and makes them dependant on him, which also justifies his actions. On the other hand, clients enter into this relation due to lack of other options and take it as granted, although they cannot claim for any compensation. As such, their interests do not intersect.

In the private farm, despite the changes, workers were subordinated to the manager, and their actions were strictly regulated by informal norms and principles. The farm is also a place where different kinds of clients continue to redefine their relations with one another and set up their own rules of negotiation and strategies. The considerable part of these rules and strategies concerns clients' position vis-à-vis their patron. The workers also need to develop appropriate attitudes, as this is an environment of instability where one's place is dependant on another's decisions within a particular checks-and-balances mechanism. The farm, therefore, becomes a place in which different clients use various tactics and strategies as tools to defend their own resources through cooperative action. In this situation, the rhetoric of "circle of trust" has been established as a "selective" mechanism, which exacerbates rivalry for having access to it.

This controversial situation, instead of bringing chaos and disorder to the farm, resulted in the emergence of self-regulating mechanisms which reflect both acceptance and a perceived threat of rejection from the "circle of trust". Thus, the farm becomes a unit of diverse interests, and consists of struggles and competitions that systematically lead clients to act according to their interests. The clients cooperate with those whose interests do not intersect, yet split up with those whose interests do intersect. This is a paradox, as "divergence of interests" may also create "joint interests". Finally, the "circle of trust" has revealed the intentions of actors by displaying them in "action": people who can creatively manage the constraints of the farm structure can establish their own rules and form their own alliances. The patronage system is not stable but blurred, because there is a "circle of trust" which creates an unintentional irony for the insiders and is challenged by new clients. This "circle of trust" is shared by the patron and his clients, both of whom have arrived at a way of coming to terms with one another on the basis of unequal power relations. This circle allows them to meet current challenges in a process that is itself in constant change, reorganization and restructuring.

Notes

1 Collective action refers to public benefit, but in this case I use the term "cooperative action" to refer to a group of individuals who work together for the private benefit.
2 Here we can see the continuity between Soviet and post-Soviet experiences.
3 See more on farmers' rights on land and property in Giovarelli (1998: 6).
4 I could use the term "*kolkhoz*" throughout the chapter, but the new workers of the farm always mentioned the former workers that this is a "private farm".
5 Interview with the head of former *kolkhoz* Mirlan.
6 See more on farmers' rights on land and property in Giovarelli (1998: 37); (Government Regulation Adopted by Resolution No. 632).
7 Therefore, the strategic plan made by the *kolkhoz* headman could not be realized, and his mission failed (Interview with the previous head of *kolkhoz*, Mirlan, 12 January 2008).
8 According to fund rules, "those who work in the fund are not allowed to apply for credit." As such, this private farm was purchased by Rahim's wife. This became evident when local people started getting their shares; they had to write a letter of request not to Rahim but to his wife.
9 In this section of the chapter, I will use the terms "private farm" and "farm" interchangeably and will not use "*kolkhoz*", as the new workers of the farm always told the former workers that this is a "private farm".
10 It has to be pointed out that his wealth was not limited to his "official" business; he also obviously also had other sources of income.
11 A unique situation arose in the case of "*dom kultura*" (house of culture), a part of the *kolkhoz* that was commonly used for public celebrations and meeting common needs (such as hairdressing and tailoring). Although land and livestock could be equally divided, the head of *kolkhoz* had difficulties in dividing the *dom kultura* among 3,000 people. In the end, it was sold to Rahim as a part of the *kolkhoz*, but then people started to face difficulties in celebrating special days such as the Victory Day without their house of culture. Before the hairdresser, circus club manager and tailors used this club for free, in return they provided cheap services for the local community. Now, they face difficulties in finding another place for themselves.
12 Instead they used kinship terminologies such as "*we are coming from your parental side (kuda)*" or "*we are your relatives from maternal side (taeke – jeen)*". They also cited well-known proverbs in order to justify their actions vis-à-vis the patron such as "*Suur jakanyn korkun achat, jeen toidun barkyn achat*" (Relatives from the maternal side can help a person to establish distant relative's positions).
13 More about migration in Kyrgyzstan can be found in Madeleine Reeves (2009), on Kyrgyz migrants in Russia, and in Ablezova *et al.* (2007), on internal migration between rural and urban areas.
14 I was allowed only to talk to people and make observations, without being given any official documentation of either workers' property or the quantity of cattle. I could only get an approximate number for the quantity of cattle from the *kolkhoz* workers. The reason was that this was a "private farm" closed for outsiders, including me.
15 Even though legally this is a private farm, Marat always refers to this place as a "*kolkhoz*".
16 Scott (1977) in his article on South Asia claimed the exchange between patron and clients are based on tangible and intangible assets. Moreover, as the interests of the patron and his clients are different, they do not intersect.

References

Aalam (2007) 18 April, Bishkek.

Ablezova, M., Botoeva, G., Tynaev, N. and Turgunbaev, T. (2007) *Conditions and State of Social Rehabilitation of Labor Migrants-Citizens of the Kyrgyz Republic Following Their Return to Homeland.* Online. Available: http://src.auca.kg/images/stories/files/Migrants_eng.pdf (accessed on 21 May 2009).

Anderson, D. (1996) "Bringing Civil Society to an Uncivilized Place", in C. Hann and E. Dunn (eds) *Civil Society: Challenging Western Models*, London: Routledge: 99–120.

Asad, T. (1970) *The Kababish Arabs: Power, Authority and Consent in a Nomadic Tribe*, London: Hurst.

Boissevain, J. (1966) "Patronage in Sicily", *Man* 1/1: 18–33.

Chuy Encyclopedia (1998) 20 February, Bishkek.

Coleman, J. (1986) *Individual Interests and Collective Action*, Cambridge: Cambridge University Press.

Csaki, C. and Lerman, Z. (1997) "Land Reform and Farm Restructuring in East Central Europe and CIS in the 1990s: Expectations and Achievements after the First Five Years", *European Review of Agricultural Economics*, 24: 428–452. Online. Available: http://erae. oxfordjournals.org/cgi/content/abstract/24/3–4/428 (accessed on 25 May 2009).

Eisenstadt, S.N. and Roniger, L. (1980) "Patron-Client as a Model of Structuring Social Exchange", *Comparative Studies in Society and History*, 22/49: 42–77.

Eisenstadt, S.N. and Roniger, L. (1999) *Patrons, Clients and Friends: Interpersonal Relations and the Structure of Trust in Society*, Cambridge: Cambridge University Press.

Ensminger, J. (2001) "Reputations, Trust, and the Principal Agent Problem", in K.S. Cook (ed.) *Trust in society*, New York: Sage: 185–201.

Firlit, E. and Chlopecki, J. (1992) "When Theft is not Theft", in J.R. Wedel (ed.) *The Unplanned Society: Poland during and after Communism*, New York: Columbia University Press: 95–109.

Foster, G.M. (1961) "The Dyadic Contract: A Model for the Social Structure of a Mexican Peasant Village", *American Anthropologist*, 63/6: 1173–1192; reprinted in S.W. Schmidt, L. Guasti, C.H. Lande and J.C. Scott (eds) (1977) *Friends, Followers, and Factions: A Reader in Political Clientelism*, Berkeley: University of California Press: 15–28.

Foster, G.M. (1963) "The Dyadic Contract in Tzintzuntzan, II: Patron–client Relationship", *American Anthropologist*, 65/6: 1280–1294.

Gellner, E. (1977) *Patrons and Clients in Mediterranean Societies*, London: Duckworth.

Gellner, E. (2000) "Trust, Cohesion, and the Social Order", in D. Gambetta (ed.) *Trust: Making and Breaking Cooperative Relations*, Oxford: Oxford University Press: 142–157.

Giovarelli, R. (1998) "Land Reform and Farm Reorganization in the Kyrgyz Republic: Report on Fieldwork Conducted in the Kyrgyz Republic", *RDI Reports on Foreign Aid and Development*, No. 96, Rural Development Institute.

Gouldner, A. (1960) "The Norm of Reciprocity: A Preliminary Statement", *American Sociological Review*, 25/2: 161–178; reprinted in S.W. Schmidt, L. Guasti, C.H. Lande and J.C. Scott (eds) (1977) *Friends, Followers, and Factions: A Reader in Political Clientelism*, Berkeley: University of California Press: 28–43.

Humphrey, C. (1998) *Marx Went Away, but Karl Stayed Behind*, Ann Arbor: University of Michigan Press.

Lemarchand, R. (1972) "Political Clientelism and Ethnicity in Tropical Africa: Competing Solidarities in Nation Building", *American Political Science Review* 66/1: 68–90; reprinted in S.W. Schmidt, L. Guasti, C.H. Lande and J.C. Scott (eds) (1977) *Friends, Followers, and Factions: A Reader in Political Clientelism*, Berkeley: University of California Press.

Mayer, A. (1977) "The Significance of Quasi-Groups in the Study of Complex Societies", in S. Leinhardt (ed.) *Social Networks: A Developing Paradigm*, New York: Academic Press: 293–318.

National Statistical Committee Data for 2007. Online. Available: www.dfid.gov.uk/Documents/kyrgyzstan-factsheet.pdf (accessed on 2 May 2009).

Nikulin, A. (2003) "Kuban *kolkhoz* between a Holding and a Hacienda: Contradictions of Post-Soviet Rural Development", *Focaal – Journal of Global and Historical Anthropology*, 41: 137–152.

Powell, J.D. (1977) "Peasant Society and Clientelist Politics", *American Political Science Review*, 64/2: 411–425; reprinted in S.W. Schmidt, L. Guasti, C.H. Lande and J.C. Scott (eds) (1977) *Friends, Followers, and Factions: A Reader in Political Clientelism*, Berkeley: University of California Press: 147–161.

Reeves, M. (2009) "Beyond Economic Determinism: Microdynamics of Migration from Rural Kyrgyzstan" [in Russian], *Neprikosnovennyi zapas*, 4: 262.

Schlee, G. (2009) *Choice and Identity*, MPI for Social Anthropology, Halle Saale.

Scott, J. (1977) "Patronage or Exploitation?" in E. Gellner and J. Waterbury (eds) *Patrons and Clients in Mediterranean Societies*, London: Duckworth: 21–39.

Silverman, S. (1977) "Patronage as Myth in Patrons and Clients in Mediterranean societies", in E. Gellner and J. Waterbury (eds) *Patrons and Clients in Mediterranean Societies*, London: Duckworth: 7–19.

Verdery (1996) *What Was Socialism, and What Comes Next?* Princeton University Press.

Zanca, R. (2000) "*Kolkhozes* into Shirkats: A Local Label for Managed Pastoralism in Uzbekistan", *The National Council for Eurasian and East European Research (NCEEER): Working Papers*. Online. Available: www.ucis.pitt.edu/nceeer/2000–814–12g-Zanca.pdf (accessed on 25 May 2009).

5   From herd breeding to land farming

Social uses of descent and kinship in a Kyrgyz village

Svetlana Jacquesson

In 1996, the last *kolkhozes* of Kyrgyzstan were dismantled. Country dwellers found themselves with small parcels of arable land and even smaller herds, the remnants of the collective ones. In an effort to facilitate the restructuring of economic activities, the government designed new types of private agricultural enterprises. This chapter examines the creation of such private agricultural enterprises in a village situated in the Aktalaa region. It analyses the social uses of descent and kinship and focuses on their role within the newly introduced economic institutions.

To this end, the chapter combines two perspectives on descent and kinship: as systems of normative relations on one hand and as networks of variously configured interactions on the other.[1] Both descent and kinship function as systems, which distribute social actors among a definite number of categories organized by a culturally specific logic. Therefore, descent and kinship generate normative representations or expectations in terms of the relations between these categories.

Since all of the ethnographic cases examined below have men as main protagonists, I will provide some indications on the expected relations between a man and his relatives. Kyrgyz kinship terminology assimilates "father's brothers" to "fathers" (*ata*) and patrilateral cousins to "elder/younger brothers" (*aga/ini*) or "elder/younger sisters" (*eje/karyndash*). Thus, patrilineal linkages and patrilateral kin are conceived of as an extended family structured by a strict hierarchy of age and gender: youngsters obey elders, women obey men. Kin on the mother's side form an entirely distinct category as indicated by the determiner *tai* preceding their names. The mother's brothers, or maternal uncles (*taike*), represent a particular category of male kin towards whom ego (*jeen*) is not bound by the hierarchy of age. Quite the opposite, for reasons that cannot be elaborated here, the maternal uncles have plenty of obligations towards promoting the male ego.[2] The husbands of sisters and daughters form still another category, marked by the determiner *kaiyn*, since the connections to them are not by blood but by marriage. They can thus be considered as relatives (by marriage) and distinguished from kin (by blood).

In varying circumstances, various kinship relations may be activated: sometimes, the interactions between siblings may appear as predominating; in other circumstances, the most significant interactions may be those between uncles and nephews. The networks of activated relations or interactions belong to the empirical domain. Their analysis makes it possible to problematize the expectations related to kinship and descent categories on one hand and the specificity of resulting interactions on the other. This is the way descent and kinship are investigated here. In addition, the chapter attempts a comparison between active networks based on the same stock of kinship and descent relations configured by different economic activities, herd breeding in the past versus land farming at present.

The genesis of a village community

The village of Togolok Moldo is situated on the northern bank of the Naryn River. At the time of my fieldwork, in 2004, it had about 3,800 inhabitants and

Table 5.1 Census of Togolok Moldo

Genealogical line	Genealogical reference[1]	Descent groups	Number of households
Chekir Saiak (Moldo Chekir)[2]	Choro	Buura	50
		Boztumak	10
		Janbul uulu	50
		Kongur uulu	59
		Baibagysh	200
		Kazak	2–3
	Kuljygach	Oidochekti	20
Saiak[3]	Kaiduulat	Chong Kaiduulat	100
		Kichi Kaiduulat	
Basyz	Kashka	–	4–5
	Kerkitamga	–	45–50
Munduz	Kokchogoz	–	30
	Jolduubay	–	20
Kalmak	–	–	40
Sarybagysh	–	–	30
Kytai	–	–	25
Kutchu	–	Kara Kutchu	20
Saruu	–	Chong Saruu	20
	–	Maida Saruu	7–8
Adigine	–	–	5–6
Mongoldor	–	–	4–5
			~740

Notes

1 I use "genealogical reference" to indicate the genealogical levels with the help of which local descent groups link themselves to genealogical lines and to the common genealogical chart of the Kyrgyz. When in a given locality the members of a genealogical line are few in number, they tend to skip both the genealogical reference and the name of their descent group and identify solely by the genealogical line.

2 Moldo Chekir is considered as the ancestor of the Chekir Saiak, cf. Figure 5.1.

3 I consider Saiak as a genealogical line different from Chekir Saiak, even if in some genealogies the two of them may be related to a common ancestor.

740 households. There was a single street in Togolok Moldo and the houses, looking all the same, were arranged in uniform quarters. When the villagers spoke of their village, they did not refer to streets or quarters but to descent lines.[3] In addition to knowing their own descent lines, they were also able to indicate the descent lines of close or distant relations and, of course, of all the village officials. Identification by descent was as widely practised as categorization by descent and both were actively used to locate social actors on the village level and beyond.[4] In a way, one hardly needed to perform a microcensus since most local residents had quite a clear idea of the number of households belonging to a given descent line and could even name all its male members. At the village level, descent lines produced descent groups with clear-cut size and membership.

Historical and genealogical setting

The village dwellers belonged to a variety of descent lines as shown in Table 5.1, but the majority of them identified themselves as Chekir Saiak. According to local traditions, the territory between the shores of the lake Song-kol in the north and the Naryn river in the south, "belonged to" or was the "ancestral land" (*yurt*) of the Chekir Saiak and, more precisely, of three of their descent lines – Kudaiberdi, Akkabak and Yman – which were also known by a common name: the Three Kurtka (*Uch Kurtka*) (see Figure 5.1). The Three Kurtka had come to their present homeland from the north after the defeat of the Dzungars by the Chinese emperor Ch'ien-lung in 1757 (Doloev 1996: 9–10). The ancestors of the villagers who belonged to other genealogical lines were said to have settled among the Three Kurtka later and for various reasons. The Basyz and Mongoldor, for example, had established themselves on the southern bank of the Naryn at the same time as the Three Kurtka occupied its northern bank, roughly in the second half of the eighteenth century, but they had come from the south, from the Fergana valley (Doloev 1996: 7–8). Nobody remembered why some Basyz and Mongoldor left their kindred, crossed the river and decided to make a living among the Three Kurtka. Other groups, such as the Saruu, the Kutchu and the Kytai, descended from slaves (*kul*) who were displaced or exchanged according to the wills and whims of the Kyrgyz chiefs. Finally, the Sarybagysh settled in the region in 1905 following a mullah, who founded the first Quranic school (Doloev 1996: 91). In Togolok Moldo members of genealogical lines other than Chekir Saiak were commonly referred to as "outsiders" (*koshulgan*).

Local knowledge on descent and genealogy was completed and enriched by a surprising abundance of published materials: families usually had a collection of newspaper clippings on genealogy, booklets containing the genealogical chart of the Kyrgyz and, in some cases, extensive published genealogies. Most of them had their descent lines written down on sheets of paper; some of them had school notebooks in which they had copied extensive passages from published genealogies trying to locate their own descent line within the genealogical chart of the Kyrgyz. The local practice of identification by descent was thus influenced by

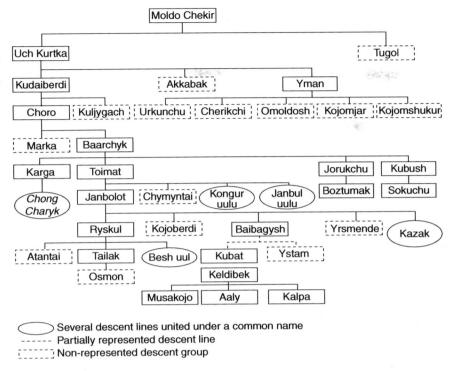

Figure 5.1 Partial genealogy of the Uch Kurtka (Chekir Saiak).

the official narratives on the genealogical relatedness of all the Kyrgyz and by a descent-based national ideology (Gullette 2008; Jacquesson 2010b). The slogan – "*Tegingdi bil, yimanyngdy sakta, ata-saltyngdy unutpa* [Know your descent, preserve your belief, do not forget your ancestral customs]" – printed on the cover page of many genealogies was well known and frequently quoted during interviews and discussions.

Colonial and Soviet social engineering

Prior to collectivization, most Kyrgyz were living in yurt camps (*ail*) of variable sizes attached to permanent winter quarters where the cemeteries – the only durable constructions – were found. The camps moved between these winter quarters and the summer pastures situated higher in the mountains (see Map 5.1). The earliest data on the composition of these camps date back to the beginning of the twentieth century when a population survey was carried out by the Russian colonial administration (Rumyantsev 1916). At that time the camps were identified by genealogical lines or by genealogical references

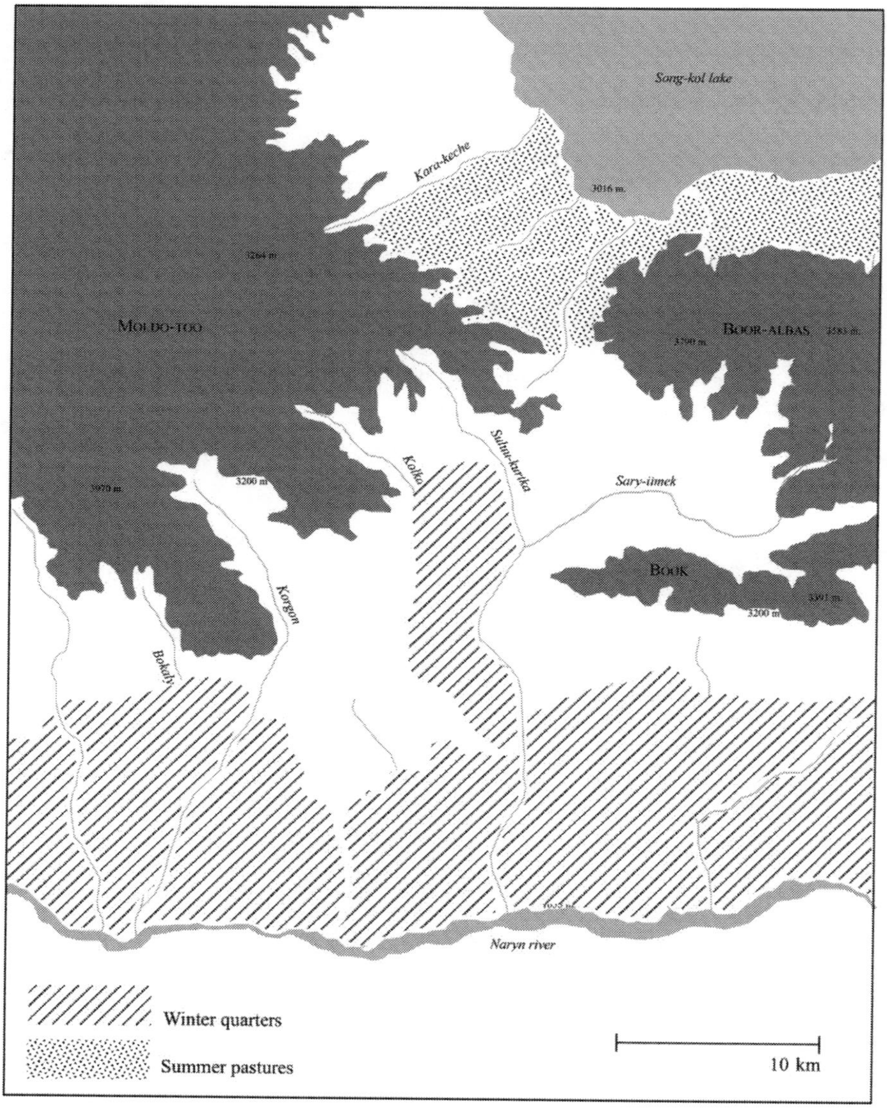

Map 5.1 Dwelling pattern on the northern bank of the Naryn river before the collectivization (© Sv. Jacquesson).

(Jacquesson 2010a). The village of Togolok Moldo, for instance, was known as the Choro camp, after the genealogical reference to the most important local descent groups. Such a method of identification and designation of camps provided the false idea that their residents were genealogically homogenous. In practice, this was rarely the case and, as the census of Togolok Moldo and the history of its inhabitants show, in most places the inhabitants belonged to a variety of genealogical lines.

The first detailed ethnographic data on the organization of kinship groups date back also to the beginning of the twentieth century (Dyrenkova 1926; Abramzon 1951: 152–156, 1971: 214–217, 241–248). According to this data, Kyrgyz lived in patrilineal units of various sizes, constituted of married couples residing in separate yurts, carrying out herd breeding and other activities together under the authority of the father or the grandfather. The order, solidarity and prosperity of these patrilineal units were based on a strict hierarchy of age and gender. Active kinship networks at that time, e.g. kin working and migrating together, as well as sharing camps and pastures, were configured by the requirements of herd breeding. Kin regrouped in such a way as to be able to form herds of a particular size and composition, and thus save labour and make the best possible use of the available pastures (Pogorel'skii and Batrakov 1930: 55–66; Sydykov 1930; Jacquesson 2010c: 99–108). In short, group making among kin was largely dependent on herd breeding and pasture use.

In contrast to other regions of Central Asia, and notably in contrast to Kazakhstan and Tajikistan, the successive waves of *kolkhoz* building in Kyrgyzstan were not accompanied by massive displacements. Actually, as the villagers themselves described it, in the 1930s they were simply trapped in their winter quarters and, as soon as 30 yurts could be brought together, a *kolkhoz* was founded (see Map 5.2). During the 1950s, these small *kolkhozes* were regrouped into larger collective farms. Most of their members used to have a dwelling in the administrative centre, but the former winter quarters were kept alive by the various production activities that took place there (see Map 5.3).

Neither collectivization nor sedentarization changed the basic dwelling pattern, although they introduced a rural type of settlement in which the *kolkhoz* was a "total social institution".[5] Within such a "total social institution", the management of herds and human labour was carried out by the administration. Consequently, kinship groups within the *kolkhoz* lost their habit of running herds, using pastures migrating together. Instead, the most active kinship networks became those based on ritual activities, such as funerals and funeral commemorations (Abramzon *et al.* 1958: 240–248; Bayalieva 1972: 151–155, 1981: 81–85).

Five years after independence, in 1996, the *kolkhozes* were dismantled by government decision and replaced by the so-called "village councils" (*ail okmoto*). Their former administrative centres, and some of their production units, became "villages" (*ail*) (see Map 5.4). The ways in which the assets of *kolkhozes*, such as arable land, animals, barns and machinery, were turned over into private use differed from one *kolkhoz* to another, but the outcome was the same all over the country: a drastic fall of herd breeding. This was more of a case in Togolok Moldo, since, in the last years of Soviet rule, the *kolkhoz* has already been heavily indebted to the state. The sheep herd of the *kolkhoz*, for instance, had diminished from 30,000 head in the early 1990s to 13,000 in 1996 (Jacquesson 2010c: 211–212). The animal shares received were insignificant. In

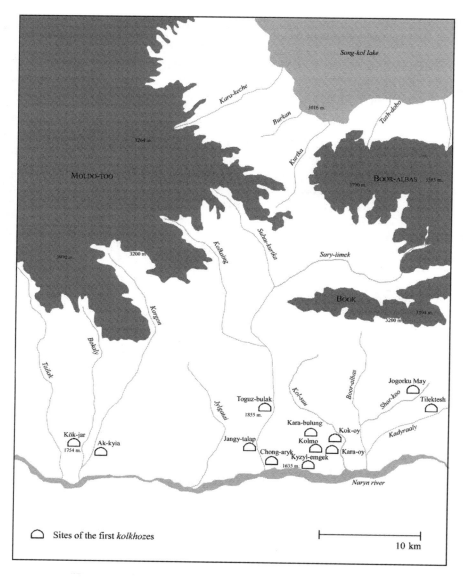

Map 5.2 Sites of the first *kolkhozes*, mid 1930s–mid 1950s (© S. Jacquesson).

terms of land shares, in Togolok Moldo each person born in the village became entitled to 0.5 ha of irrigated land. However the quality of some land plots was poor, the irrigation system badly needed repair and tractors and ploughing machines were either broken or too expensive to use. As the outcome of a century of colonial rule and Soviet social and economic engineering, the inhabitants of

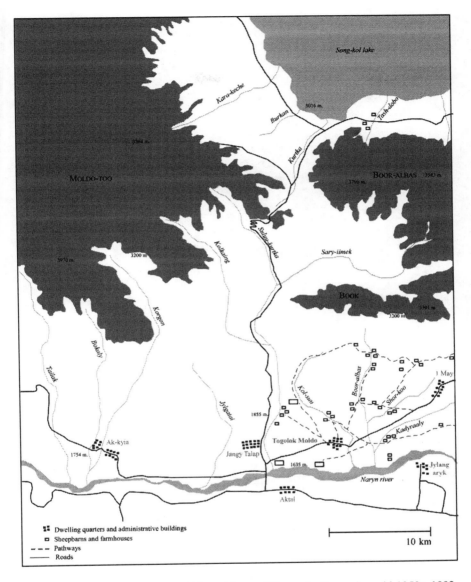

Map 5.3 The *kolkhoz* Togolok Moldo and its satellite production units, mid 1950s–1992 (© S. Jacquesson).

Togolok Moldo found themselves poorly bestowed in animals and land, and were faced with inadequate supply of agricultural machines and severely deteriorated infrastructure. They were also far away from urban and market places and the only means of communication were dirt roads.

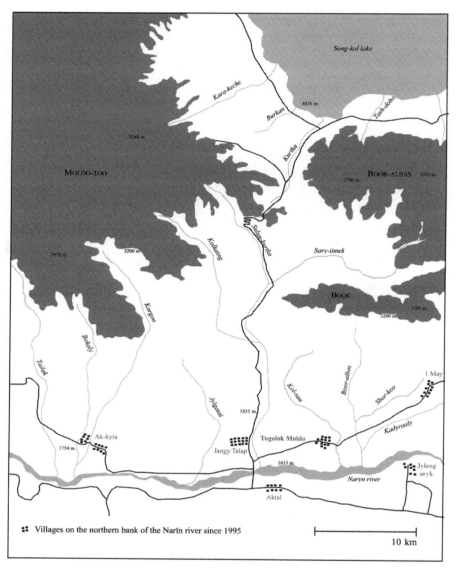

Villages on the northern bank of the Narîn river since 1995

10 km

Map 5.4 Kyrgyz villages on the northern bank of the Naryn river since 1995 (© S. Jacquesson).

From herd breeding to land farming

In an attempt to apprehend the post-*kolkhoz* economic disorganization, the government had designed a new legal framework for carrying out self-sustainable farming at the very beginning of the land reform in 1991 (Bloch *et al.* 1996: 11–13; Bloch 2002). This legal framework offered a reasonably wide choice of alternatives in terms of the size of agricultural enterprises. Yet, wittingly or unwittingly, it also promoted land farming as the most significant economic activity and family as the basic production unit. The various types of private agricultural enterprises were in fact all defined by the size of arable land plot and by the number of families which cultivated it. Thus, an "individual household enterprise" consisted of a household plot and a single family; a "farm enterprise" was also operated by a single family but cultivated at least 5 ha of land; finally, a "peasant enterprise" corresponded to two or more families farming from 5 ha to 100 ha of land (Giovarelli 2001: 93). In a country which had specialized in herd breeding for at least 70 years, such legislation was rather unexpected. What about herd breeding, migration and pastures? What about those regions where land farming was next to impossible? Answers to these questions were not provided by government regulations at that time and, in a way, they are still unanswered today.[6]

The government regulations redefined the status of herd breeding and land farming. In Soviet times, the prosperity of Togolok Moldo depended on a highly specialized and highly productive fine-wool sheep breeding. Without the *kolkhoz* and the state subsidies, fine-wool sheep breeding collapsed. Families went back to small, mixed herds comprised of local, low-productive livestock. In the absence of any official regulations, animal keeping came to be carried out in three different ways: on a contractual basis in summer when a certain fee per animal and per month was paid to a herdsman who took the livestock to the summer pastures; by rotation in autumn when the village dwellers took turns in looking after the animals of a street or a neighbourhood; and, finally, in winter each family taking care of its own animals. In a way, animal keeping became a subsistence activity of secondary importance, abandoned to private initiatives without any formal institutional frame.

Getting kin and land together

The privatization wave left most village dwellers poor in terms of the number of animals. Instead, the villagers became entitled to small land shares. They could only be farmed effectively when regrouped. All of the agricultural enterprises that were set up and officially registered in Togolok Moldo took up land farming. These were entirely new circumstances for northern Kyrgyz, among whom cooperation and group making have been configured by herd breeding and pasture use. The absolute majority of agricultural enterprises in Togolok Moldo were "individual household enterprises", e.g. single families of various size making a living together. In the following section, I will analyse only "farm enterprises" or "peasant enterprises", e.g. enterprises extending beyond a single family, set up in the village.[7] I will focus more particularly on the kinship and descent categories, which had been put into use by their founders.

Father and sons (ata uul)

The Mambetov enterprise was managed by an elderly couple: Kubanychbek and Altyn. Kubanychbek (born in 1940) was in control of all the production activities. Altyn was about the same age as her husband and she was the pillar of the family order. They had worked together from 1958, when Kubanychbek had taken over from his father one of the horse herds of the *kolkhoz*, until 1996, when the *kolkhoz* was dismantled. The eldest, divorced son and the two daughters of Kubanychbek lived and worked in Bishkek (see Figure 5.2). After losing his job and divorcing his wife, the fourth son returned from the capital to the village. In 2002, he married again but, in contrast to his first wife who was from Osh, his new wife was a neighbour's daughter.

The Mambetov enterprise was divided into three living quarters: the second and third sons had their own houses situated on the outskirts of the village, while the fourth and the fifth sons shared the same courtyard as Kubanychbek. In this courtyard, Kubanychbek, Altyn, their unmarried sons and most of the children lived in the old house, while the new house was divided in two equal parts between his fourth and fifth sons.

The family herd, comprising 20 horses, 70 sheep, 15 cows and a camel, was managed by Kubanychbek. The milk and meat were processed and distributed under the supervision of his wife Altyn. Each of the married sons knew exactly

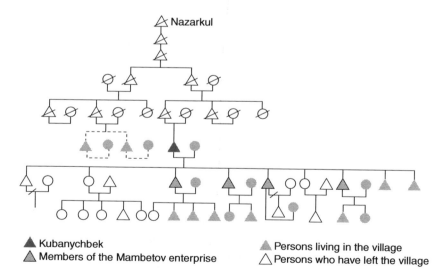

▲ Kubanychbek
△ Members of the Mambetov enterprise

▲ Persons living in the village
△ Persons who have left the village

Figure 5.2 Descent and kinship groups of the head of the Mambetov enterprise.

how many animals belonged to him but they all agreed that, as long as their father was alive, the animals would remain in the family herd. The Mambetov enterprise rented 119 ha of pastures and cultivated 10 ha of land corresponding to the land shares of the family members.[8] They grew fodder, wheat and barley.

The enterprise did not hire external labour, it produced for its own consumption, and wheat and animals were sold only when certain expenditures had to be met. The most important among them were electricity, wood and charcoal (for the winter period), and pasture and land taxes. Like most of the newly established agricultural enterprises in Togolok Moldo, this one used the market to convert animals and wheat into cash, but market demands did not influence the organization of its production activities. In the village, the Mambetov enterprise was considered successful. Its head, Kubanychbek, was highly respected and even admired, since few villagers had succeeded in making their married sons work together. In Togolok Moldo the Mambetov enterprise was an exception, both because of the unusually long cooperation between a father and his married sons, and because herd breeding was the main activity of the enterprise.

Genealogy was not among the topics Kubanychbek was talkative about. He was a Basyz and belonged thus to one of the groups considered as "outsiders" to the locality. Within the Basyz, he related himself to the Kashka descent line and there were only five households from the same descent line in the village. A look at the genealogy of Kubanychbek (see Figure 5.2) reveals the small size of his descent group. He was not only a single son but also a single child. Moreover he was an adopted one. Kubanychbek had just two patrilateral cousins twice-removed in the village.

His wife Altyn identified herself as Munduz. The Munduz, like the Basyz, were "outsiders" to the locality. They had two major descent lines in the village – the Kokchogoz and the Jolduubay (see Table 5.1). Altyn belonged to the Jolduubay. The parents of Altyn and her three elder brothers had passed away. Therefore, Kubanychbek's in-laws belonged to the generation of his own children. His relations with them were limited to occasional invitations for the lifecycle rites. As far as Kubanychbek's sons were concerned, they had no maternal uncles and just a few distant patrilateral cousins.

As I have mentioned above, the Mambetov enterprise was considered as an exception in the village. I believe that this exceptional status was largely explained by the choice of herd breeding as a main activity. Kubanychbek could do so because, when the *kolkhoz* herds were divided among the *kolkhoz* members, he managed to preserve not only his own animal share but also the animal shares of his wife and children. Further, as a family head, he could keep all the family animals in a common herd. Finally, since he had provided the bride price for their marriage, his married sons could not take away their animal shares without "breaking the custom" (*salt buzgan*) and facing general approbation in the village. Willingly or unwillingly, they stayed dependent on their father.

Kubanychbek's sons were well aware of this dependence. Therefore, they all welcomed a young and wealthy businessman when the latter asked Kubanychbek to become his adoptive father. This fictive kinship relation had an additional significance given the fact that the young businessman was a single and orphaned son and that he belonged to the same descent line of the Basyz as Kubanychbek. Thanks to their adoptive brother, the sons of Kubanychbek came to be seasonally employed as construction workers in the capital. The cash income allowed the family herd to be increased and helped stabilize the family enterprise. Consequently, the second son of Kubanychbek could leave it and start working independently as a contractual herder taking care of other people's animals.

Siblings (bir tuugan)

Unlike Kubanychbek, Berdibek (born 1950), the head of the Imanaaly enterprise, knew his genealogy perfectly well and liked to discuss it: he belonged to the Baibagysh line, which was the descent line of the local chiefs of the pre-Soviet period, and he was proud of it. Berdibek's family, however, was a modest one: his father (died in 1985) and his mother had worked as shepherds in the *kolkhoz*. Berdibek's father had had a younger brother, who died in the Second World War, and an older sister, who married in the Yssyk-kol region. The kinship groups of Berdibek and Kubanychbek were similar as both of them had few patrilateral kin in the generation of their fathers (see Figure 5.3).

Berdibek had five brothers and six sisters. He and his fourth brother, Kachy, had only secondary education because Berdibek had to take care of his younger

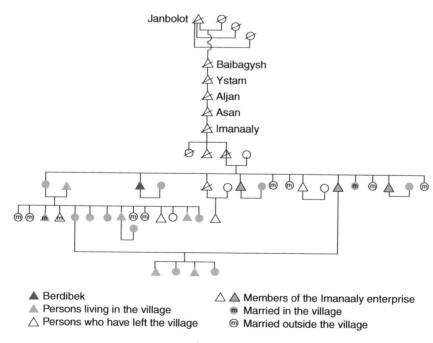

Figure 5.3 Descent and kinship groups of the head of the Imanaaly enterprise.

brothers and sisters while Kachy replaced his father as a shepherd in the *kolkhoz*. The other brothers and sisters had higher education. One of the brothers was making a living in the capital and two others were state employees in the regional centre Baetovo. The youngest one had graduated from the State Ped-agogical University in the capital but he was not working as a teacher, since teachers were poorly paid. Following the custom, he was taking care of his widowed mother and living with her in the village. Three of the sisters were married in Baetovo, two in Togolok Moldo and one in the Yssyk-kol region. It should be mentioned here that the land shares of those women who were born in the village but married outside of it were not given to their families, represented in most cases by their brothers, but became part of a special land reserve on the village level called "Unused Land".

Even if Berdibek was shy about his working career, he had directed one of the sheep farms for more than ten years and was thus one of those villagers who, thanks to the *kolkhoz*, had acquired good managing skills. When the *kolkhoz* was dismantled he took the initiative of setting up a "peasant enterprise". The latter was named after his ancestor in the third degree – Imanaaly – following a newly established local fashion of perpetuating ancestors' names by using them to identify any private enterprise of some significance.[9]

The family land shares amounted to 4.5 ha; in addition, the enterprise rented 25.5 ha from the Land Redistribution Fund.[10] The crops grown in the enterprise comprised of wheat, lucerne, flax (for the production of oil) and tobacco. All the brothers were official members of the enterprise, but only those living in the village actually worked in it. In contrast to Kubanychbek, Berdibek was more of a manager than a real head of enterprise. The important decisions were taken in common by all the brothers, and Berdibek just carried them out. He was the eldest brother and this had certainly helped him becoming the manager of the family enterprise. Equally important, however, was the fact that he was living in the village where the arable land was located.

Like the Mambetov enterprise, the Imanaaly enterprise produced for their own consumption and the crop was sold only for cash. But the latter did not deal with animal keeping: each brother took care of his own animals independently. For instance, the brothers who lived in Bishkek and Baetovo paid contractual herdsmen and from the family enterprise they received only the fodder necessary to feed their animals in winter. When I asked Berdibek why the family enterprise did not engage in animal keeping, he gave an unambiguous answer: animal keeping was a constant source of trouble; each time an animal died or was lost, the good relations between the brothers were threatened. The absence of a father, and thus of an undisputed authority in terms of herd management, had made keeping animals together impossible.

Finally, Berdibek described the interactions among the members of his descent group, which was one of the most numerous descent groups in the village, as following the rules of "unity" (*yntymak*) and "support" (*jardam*). These rules, however, worked only on the occasions of funerals and funeral feasts. As for other types of support, such as providing a ploughing machine or procuring petrol in periods of shortage, Berdibek relied mostly on his siblings (*bir tuugan*). Nevertheless, he also admitted that plenty of tasks could be carried out thanks to friends, no matter whether they were kin or not.

As far as his "peasant enterprise" was concerned, he shared the same opinion as Kubanychbek: there was no place to think of it as "business" (*biznes*), that is to say a profit-making activity; it was just a means to make a living (*jan baguu*). He underlined repeatedly that for him and his brothers, coming together within a single enterprise was conditioned by the fact that if land shares were not made use of, one could lose them. Consequently, the family enterprise was not a *biznes* but just a way to help each other out and preserve the newly acquired land property rights.

Uncle and nephews (taike-jeen)

The Chong Saruu enterprise is an example of a failed enterprise, since it functioned for only two years (1998–1999). Its founder, Deken Satyndiev (born in 1932), had been employed as the chief of one of the sheep farms of the *kolkhoz* but also as a history teacher at the local school. Accordingly, Deken was a fan of history in general and of that of his descent group in particular.

As a matter of fact, the Chong Saruu was a small descent group comprising about 20 households (see Table 5.1). Deken balanced the small size of the group with a meticulous record of all its male members, including those of the collateral lines, and by long and detailed descriptions of their lives and deeds. According to his descriptions, the common ancestor Toloko succeeded in becoming the chief (*eluu-bashy*) of a minor administrative division in the colonial period; the sons of Karymshak, Omuraaly and Otur, made a fortune by trading with the Fergana valley and the son of Omuraaly, Nurmat, became the president of one of the first *kolkhozes* in the region. In Togolok Moldo, however, the Chong Saruu were often derided since they were the descendants of slaves (*kul*).

Deken's father, Satyndy, was a single son who had had just two sons and a daughter. Similarly, Deken and his brother had few male descendants: Deken had only two sons whereas he had seven daughters; his brother Ayilchy had also just two sons. The other descent lines of the Chong Saruu – those of Tileke, Karyke, Kalyibek and Karymshak – had been interrupted since there had been no male descendants in the last three generations (see Figure 5.4).

The elder son of Deken worked in Bishkek and had two; Deken referred to them as "half Russian" (*chala orus*) since they spoke Russian and were not at ease with village life. All of Deken's daughters were married outside of Togolok Moldo; therefore, he had no sons-in-law in the village. Deken lived with his younger son Mirbek who had three daughters and a baby son.

When the land was privatized, Deken took the land shares of his children for his own use and decided to set up a private enterprise. But he found himself short of associates. Deken did not turn to his elder brother whom he considered as a "rough guy" (*karapaym*). He co-opted instead a nephew who was the son of a woman from the Karymshak line but, for reasons which remained unclear,

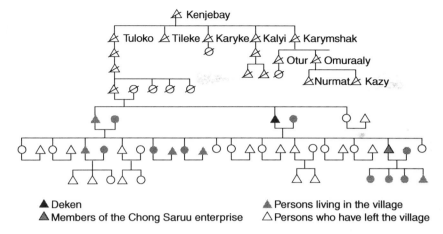

▲ Deken   ▲ Persons living in the village
▲ Members of the Chong Saruu enterprise   △ Persons who have left the village

Figure 5.4 Descent and kinship groups of the head of the Chong Saruu enterprise.

identified himself as Karymshak and Chong Saruu, e.g. as belonging to the descent line of his mother and not to that of his father. The working force of the Chong Saruu enterprise comprised Deken, his son Mirlan and his nephew. They engaged in farming 6.5 ha of land. Notwithstanding its modest size, the enterprise was given the name of a whole descent line – the Chong Saruu.

In spite of Deken's enthusiasm, the enterprise functioned for just two years. Deken admitted himself that he did not succeed in establishing suitable working relations with his nephew. As he remarked jokingly, *taike jeen el bolboit, jelke tas bolboit* "an uncle and a nephew go together like baldness and scabbiness" or *jeen kelgenche jeti boru kelsin* "better face seven wolves than a single nephew". In fact, these were not just jokes. Because of the abundance of women in the last three generations of the Chong Saruu, Deken had plenty of classificatory nephews[11] in the village and they kept interfering with his affairs. One of them, for instance, had asked to take care of Deken's mares and Deken had agreed. The nephew, therefore, kept the mares, milked them and sold the milk to earn a living. The only profit for Deken was that he did not have to worry about the feeding of the mares. Since these mares were kept in order to be sacrificed at funeral feasts, it was, after all, not such a bad deal even if Deken was deprived of mare's milk. Another nephew had borrowed a cow from Deken. When the cow calved, the nephew asked to sell the calf to his own profit and Deken allowed him to do so.

These nephews, however, were never envisaged as working partners by Deken. After the failure of the "Chong Saruu enterprise", he remained alone with his son Mirlan. The enterprise stayed registered at the local administration but it had only the label of an "enterprise"; like the Mambetov and the Imanaaly ventures, Deken and his son were just making a living and keeping a hold on the family's land shares.

Conclusions

Identifications and categorization by descent are still widely practiced in rural Kyrgyzstan. Backed by a state ideology of descent-based nationalism, they contribute to the perception of descent groups as the strongholds of trust, support and cooperation. This newly recovered pride in descent is manifested in various ways, the widespread fashion of giving ancestors' names to private ventures being one of them.

Social actors whose descent groups are of small size, like Kubanychbek and Deken, are aware of a lack of social capital, although their ways to remedy this differed significantly, at least on the discursive level: in the case of Kubanychbek, the descent factor was underplayed and found not worthy of lengthy discussions; in the case of Deken, the history of the descent group was augmented as if to remedy for its small size and for the fact that it was comprised of the descendants of former slaves.

When it came to the members of sizeable and prestigious descent groups, the pride and the confidence derived from such membership were commonly manifested in discourse. The only duty of a descent group's members that was taken for granted however was the support for funerals or funeral feasts. As far as the practicalities of earning a living were concerned, a descent group's members were not expected to act differently from other villagers.

The commitment to descent depended to a large extent on individual actors: some people, like Kubanychbek, had nothing to say on descent and they hardly knew their own ancestors; others, like Deken, took pride in descent and could speak of ancestors for hours. In the first case, interactions and relations were rarely interpreted in terms of descent, while in the second case nearly all social intercourse tended to be perceived through the grid of descent. The varying attitudes to descent did not seem to depend on the social status of the actors since former shepherds could share the same discourse on descent as former secretaries of the Communist Party.

As outlined in the introduction, the Kyrgyz kinship system is patrilinially biased. Further, the active kinship networks among northern Kyrgyz in the pre-Soviet period were largely shaped by herd breeding. The patrilineal bias still exists but it is mostly discursively manifested, by the knowledge of one's ancestors, the pride in one's descent group and its history and the maintenance of ritual groups focused on funeral. In Togolok Moldo there were no extended families functioning as herding groups or as farming ones.

Whether dealing with herd breeding or with land farming, the newly established enterprises could hardly mobilize kin beyond the family. In terms of family configuration, in the Mambetov case, the father has succeeded in making his married and unmarried sons work together for a while, in the Imanaaly case, an elder brother pulled together the land shares of his siblings. One may suggest that if the land parcels obtained by pulling together a family's land shares are big enough, or of an optimal size, there is no need to try to look for more partners. In the case of the Imanaaly entreprise, however, the brothers rented land from the land redistribution fund, which means that their land shares alone were insufficient. Yet, they obviously deemed it more rational to pay a land rent instead of attempting to mobilize other kin.

Sisters and daughters, even when they lived in the village, were not involved in the agricultural enterprises set up by their brothers or fathers. In the case of daughters, a custom has already been established in order to retain their land shares once they got married, namely their dowry was augmented by two or three head of cattle in exchange for their land share. As for sisters, in the three cases analysed here, either they did not exist (Kubanychbek), or they were married outside of the village (Berdibek and Deken), or they were older than their brothers, had a family of their own and were members of the individual household enterprises of their husbands. As I have mentioned above, the land shares of those women born in the village but married outside of it were not given to their brothers, but kept as a special reserve land fund. In a way, both the official regulations and the local practices put some limits on the kinship categories viewed as compatible in term of economic cooperation.

One of the reasons for the observed preference of patrilineal kin might be the clear hierarchies within patrilineal categories and thus the possibility to introduce certain logic of power relations, or a familiar mode of authority, e.g. sons obeying the father, younger brothers being under the supervision of an elder one, within the newly established agricultural enterprises. Whether they were fathers, elder brothers or uncles, those who initiated the regrouping of land shares were also always those on whom authority was already bestowed by their position in the kinship system.

However, the attempts to put patrilineal kinship into practice could fail, first and foremost, for the simple reason that some kinship categories could be empty or poorly provided in terms of individual actors as a consequence of the hazards of human reproduction. Evidence of this can be found in the Chong Saruu case where the abundance of women during the last three generations accounted for the lack of brothers or sons as potential partners. Occasionally, fictive kinship could be put into practice in order to fill in empty kinship categories. It is somehow significant that fictive kinship is almost exclusively formed within patrilineal categories: cases of ritual godfatherhood or brotherhood were numerous, while no mention was ever made of a ritual sisterhood.

Finally, as far as the changed status of herd breeding and land farming are concerned, I believe that land farming has not had a noticeable impact on kinship networks. To put it differently, the kinship categories activated in order to create agricultural enterprises remain the same as those which used to support herd breeding activities in the past. In fact, instead of the creation of new kinship networks, we observe a withdrawal to the family. Such a withdrawal may be related to the government regulations and their emphasis on the family as the basic production unit or, more pragmatically, to the lack of agricultural machinery, and thus the lack of stimulation for further regrouping of land shares. Whether the changing conditions of land farming will lead to a shift away from the family and in which direction is a research topic for future investigations.

Notes

1 On such an approach to kinship see also Fliche (2006) and Heady and Schweitzer (2010).
2 On the relations between uncles and nephews, see Dyrenkova 1926: 10–13.
3 Descent reckoning among Kyrgyz is patrilineal. Categories based on descent can have various extensions or sizes. The Kyrgyz distinguish between two major categories: local descent groups (*uruk*) and genealogical lines (*uruu*). There are 40 genealogical lines recognized as Kyrgyz both by the genealogies (*sanjyra*).
4 On categorization and identification see Jenkins (1996: 23, 89); Brubaker and Cooper (2004: 41–44).
5 On the *kolkhoz* as a total social institution, see the key monograph of Caroline Humphrey (2001).
6 On the most recent attempts of the government to introduce some regulations on pasture use and herd breeding, see Jacquesson 2010a.
7 Besides the three cases analysed here, there were two more "peasant enterprises" in the village: the first one was set up by the last president of the *kolkhoz* and the second one by a Bishkek lawyer who had recently returned to the village. Because their founders had previously been members of the *nomenklatura*, these enterprises could hardly be considered as representative of the restructuring process in the village. For more information, see Petric *et al.* 2004.
8 Comprised of the land shares of Kubanych and Altyn, the land shares of all of their children (even those who were living and working in Bishkek) and the land shares of those grand-children who were born in Togolok Moldo. See Figure 5.2.
9 Such private enterprises range from wholesale markets of regional importance (Dordoi) to shops, cafés and even feature magazines (*Jetigen*).
10 A local reserve comprising 25 per cent of the available arable land established after the dismantlement of the *kolkhoz* in order to meet land shortages in particularly specified circumstances.
11 Sons of women belonging to the Tuloko branch.

References

Abramzon, S. (1951) "Formy rodoplemennoi organizatsii u kochevnikov Srednei Azii [Clan and tribal organizations among the nomads of Central Asia]", *Trudy instituta etnografii*, XIV: 132–156.

Abramzon, S. *et al.* (1958) *Byt kolhoznikov kirgizskikh selenii Darkhan i Chichkan* [Kolkhoz life in the Kyrgyz villages of Darkhan and Chichkan], Moscow: AN SSSR.

Abramzon, S. *et al.* (1971) *Kirgizy i ikh etnogeneticheskie i istoriko-kul'turnye svyazi* [Ethnogenetic and cultural history of the Kyrgyz], Leningrad: Nauka.

Akmataliev, A. (1993) *Baba salty ene adebi* [Ancestral mores and customs], Bishkek: Balasagïn.

Baialieva, T. (1972) *Doislamskie verovaniya i ikh perezhitki u kirgizov* [Pre-Islamic beliefs and their survivals among the Kyrgyz], Frunze: Ilim.

Baialieva, T. (1981) *Religioznye perezhitki u kirgizov i ikh preodolenie* [Kyrgyz religious customs and the ways to overcome them], Frunze: Ilim.

Bloch, P. (2002) "Kyrgyzstan: Almost Done What Next?" *Problems of Post-Communism*, 48/1: 53–62.

Bloch, P., Delehanty, J.M. and Roth, M.J. (1996) *Land and Agrarian Reform in the Kyrgyz Republic*, LTC Research Paper 128, Madison: University of Wisconsin, Madison Land Tenure Center.

Brubaker, R. and Cooper, F. (2004) "Beyond Identity", in R. Brubaker, *Ethnicity without Groups*, Cambridge, London: Harvard University Press: 28–63.

Doloev, Ö. (1996) *Aktalaa – kuttun jergesi* [Aktalaa – the land of the blessed], Bishkek.

Dyrenkova, N. (1926) "Brak, terminy rodstva i psikhicheskie zaprety u kirgizov [Marriage, kinship terminology and psychological taboos among the Kyrgyz]", in *Materialy po svad'be i semeino-rodovomu stroyu narodov SSSR* [Materials on marriage and family and kinship structure amongst the peoples of the Soviet Union], Leningrad: Kommissiya po ustroistvu studentcheskikh etnograficheskikh ekskursii.

Fiel'strup, F. (1925 [2002]) *Iz obryadovoi zhizni kirgizov nachala XX veka* [On the ritual life of the Kyrgyz at the beginning of the 20th century], Moskva: Nauka.

Fliche, B. (ed.) (2006) "The Social Practices of Kinship: A Comparative Perspective", *European Journal of Turkish Studies*, 4. Online. Available: www.ejts.org/document629.html (accessed on 12 September 2007).

Giovarelli, R. (2001) "Land Reform and Farm Reorganization in the Kyrgyz Republic: A Legal Perpsective", in K.E. Engelmann and V. Pavlaković (eds), *Rural Development in Eurasia and the Middle East: Land Reform, Demographic Change and Environmental Constraints*, Seattle and London: University of Washington Press.

Gullette, D. (2008) "A State of Passion: The Use of Ethnogenesis in Kyrgyzstan", *Inner Asia*, 10/2: 261–279.

Heady, P. and Schweitzer, P. (eds) (2010) *Family, Kinship and State in Contemporary Europe*, 3 vols, Frankfurt, New York: Campus Verlag.

Humphrey, C. (2001) *Marx went away but Karl stayed behind*. Updated edition of *Karl Marx Collective: Economy, Society and Religion in a Siberian Collective Farm*. Ann Arbor: The University of Michigan Press.

Jacquesson, S. (2010a) "Reforming Pastoral Land Use: From Clan and Custom to Self-Government and Tradition", *Central Asian Survey*, 29/1: 103–118.

Jacquesson, S. (2010b) "A Power Play among the Kyrgyz: State versus Descent", in I. Charleux *et al.* (eds) *Representing Power in Modern Inner Asia: Conventions, Alternatives and Oppositions*, Bellingham: Western Washington University Press, 221–236.

Jacquesson, S. (2010c) *Pastoréalismes: anthropologie historique des processus d'intégration chez les Kirghiz du Tian Shan*, Wiesbaden: Dr. Ludwig Reichert Verlag.

Jenkins, R. (1996) *Social Identity*, London and New York: Routledge.

Petric, B., Jacquesson, S., Gossiaux, J.-F. and Bourgeot, A. (2004) "L'émergence de nouveaux pouvoirs locaux sur les cendres d'un kolkhoze Kirghize (oblast de Naryn)", *Cahiers d'Asie centrale*, 13–14: 21–44.

Pogorel'skii, P. and Batrakov, V. (1930) *Ekonomika kochevogo aula Kirgizstana* [The economy of migrating camps in Kyrgyzstan], Moskva: Sovnarkom KirASSR.

Rumyantsev, P. (ed.) (1916) *Materialy po obsledovaniyu tuzemnogo i russkogo starozhil'cheskogo khozyaistva i zemlepol'zovaniya v Semirecheskoi oblasti. Tom VIII: Przheval'skii uezd, kirgizskoe khozyaistvo. Vyp. 1: Tablitsy.* [Survey of native and Russian households and land use in the Semirech'e oblast. Volume VIII: Kyrgyz households in the district of Przhevalsk. Issue 1: Tables], Petrograd: Pereselencheskoe upravlenie Ministerstva zemledeliya.

Sydykov, A. (1930) "Organizatsiya vypasa skota v kochevoi gruppe [The organization of pasturage in migrating camps]", in N. Kazhanov (ed.) *Organizatsiya gorno-kochevogo khozyaistva Narynskogo kantona Kirgizskoi* [The organization of the nomad economy in the Kyrgyz Naryn region], ASSR, Tashkent: Narkomzem KirASSR: 233–269.

6 Religious conversion and its impact on ethnic identity in post-Soviet Kyrgyzstan

David Radford

The collapse of the Soviet Union and subsequent independence of Kyrgyzstan in 1991 resulted in rapid social and economic change and a greater openness to new ideas. This chapter will focus on the phenomenon of religious revitalization that has taken place in Kyrgyz society as part of this new openness and change in the post-communist era. In particular, this chapter will consider the impact that Christianity has had within the Kyrgyz community as growing numbers of Kyrgyz have embraced the Protestant Christian faith. This has challenged a common assumption in Kyrgyzstan regarding Kyrgyz identity that "to be Kyrgyz is to be Muslim". For the purposes of this chapter, I define "Protestant" as those non-Russian Orthodox and non-Roman Catholic elements of the Christian faith that are generally considered part of mainstream Christianity, such as Evangelical and Pentecostal, but not "sects", such as Jehovah's Witnesses or Mormons.

I argue in this chapter that Kyrgyz Christian believers do not see themselves as any less Kyrgyz than other Kyrgyz people. While there is recognition that not all of their Kyrgyz traditional ways fall in line with their new Christian faith, these believers value their sense of "Kyrgyzness" and have found ways to identify and develop continuity between their new religious faith and Kyrgyz traditional values, history and community, and beyond a strictly Muslim framework. I also argue that this view is consistent with recent sociological findings concerning the growth of new religious movements (Stark and Finke 2000) and the rapid growth of Christianity in non-western contexts (Jenkins 2002). In addition, I affirm the reality that ethnic identity is not fixed but is dynamically affected by its constant interaction with external changes and new opportunities. A qualitative approach involving in-depth interviews conducted in 2007 with Kyrgyz Christian believers from different backgrounds (ages, gender, location, length of Christian allegiance) is used to discuss their personal experiences. An analysis of these interviews forms the basis for this chapter.

Context: large-scale changes since independence

Kyrgyzstan has undergone large-scale changes since 1991. Independence from the Soviet Union was immediate and rapid and it affected many areas of society. This paved the way for a great openness to new ideas that were no longer confined to the authorized communist ideology of the Soviet Union. A new constitution was drawn up that included several articles on democracy, secularism and religious freedom (Anderson 1999). Repressive measures for maintaining the status quo were removed. Foreign or "western" ideas were no longer "bad" but were in fact "in". While there had been some privilege given to the titular Kyrgyz in the Soviet era, after independence this was further promoted without any need to uphold special status for the Russian language or people. In fact, as in other Central Asian states, laws were passed that gave sole state status to the Kyrgyz language (Smith *et al.* 1998). There is a perception that the situation has changed less favourably for Russians in the post-independence environment in Kyrgyzstan although the Russian language, even today, still plays an important role in education, media and commerce. This, amongst other reasons, has led to a major exodus of Russian and German people back to their "homelands" of Russia and Germany (Anderson 1999).

The decrease in the Slavic and German populations has had a significant impact on the Kyrgyz economy, as it was this segment of the population that represented a large part of the skilled labour force (Anderson 1999). This group was part of the elite section of urban society – local ethnic Kyrgyz accounted only for 8 per cent of the skilled labour force and only 3 per cent of engineers and technicians (Filonyk 1994). In some of the initial period, there were barely enough food supplies in shops. Many survived by bartering goods in the bazaars, or living off the produce of their land. Over the course of the years since 1991, there has also been a greater emphasis on learning English as a desired spoken language. The hope of the future was no longer dependent on Russia; it was perceived as now lying also in Europe and America.

While these have all been important factors, for my purposes, the changing religious landscape and the openness to new religious ideas have had a marked effect on the nation and the Kyrgyz people. The new constitution guaranteed freedom of religious ideas, expression and practice. A 70-year suppression of all things religious under Soviet atheism opened a floodgate of spiritual awakening (Tabyshalieva 2000). People no longer had to practice their traditional religion in secret. Many who had no or little interest in religious issues and rites were now becoming more interested. Public observance of Islam led to a sudden proliferation of new mosques and mosque attendance. Since independence, there has been a sharp increase in the number of mosques (from 59 in 1991 to more than 1,000 five years later) and in mosque attendance, although it is still small compared with the population as a whole (Anderson 1999).

In this era of sudden change and openness, there was also a large influx of new religious ideas not common to most of the Kyrgyz people up until that time. Religious groups as diverse as the Hare Krishnas and the Jehovah's Witnesses flooded in together with various Protestant Christian groups. (I do not include here the Russian Orthodox Church, which has been part of the Slavic, especially Russian, community since Tsarist days and which, until today, had only negligible, if any, direct influence on Kyrgyz people.) People were now open to these new ideas. From a situation where there were apparently only a handful of known Kyrgyz Protestant Christians before 1991, today there are many thousands. Exact numbers of Kyrgyz Christians vary but an estimate of around 20,000 is generally accepted (Pelkmans 2007). One Protestant group alone claims over 3,000 Kyrgyz adherents (Rotar 2004). While there were missionary efforts beginning from the early 1990s, this rapid social and religious phenomenon has continued over the following ten to 20 years. Of particular interest here is that this change has occurred amongst a people who have been traditionally identified as being Muslim. This is important for at least two major reasons. First, there have not been significant numbers of indigenous Christians since the thirteenth to fourteenth centuries and, second, it challenges the common perception that "to be Kyrgyz is to be Muslim".

Kyrgyz Christian believers – continuity with Kyrgyz culture, traditions and history

The idea that Kyrgyz can be anything other than Muslim, in terms of religious identity, is a growing reality for many Kyrgyz. These "Kyrgyz believers" (*mashayakche* in the Kyrgyz language) for the most part do not see themselves as any less Kyrgyz in their self-sense of ethnic identity than other Kyrgyz. Some, especially those who grew up in villages, towns and cities where there was great diversity of nationalities, place less importance on a sense of being Kyrgyz vis-à-vis other ethnic groups, but nevertheless do not consider themselves as having any other ethnic identity. By accepting the Christian faith as their own, these Kyrgyz do not feel that they have in any way ceased being Kyrgyz or have changed their ethnic identity.

Consistent with the data collected from a survey done in conjunction with the interviews, Kyrgyz Christians largely come from the age groups of adult (26–39 years – 39 per cent) and middle age (41–55 years – 33 per cent), although there is a reasonable number from the younger age cohort (<26 years – 15 per cent) as well. This would suggest that Kyrgyz conversion to Christianity is not simply a youth phenomenon. Unlike the census figures which indicate that there is roughly a 1:1 gender ratio between females and males, the Kyrgyz Christian ratio is nearly 2:1 although this is consistent with the literature on religion which consistently notes that women are generally more religious than men (Sherkat and Ellison 1999). Kyrgyz Christians also have a reasonably high level of education, with the great majority completing high school and about 20 per cent completing university. There is a high level of unemployment (21 per cent) but this is also consistent with the general population (18.5 per cent) (Indexmundi 2010).

In the interview process with 49 Kyrgyz Christian believers, several key issues relating to the Kyrgyz identity and Christianity have emerged. Surprisingly, a few of those I interviewed had either no knowledge or very limited knowledge of Christianity or Jesus Christ before they were introduced to Protestant Christianity. Therefore, the introduction of the Christian faith into their lives was virtually a brand new idea. There was little or no bias against Christianity because they just had never heard of it before. There was an openness to hear about something new, as one would generally be open to hear about something such as technology. In an era of dramatic change and new ideas, such as democracy as an alternative political system, this was initially also another idea, albeit a religious one, to listen to.

For those Kyrgyz who had already heard about Christianity or Jesus Christ prior to 1991, there was a perception, still prevalent today, that Christianity is a Russian religion and that Jesus Christ is the "Russian God". These ideas were associated with the connection that Russian people attended the Russian Orthodox Church. They have images (icons) of Jesus Christ and he was their god. If it was Russian, it was foreign, so not for the Kyrgyz people. The Russian Orthodox Church also had a deliberate policy of non-interference or non-evangelization of the Kyrgyz or other Central Asian ethnic people groups, which further encouraged a separation between the different "religious communities" (Roy 2000; Soucek 2000; Vladmir 2000). Many Russians had a strong social prejudice against the Kyrgyz (Haghayeghi 1996; Allworth 1998), they looked down on them as less civilized, as somehow lower in status, and this often meant that little deep or intimate interaction or relationship actually took place between members of these communities. This reinforced an ethnic differentiation between the Russians and the Kyrgyz so that it was natural for many Kyrgyz to associate Christianity, albeit Russian Orthodoxy, with Russian ethnicity and identity, especially in the post-Soviet era. It also reinforced the idea, both consciously and subconsciously, that if you were ethnically Kyrgyz you were Muslim because that was the ethnic association. Some people whom I interviewed had never really thought about any theological reasons why Kyrgyz were considered Muslim; they simply suggested that because their "ancestors" were Muslims, so were they.

Some that I interviewed had heard about other kinds of Christians, called "Baptists". It appears that this identification as "Baptist" was not so much an ethnic identity, although it was still associated with mostly the Russian or German communities, as it was a derogatory term that the Soviets promoted against some Christian groups who were non-Russian Orthodox and non-Roman Catholic. Who were the "Baptists"? Rumours circulated claiming that "Baptists" were Christians who engaged in secret sexual rites, even between members of the same family, and that they were cannibalistic (Wanner 2003). As one respondent put it: "They said, 'The Baptist Christians they are eating babies or people.'" To be called a "Baptist" was to invite persecution during Soviet times and, even today among some Kyrgyz, invites derision, mockery and ostracism [to be called a "betrayer", a *kafir*] – a pariah of normal Kyrgyz society.

Nevertheless, in the post-Soviet era, thousands of Kyrgyz have crossed these barriers of prejudice and embraced the Christian faith in the Protestant tradition. What changes have taken place and how have these changes affected their sense of ethnic identity, given that it was commonly understood that Kyrgyz were Muslims? A number of key elements have contributed to this. At the outset, it is important to note that for Kyrgyz who have embraced the Christian faith, there is no doubt that they still perceive themselves to be Kyrgyz. This is no less so now than before they embraced the Christian faith, and in fact in some cases, there is even a heightened sense of "Kyrgyzness". A noticeable feature of these Kyrgyz Christians is the way they refer to themselves. Many of those I have interviewed do not call themselves "Christians" as such but rather *ishengen* (literally "believers") or *mashayakche* (literally "one who follows the Messiah"), self-describing themselves in terms that are congruous with the Kyrgyz language, culture and tradition. They do not see themselves as having left the Kyrgyz community, but rather that within it they are "believers". Rather than referring to Jesus in Russian terms (*Iisus Khristos*), they describe themselves as believers in the Messiah (*Mashayak*), *Isa*, a Prophet (*Paigambar*) recognized by their Muslim religious tradition. It seems there has been an intentional effort to combine both Muslim and traditional Kyrgyz elements in the addressing of Jesus as *Isa Mashayak*. *Isa* is the Arabic word for Jesus in the Quran, which has also been accepted as the word for Jesus in the Kyrgyz language. Yet, unlike Christian believers in other parts of Central Asia, they have dropped the Arabic title for Jesus, *Masih*, in favour of the Kyrgyz word, *Mashayak*. They "believe" in *kudai* (literally "God"), otherwise referred to as *tengir* (literally "God the Lord", "Creator"). *Kudai* in Kyrgyz is a Central Asian word, originally Iranian, *khudo*, which came with Islam. *Tengir* is a purely Kyrgyz word related to a pre-Islamic religion incorporating mountains and the sky, and shamanistic practices. These terms are steeped in the traditional Kyrgyz world-view and are now incorporated into the expression and understanding of believers' new Christian faith. It is not a different God that they now worship but a different understanding of *kudai* interpreted through their new Christian experience and new scripture, the Bible. Remarkably, there seems to have been relatively little difficulty for many Kyrgyz to directly associate Jesus Christ as *kudai*, though this is anathema (*shirk*) for orthodox Islamic theology. This is perhaps a reflection that for the Kyrgyz it is the "affection" of religion rather than the "ideology" that underlies their sense of religiousness or spirituality.

Those I interviewed (49 respondents) had various approaches to their traditional cultural traditions and practices now that they have become *mashayakche*. Many (23 respondents) commented that it was important for *mashayakche* to continue to attend life-cycle ceremonies (e.g. birth, circumcision, marriage and death) even though they include elements of Islamic religion. Some commented that they attend but do not participate in Quranic prayers (recitations), while others attend but will pray Christian prayers silently. One respondent, when asked to lead the prayer, prayed out a memorized Bible verse without any opposition. A few do not attend these important functions. This is either because they feel there is too much association with Muslim religion or because of difficulty with family members who know they are *mashayakche*. One or two have either not told their family of their new faith, or have told one or both of their parents who, while not being happy with the situation, have asked the *mashayakche* not to let other members of the family know for the shame it will bring in the community. They attend family/community functions but others do not know they are *mashayakche*. The overriding reason cited for attending or not attending these life-cycle rituals was not so much to do with religion per se as it was to do with "being a part of the community/family". It was very important to maintain participation because it was important to be seen to be part of the family and the community. Being a *mashayakche* did not mean leaving the family or community and it was important to show this even if their family did not agree with their new faith.

Some (12 respondents) placed great emphasis on the many similarities between Kyrgyz cultural practices and traditions and their new Christian faith. Some others referred to particular words used in the Kyrgyz language relating them to Old Testament stories and cultural practices. For example one respondent suggested the following:

> Even if we take *boz ui* [yurt], God commanded [the Israelites] to put the sign of the blood on the entrance to protect the people from His judgment.... We still keep this because the entrance of *boz ui* is always painted with red. The wood of the entrance is supposed to be painted with red. The *tunduk* [top of the yurt] has three pieces of wood [criss-crossing] and symbolizes the cross. And also it symbolizes the trinity – God, Son and the Holy Spirit. It symbolizes the Triune God. And light comes through the Trinity. Our women are supposed to wake up early and open the roof in the morning to receive blessing. And before the sun rises we are supposed to get the blessing.

A couple of people further suggested that there is a strong link between the Kyrgyz people and the Jewish people, and that perhaps the Kyrgyz were even one of the "lost tribes of Israel".

Generally, those who grew up in towns or communities that had mixed nationalities (e.g. Russian, German, Uzbek and Kyrgyz) did not place as much importance on being Kyrgyz as those from more homogenous communities. They were Kyrgyz because they were born so, as were their fathers, and they speak Kyrgyz. Their sense of Kyrgyz identity is clearly related directly to blood, language and land, but not necessarily to religion.

It must also be pointed out that according to some scholars, before the arrival of Islam, the Kyrgyz people had other religious affiliations associated with Shamanism and Animism (Abramzon 1971; Lewis 2000; Tabyshalieva 2000). There is some historical evidence that there has been significant Christian (Nestorian and perhaps even earlier Syrian) presence in areas located within present-day Kyrgyzstan at least around the twelfth to fourteenth centuries, possibly numbering into many thousands (Rashid 1994; England 1996; Foltz 1999). This was also mentioned by some of the interviewees (13 respondents), a few of whom made reference to the fact that Kyrgyz were not always Muslims. Some indicated that they were shamans before, others said that the Kyrgyz were Christians even before they were really Muslims. So, for these Kyrgyz Christian believers, to be *mashayakche* today is only to return to what many Kyrgyz once were. As put forward by one respondent:

> We are Kyrgyz but now we are Kyrgyz Christians. The good news about Jesus did not only come to us today. It came to Central Asia before Islam

and history can prove it. It is why I think that we do not come to new faith, our old faith came back to us. Maybe we even became Christians before Americans.

Some saw Islam as being associated with Arabic, and not Kyrgyz culture, and as such, their Christian faith was closer to their sense of Kyrgyzness. When asked, for example, "what does it mean for you to be a Kyrgyz?" one respondent said:

> I told the mullah, "I wasn't born as an Arab. I wasn't born English. I was born Kyrgyz. And I was [born] in Kyrgyzstan, in the mountain." That's why God is for me here. God created me Kyrgyz therefore he understands Kyrgyz. It's no use for me to memorize words in Arabic. There is no need for me to grow a beard. I can't grow a beard, that's how God created me. God created me like that I should be like this.... Our ancestors are supposed to have had a box. Even when there were difficulties they wouldn't leave that box behind because the holy book was in there. It proves that we believed in God a long time ago ... later we lost contact with God. And then the difficulties came.... We had to flee to China and we had many other difficulties. And now many people think that this religion is coming from the west and from a foreign country. I think when we turned our back to God he was offended by us. But he didn't destroy us completely and he came with foreigners. I think God is working here, I think we are like rebellious children but I believe that eventually everybody will come to God.

Nevertheless, there was general agreement among all those I interviewed that not all Kyrgyz traditions were good. Now, as *mashayakche*, some aspects of their culture were no longer appropriate and needed to be changed. In particular, practices and ideas associated with "spiritual dynamics" were not necessarily associated with Islam as a religion but commonly thought of as relating to the Kyrgyz shamanistic past. These include things such as going to fortune tellers (*kozu achyk*) and shamans (*bakshy*) to help with sickness, questions about the future, or dealing with evil; and offering food and prayers for their dead ancestors (*arbak*), particularly the Thursday ceremony, where various breads and *plov* (a staple dish of lamb and rice) are made. Most acknowledged that before becoming *mashayakche*, they also had experienced visitations of an oppressive black spirit (*basyryk/albarsti*). While most commented that after becoming *mashayakche* these visits stopped, a few mentioned that these had resumed but that praying in the name of Isa had released them from it.

Response of the Kyrgyz community to conversion

The wider non-Christian Kyrgyz community have responded in a number of different ways to Kyrgyz conversion. Certainly, Christianity as a religious choice and identity is considered not normative for the Kyrgyz and so those who embrace this identity, whether "Christian" or *mashayakche*, face social pressures and sanctions. The main opposition comes from immediate and extended family but also from the general community. This opposition stems largely from the sense that in some way Kyrgyz Christians have "betrayed" the family, the community, the ancestors and the Muslim faith. The verbal accusations and gossip from the community have labelled Kyrgyz Christians as people who have "sold their faith", of "being bought by foreigners", of "becoming Russians" and of being "*kafirs*". The goal appears to be to shame Kyrgyz Christians into leaving their Christian faith and returning to the Muslim fold of the Kyrgyz community. It also appears to be aimed at shaming the family into taking action. Younger Kyrgyz Christians have had Christian literature and Bibles taken away from them and have been refused permission to attend Christian gatherings.

There have been reports of physical intimidation, though only one of the respondents I interviewed had experienced this. Ostracism from the family or community does occur but it does not appear to be the main response taken. Apart from the verbal threats and labelling the main opposition comes from the extended family and community which sometimes refuse to invite Kyrgyz Christians to attend important family and community events such as weddings and funerals. Tensions are particularly evident when it comes to the burial of a Kyrgyz Christian. The community cemetery (usually situated near the village) is an important symbolic representation of Kyrgyz identity and community linking a Kyrgyz to their family, the community, the ancestors and the Muslim faith. Some communities have refused permission for Kyrgyz Christians to be buried in the community cemetery, resulting in significant tension between Muslims and Christians in the Kyrgyz community drawing media attention (Murzakhalilov 2004; Pannier 2008).

While there clearly is opposition towards Kyrgyz Christian conversion, the data from my research indicates that in actual fact this opposition reduces over time. The family and community come to some level of rapprochement and toleration with Kyrgyz Christians, to the point where many Kyrgyz Christians are still invited to attend family and community events. Further, the narratives show that a number of family members have also become Christians. One respondent indicated that over 30 members of his family had become Christians, covering three generations. This suggests that when it comes to the bottom line it is blood, or family, that has greater salience than religion for the Kyrgyz.

As noted earlier, a new constitution was put into effect following independence, in 1991, which guaranteed the freedom to believe, practise and promote religion (Anderson 1999). This political or legal freedom remained in place until the beginning of 2009 when, under President Kurmanbek Bakiev, some restrictions were imposed on religious freedom based on what were considered the excesses of both Muslim and Protestant Christian groups (Bayram 2009). The research for this chapter took place between 2004 and 2008 and explains why there is little reference to the activities of government authorities in restricting or controlling Christian activity.

One final note of interest regarding opposition is that the role of mullahs in garnering opposition to Kyrgyz Christians seems to be relatively minor. The main oppositional function of the mullahs, based on the narratives, is when the family or community invite mullahs to convince Kyrgyz Christians to leave their Christian faith or in their refusal to give burial rights to Kyrgyz Christians. The minimal role of the mullah reflects the reality that Muslim religious figures and institutions were severely weakened during the Soviet period (Ro'i 1995; Glenn 1999). This research has no data on the influence of Muslim religious groups such as the Hizb-ut Tahrir on community responses.

Theoretical propositions for "new religious movements"

Stark and Finke (2000) have proposed an extensive theoretical model for under-standing what has come to be called "new religious movements". Who joins these movements? How do people become a part of the process and why? Such questions are thoroughly researched and a number of propositions have been developed. I believe that the rise and development of Protestant Christianity amongst the Kyrgyz people of Kyrgyzstan represents an example of a new religious movement. Likewise, a consideration of some of Stark and Finke's findings, including Stark's earlier work *The Rise of Christianity* (1996), provides a valuable tool for understanding the growth of this movement and the changing identity of these Kyrgyz *mashayakche*. While Protestant Christianity is not a new religious movement in a historical sense, it is new as far as the Kyrgyz people of Kyrgyzstan are concerned. As was mentioned above, the religious milieu up to 1991 included traditional forms of Islam (I include here all varieties of Islam – orthodox and heterodox) and the Russian Orthodox Church form of Christianity. There were examples of "Baptist" churches but these were few in number and members were virtually exclusively non-Kyrgyz. Due to the nature of this chapter, I have selected a few of these propositions and have applied them to these *mashayakche*, particularly in the way these affect the possibility of identity change.

According to the first proposition, "people are more willing to adopt a new religion to the extent that it retains cultural continuity with conventional religions(s) with which they are familiar" (Stark 1996: 55).

In the examples I have already given above, these *mashayakche* have made some clear differentiations about the Protestant Christian faith. While it did not originate in Kyrgyzstan, they have been able to separate it quite clearly from Russian culture, Russian ethnicity and the Russian Orthodox Church, a previous barrier for Kyrgyz acceptance of Christianity. They have found that this new "Protestant Christianity" has "cultural continuity" with many elements of their perception of Kyrgyzness, even to the point of claiming that some elements are Biblical in origin. They do not have to "give up, leave or reject" many aspects of their Kyrgyzness, therefore their conversion enables them to remain within the same cultural milieu as their family and community despite embracing a new ideological faith. "The principle of cultural continuity", Stark maintains, "captures the human tendency to maximize – to get the most for the least cost. … To the extent that potential converts can retain much of their original cultural heritage and merely add to it, cost is minimized" (ibid.). This is not to say that some varieties of this Protestant movement do not show expressions of other non-Kyrgyz cultural elements. Some aspects of form and worship are different, while many Kyrgyz who participate in Kyrgyz language churches are happy to participate in either Russian or Russian/Kyrgyz language mediums. This sense of cultural continuity reinforces an acceptance that these *mashayakche* consider themselves both Kyrgyz and Christian believers, separate from a Muslim religious association. This is a major shift in just 15 years.

According to the second proposition, "in making religious choices, people will attempt to conserve their social capital" (Stark and Finke 2000: 119).

Stark and Finke point out that "social capital" refers to both relationships within a community and the cultural "bundle" that people learn and become attached to through the socialization process (ibid: 120). I have briefly addressed the "cultural" issue above. But a further aspect that Stark and Finke addressed is that people generally attempt to maintain the social network (family, friends, etc.) as much as possible when making religious choices, such as embracing the Christian faith. It is clear that an important value for these *mashayakche* is the maintenance, as far as possible, of the network of social relationships that they already have – especially as it relates to the participation in traditional life-cycle rituals and other important family events. To break these relationships is to isolate themselves from a strong network to which each one turns, especially in times of need such as sickness, death and financial debt.

According to the third proposition, "attachments lie at the heart of conversion and therefore that conversion tends to proceed along social networks formed by interpersonal attachments" (Stark 1996: 18, 20; also Loftland and Stark 1965).

Almost without exception, every person I have interviewed has been directly influenced into becoming a *mashayakche* by a family member, a close (Kyrgyz) friend or by another Kyrgyz. The importance of this process of "recruitment" by these strong interpersonal attachments cannot be overstated. To a large extent Kyrgyz are becoming *mashayakche* through other Kyrgyz. Or at least, are very quickly introduced to other Kyrgyz *mashayakche*, or a Kyrgyz church or a group, usually where the Kyrgyz language is widely spoken or used, and where Kyrgyz songs are employed in worship. The early identification of their new faith, for these *mashayakche*, is very quickly associated with other Kyrgyz and with forms and language that are their own. This has the effect of reinforcing the idea that it is normal, it is natural and it is fine to be a Kyrgyz and a *mashayakche*. The breaking down of traditional thinking relating to the boundaries defining ethnic identity is apparent among these *mashayakche*. To reinforce this idea the large majority of those interviewed could number several members of their extended family who were also *mashayakche*. In one case, the interviewee numbered nearly 30 people crossing three generations. A situation in which significant numbers of Kyrgyz openly declare a new religious allegiance, where significant numbers are either family members or people within their social networks are also *mashayakche*, and where they maintain large elements of continuity with their Kyrgyz culture, will create an environment which reduces the effect and isolation of "deviant" behaviour affirming its legitimacy in terms of ethnic identity.

A final comment seems relevant in regards to those who first introduced Protestant Christianity to the Kyrgyz. While there were attempts by a few individuals (e.g. Yanzen 1993) to evangelize ethnic Kyrgyz during the Soviet period, the initial credit for the recent development seems to be given to an ethnic German from one of the "Russian Baptist" churches who independently moved to a Kyrgyz town to evangelize the Kyrgyz ("A Ray of Hope" 2004). The church grew through Kyrgyz networks as well as through the activities of other nationalities such as ethnic Russians and Germans (for the example of the Church of Jesus Christ, see Rotar 2004). After 1991, foreign missionaries from North America, Europe and South Korea also arrived in Kyrgyzstan and have played some role in the process (Anderson 1999; Peyrouse 2004). Some have been involved in evangelism and training, while others have focused on areas of social concern such as community development and English language teaching.

Conclusion

The Next Christendom (2002) is one of the most significant books concerning the place of Christianity in the twenty-first century. Its author, Phillip Jenkins, points out that the centre of gravity for this religious movement is no longer the northern hemisphere nations associated with North America and Europe, but with the southern hemisphere regions of South America, Africa and Asia. He further comments that "non-Western converts are very soon absorbed and adapted the religion according to their own cultural needs" (2002: 16). This process, which included the use of local languages and local religious leaders, has significantly contributed to the growth of Christianity outside of Western cultural environments and, as indicated in this chapter, has contributed considerably to the growth of the Protestant Christian faith among the Kyrgyz. This process of "indigenization and adaption" has further strengthened the sense, for many Kyrgyz Christians, that "to be Kyrgyz is also to be a *mashayakche*" – not just a Muslim.

References

Abramzon, S.M. (1971) *Kirgizy i ikh etnogeneticheskie i istoriko-kul'turnie svyazi* [The Kyrgyz and their ethnogenetic, historical and cultural ties], Leningrad: Nauka.
Allworth, E. (1998) "Commensals or Parasites? Russians, Kazakhs, Uzbeks and Others", in B. Manz (ed.) *Central Asia in Historical Perspective*, Boulder: Westview: 185–201.
Anderson, J. (1999) *Kyrgyzstan: Central Asia's Island of Democracy*, Amsterdam: Overseas Publishers' Association.
"A Ray of Hope" (2004) *M.B. Herald*, 36/13. Online. Available: http://old.mbconf.ca/mb/mbh3613/ray.htm (accessed 1 October 2004).
Bayram, M. (2009) "Kyryzstan: Will Restrictive Provisions of New Religion Law be Removed?" Online. Available: www.forum18.org/Archive.php?article_id=1301 (accessed 23 July 2009).
England, J.C. (1996) *The Hidden History of Christianity: The Churches of the East before 1500*, Delhi: ISPCK.

Filonyk, A.O. (1994) *Kyrgyzstan*, Florida: University Press.

Foltz, R.C. (1999) *Religions of the Silk Road: Overland Trade and Cultural Exchange from Antiquity to the Fifteenth Century*, New York: St. Martin's Griffin.

Glenn, J. (1999) *The Soviet Legacy in Central Asia*, New York: St. Martin's Press.

Haghayeghi, M. (1996) *Islam and Politics in Central Asia*, New York: St. Martin's Press.

Indexmundi (2010) Online. Available: www.indexmundi.com/kyrgyzstan/unemployment_rate.html (accessed 15 November 2010).

Jenkins, P. (2002) *The Next Christendom: The Coming of Global Christianity*, Oxford: Oxford University.

Lewis, D.C. (2000) *After Atheism: Religion and Ethnicity in Russian and Central Asia*, Richmond: Curzon.

Loftland, J. and Stark, R. (1965) "Becoming a World Saver: A Theory of Conversion to a Deviant Perspective", *American Sociological Review*, 30/6: 862–875.

Murzakhalilov, K. (2004) "Proselytism in Kyrgyzstan", *Central Asia and the Caucasus – Journal of Social and Political Studies*, 25/1: 83–87.

Pannier, B. (2008) "Kyrgyz Converts from Islam Ask, "Where Can We Bury Our Dead?'" Online. Available: www.rferl.org/content/Kyrgyz_Converts_From_Islam_Unable_To_Bury_Dead/1186456.html (accessed on 4 August 2009).

Pelkmans, M. (2007) "'Culture' as a Tool and an Obstacle: Missionary Encounters in Post-Soviet Kyrgyzstan", *Journal of the Royal Anthropological Institute*, 13/4: 881–899.

Peyrouse, S. (2004) "Christianity and Nationality in Soviet and Post-Soviet Central Asia: Mutual Intrusions and Instrumentalizations", *Nationalities Papers*, 32/3: 651–674.

Rashid, A. (1994) *The Resurgence of Central Asia: Islam or Nationalism*, Karachi: Oxford University Press.

Ro'i, Y. (1995) *Muslim Eurasia: Conflicting Legacies*, London: Frank Cass.

Rotar, I. (2004) "Kyrgyzstan: Campaigning to Close down Pentecostal Church?" *Forum 18*, 4 May. Online. Available: www.forum18.org/Archive.php?article_id=83 (accessed 25 June 2009).

Roy, O. (2000) *The New Central Asia: The Creation of Nations*, Washington Square, NY: New York University.

Sherkat, D.E. and Ellison, C.G. (1999) "Recent Developments and Current Controversies in the Sociology of Religion", *Annual Review of Sociology*, 25: 363–394.

Smith, G., Law, V., Wilson, A., Bohr, A. and Allworth, E. (1998) "The Central Asian States as Nationalising Regimes", *Nation-Building in the Post-Soviet Borderlands: The Politics of National Identities*, Cambridge: Cambridge University Press: 139–166.

Soucek, S. (2000) *A History of Inner Asia*, Cambridge: Cambridge University.

Stark, R. (1996) *The Rise of Christianity*, San Francisco: Harper Collins.

Stark, R. and Finke, R. (2000) *Acts of Faith*, Berkeley: University of California.

Tabyshalieva, Dr. A. (2000) "The Kyrgyz and Spiritual Dimensions of Daily Life", in R. Sagdeev and S. Eizenhower (eds), *Islam and Central Asia*, Washington D.C.: Center for Political and Strategic Studies: 27–38.

Vladmir, A. (2000) "Christianity and Islam in Central Asia", in R. Sagdeev and S. Eisenhower (eds), *Islam and Central Asia*, Washington D.C.: Center for Political and Strategic Studies.

Wanner, C. (2003) "Advocating New Moralities: Conversion to Evangelicalism in Ukraine", *Religion, State and Society*, 31/3: 273–287.

Yanzen, German (1993) *V Dalekom Turkestane* [In Faraway Turkestan], Bishkek: Luch Nadezhdy.

Part III
Education

7 Everyday realities of a young teacher in post-Soviet Kyrgyzstan

The case of a history teacher from a rural school

Düishön Alievich Shamatov

Introduction

While becoming a teacher anywhere is a complex process, in Kyrgyzstan this process has the added challenges of the country's present socio-political and economic upheavals. In recent years, teachers with fewer than ten years of teaching experience constitute a significant and growing proportion of school staff. In addition to the typical personal and institutional challenges of adjusting to school culture, rules and regulations, children with various needs, and classroom management problems, these newer teachers face unique challenges that are specific to the socio-economic realities that have emerged in Kyrgyzstan since the collapse of the USSR. These include insufficient resources for schools, poor teacher retention, poorly qualified and inexperienced colleagues, high student dropout rates, a curriculum that is undergoing constant change, a lack of textbooks, and low salaries.

This chapter contributes to the discussion of who beginning teachers are as learners, what they need to learn and how that learning can be fostered (Feiman-Nemser and Remillard 1996) with particular emphasis on how beginning teachers influence their own development and what kind of teachers they become. A better understanding of beginning teachers' learning can help teacher educators do a better job of preparing future teachers (Olson and Osborne 1991). Through the case study of a beginner history teacher, this chapter explores all these issues within the unique framework of the systemic and socio-economic challenges to beginning teachers' professional socialization in the context of post-Soviet Kyrgyzstan.

Methodology

Conventional education research in the former USSR has tended to reduce teachers to statistics in the educational landscape, with no information on their views and their practices amassed through large-scale school surveys (Niyozov 2001). Little research has been done to better understand the experiences of beginning teachers in countries experiencing the transition from socialism to free-market democracies (Niyozov 2001). Additionally, education research in the region has traditionally utilized quantitative research methods, which have certain limitations in the study of teachers' experiences. Specifically, quantitative methods can be limited in eliciting the practical concerns of teachers as they experience them; the research methods are not effective in describing the classroom practice of teachers; quantitative methods can impose the views of educational researchers onto the experiences of teachers, which can be exploitative (Hammersley 1993).

Given these limitations, this research project moved beyond conventional practice in the region, and utilized qualitative research methods. Qualitative studies that explore the lives and experiences of teachers, and allow for the subjective expressions of those experiences can provide much needed insight into the reality of teaching in the former USSR. Events and experiences, both past and present, that take place at home, school and in the broader social sphere help shape teachers' lives and careers. Researchers, policy makers and educators should learn from the biographies of beginning teachers to understand their experiences and develop effective models for teacher development and support.

"Qualitative researchers depend on a variety of methods for gathering data. The use of multiple data-collection methods contributes to the trustworthiness of the data", provided that the method involves not merely "the simple combination of different kinds of data, but the attempt to relate them so as to counteract the threats to validity identified in each" (Glesne 1999: 31). For this study, in-depth case studies (Cohen and Manion 1997; Merriam 1998; Yin 1989) of beginning teachers in Kyrgyzstan were developed between 2001 and 2005. A case study "is a detailed examination of one setting, or a single subject, or a single depository of documents, or one particular event" (Bogdan and Biklen 1998: 54) and it enables "intensive, holistic description and analysis of a bounded phenomenon" (Merriam 1998: xiii). Merriam (1998: 27) added that case study research is characterized by "delimiting of the object of the study"; a case thus constitutes a single entity, a unit around which there are boundaries. The boundaries are defined by "temporal, geographical, organisational, institutional, and other contexts that enable boundaries to be drawn around the case" (Cohen *et al.* 2000: 182).

Purposeful sampling was used "to increase the utility of information to be obtained from small samples. The power and logic of purposeful sampling is that a few cases studied in depth yield many insights about the topic" (McMillan and Schumacher 1997: 397). For the case study described in this chapter, a history teacher from a village school was selected.

To provide an understanding of the context of the case study, informal conversations were conducted with representatives of the wider community. Once again, purposeful sampling was used, to identify experienced teachers and officials from *oblono* (Regional Board of Education), *gorono* (Town Board of Education) and *raiono* (District Boards of Education), professors of teacher training institutions, foreign education specialists, government officials, community members from town and villages, and parents. These informants provided insight into the complexities of the context in which the new teachers were working and also provided different perspectives on issues such as the relevance of education, schooling, and teachers' work and life.

Fieldwork was conducted from 2001 to 2002. Data collection was a prolonged and challenging experience, involving a lot of travel to meet and interview people, record events, conversations and interviews, observe and reflect, and plan further activities. Data collection was conducted with the awareness that the data was not simply waiting passively to be gathered through interviews and observations (Ball 1993: 45). Rather, the data was considered a dynamic and meaningful outgrowth of the research process itself which encompasses the researcher's skills and imagination, and the interactions between the researcher and the researched (Morgan and Smircich 1980; Niyozov 2001). To minimize the influence of the researcher's subjectivity, an effort was made to be aware of any preferences (Bogdan and Biklen 1998), minimize them and approach the data as open-mindedly as possible. Data was collected using interviews and observations. It was recorded on audiotapes and in field notes and memos on a regular basis.

Data analysis is a rigorous continuous process of systematically searching and arranging the accumulated data (interview transcripts, field notes and memos, reflections and other materials) in order to increase one's understanding of them (Bogdan and Biklen 1998; Merriam 1998; Niyozov 2001). A combination of techniques were used, including noting patterns and themes, testing plausibility, clustering, counting, making metaphors, making contrasts and comparisons, and noting relations between variables, to analyse the data and generate meaning from them (Miles and Huberman 1994).

Contextual background

The Soviets achieved remarkable progress in education in Central Asia in a relatively short span of time (Holmes *et al.* 1995; Maksimov 1974; Medlin *et al.* 1971; Naumkin 1993; Soktoev 1981; Tabyshaliev 1979). In 1913, about 95.4 per cent of the Kyrgyz population was illiterate, and there were only 195 primary schools and only 220 qualified teachers (Abazov 2004). In 1919, after Soviet rule was established, Lenin issued a decree on mass education and the eradication of illiteracy (Tabyshaliev 1979). The Soviets realized that the tempo of societal progress depended on the development of science and education. With massive campaigns, the literacy rate in Kyrgyzstan grew from 3.5 per cent among people nine to 49 years old in 1920 to 16.5 per cent in 1926, and then to a phenomenal 99.8 per cent in 1979 (Ibraimov 2001). Schools were built in the most remote areas of the country; by 1978 there were 1,757 schools with 854,000 pupils, and around 50,000 teachers (Tabyshaliev 1979).

At the same time, there were problems with Soviet education. All students were exposed to the same centrally designed curriculum, with minor local adaptations to accommodate each Soviet republic (De Young 2001; Heyneman 2000).[1] The state controlled educational institutions, teaching appointments, syllabuses and textbooks to ensure that all learners were exposed to the same outlook, knowledge and attitudes (Heyneman 2000). While Soviet education overtly promoted internationalism above nationalist and ethnic identities, many scholars argue that in practice it promoted Russian identity over other national identities within the USSR.[2]

After the break-up of the USSR, Kyrgyzstan began experiencing severe problems in all public spheres, including education. It became difficult to sustain the level of education achieved during the USSR at all levels. Due to lack of funding, many educational institutions, such as a number of *internats*[3] (boarding schools), were closed. Pre-school enrolment declined catastrophically during the 1990s; of 1,604 in 1991, only 416 pre-school institutions remained by 2000[4] (DeYoung 2004). In 1993, about 83.6 per cent of the population of Kyrgyzstan had completed secondary education. This decreased to 76.4 per cent in 1996, and further to 69 per cent in 1999 (DeYoung 2001).

Schools have started experiencing severe shortages of funding. The central government has turned over the costs of school building maintenance and repair to *ail okmotus*[5] (local governments), which cannot afford existing school-related expenses, such as heating and equipment, let alone new expenses due to their low budgets (OSI-ESP 2002). Most school buildings remain in very poor condition (DeYoung and Santos 2004). Schools have begun adopting alternative measures to generate funds for building repairs, such as collecting money from parents and other community members (OSI 2002). In 2003, out of 92 million *som*[6] spent on school repairs, 76 million was collected from parents and private donors. *Ail okmotus* could only provide 16 million *som* (DeYoung and Santos 2004; Karym Kyzy 2003). Not surprisingly, parents and community members, who are also struggling financially, resent the frequent collection of money by schools (paradoxically called "voluntary contributions"), as well as the lack of transparency of how the collected money is used (UNDP 2003).[7]

Since *perestroika*, new, innovative schools have emerged in Kyrgyzstan, such as academic lyceums, gymnasiums and schools for gifted children (DeYoung *et al.* 2006; Sutherland 1992). This diversification is officially endorsed through educational reform. Overall, there are 73 private schools in Kyrgyzstan, according to the Ministry of Education and Science. While most people are struggling with everyday constraints, a small number can now choose quality education for their children (EFA 2000). The "new type" schools provide extra academic services to pupils by offering advanced coursework. They generally provide a better and more comprehensive education than "ordinary" state-funded schools. They charge parents for extra services such as additional lessons in academic subjects. The pupils of these schools have a better chance to enter prestigious higher education institutions upon completing school.[8] As a rule, private and "new type" schools are located in urban areas where wealthier families live who can afford to pay for their children's schooling (OSI 2002).

However, almost 70 per cent of Kyrgyzstan's population lives in rural areas and 83 per cent of schools are in rural settings (UNDP 2003). Rural schools in post-Soviet Kyrgyzstan are experiencing major challenges (Shamatov 2005)[9] and lack funds and support from the government. Moreover, they generally serve impoverished communities, and lack resources and facilities. Rural community members normally have a low opinion of education and teachers and have urgent economic priorities such as farm work that do not allow them the time to focus on education. Pupils from rural areas also have access to less in-depth schooling, and are frequently distracted by agricultural work. The pupils normally score poorly during Olympiads[10] held in different subjects locally, regionally and nationally (Bekbolotov 2000), and find it difficult to score high in National Scholarship Tests leading to university entrance and scholarships (Shamatov 2012). A large number of pupils from rural areas cannot attend school (OSI 2002). The high dropout rates are a by-product of economic collapse and declining support for the social sector; the main reasons include poverty, insufficient food, lack of adequate clothing and an inability to afford learning material materials, the increasing cost of education, the decline of prestige and value of education among community members, and negative attitudes towards education (OSI 2002). Independent sources estimated that about 30,000 pupils dropped out in the 1990s (Eversmann 2000), and by the beginning of the 1996–1997 school year, about 16,500 children stopped going to school (Karym Kyzy 2003). According to official sources, over 2,500 school-age children dropped out of school in 2001; however, unofficial reports suggest that the actual number is double this (DeYoung and Santos 2004). Of those who cannot attend school, 79 per cent are from rural areas (UNDP 2003).

Teachers in Kyrgyzstan struggle with many problems, including teacher shortages, unqualified colleagues, low salaries, few teaching resources, and working and living in worsening conditions. Not surprisingly schools face harsh teacher shortages because many teachers have left teaching. Official figures claim 2,863 vacant teaching positions in Kyrgyzstan, although the actual numbers are estimated as double that (DeYoung and Santos 2004). According to a specialist at the Ministry of Education and Science, teacher shortages remained between 3,000 and 4,000 each year from 2002 to 2007 (Shamatov and Sainazarov 2010). At the same time, the percentage of young new teachers entering the profession is decreasing; in 2005, they made up 60 per cent of the teaching force. In 2007, the percentage had fallen to 35 per cent. Many students in pre-service education programmes in higher educational institutions do not actually want to become teachers upon graduation. Every year, between 1,000 and 1,500 students graduate from pre-service teacher education institutions, both state-funded and self-funded. However, only half of those who graduate from state-funded courses go on to teach at schools according to their placements (Bekbolotov 2000) and only about 30 per cent of all graduates take teaching jobs at all (OSI 2002).[11]

Teacher shortages are especially acute in schools in villages and remote areas, since many university graduates, including graduating teachers, prefer to stay in towns and cities (Bekbolotov 2000). There is a long-standing shortage of teachers for English, Kyrgyz, mathematics, informatics (computer sciences), history, chemistry and biology, and village schools experience a serious shortage of teachers of English and Russian (DeYoung and Santos 2004). Due to the shortage, rural and remote mountain schools have to resort to recalling retired teachers, and hiring part-time university students with incomplete training. These alternatives often lack either the energy or qualifications that young, beginning teachers bring to schools.

The 30 per cent of graduating teachers who actually take jobs in the teaching profession begin at the lowest salary scale and without *kategoriya* (category).[12] They face frequent delays in salary payments due to budget constraints, and many have to take on extra work on farms or small businesses to earn more money. Teachers have also lost subsidies they used to get to cover electricity and heating. A standard teaching assignment is 16 to 18 teaching hours per week, but to earn more, many teachers teach 25 or more hours per week, sometimes at more than one school and, have little or no time for professional development. Teachers also work in difficult conditions. There are regularly scheduled cuts to electricity, and most schools no longer have central heating in winter. Due to these conditions, many qualified teachers leave the school system altogether for better-paid jobs that enable them to provide their families with basic necessities (Niyozov 2001; Niyozov and Shamatov 2006; Shamatov 2005).

The government is trying to attract and retain more young teachers at schools to rectify teacher shortages. Officials are trying to attract new teacher education graduates to rural schools by promising better working conditions, or by providing the teachers with plots of land from the village governments. To retain young teaching graduates to work in rural public schools, the Government of Kyrgyzstan introduced a new project called "Deposit for Young Teachers" in 2004 (Kanimetova 2005). To execute this programme, the Ministry of Education of the Kyrgyz Republic organized a competitive recruiting campaign to select beginning teachers. In 2004, 200 beginning teachers were selected and signed a contract. In addition to their salaries, they were credited 2,000 *som* a month, to a total of 76,000 *som* each, to be withdrawn only after completing their contracts. The selected teachers underwent training and were under contract to work for three years at the schools to which they were assigned. Government officials hoped, perhaps unrealistically, that retaining these young teachers at village schools for three years would lead to their adaptation and continued commitment to teaching at the same schools.

Teaching history

History was a core subject in Soviet schools and it was used to promote Soviet values based on Marxism-Leninism and a communist worldview (Davies 1989; Ibraimov 2001; Lisovskaya and Karpov 1999; Medlin 1976; Nersesova 1973: 68). The history curriculum included courses on History of the World and History of the USSR. Beginning in the 1930s, Soviet history teaching adopted a five-phased paradigm that reflected a Marxist analysis of the socio-economic stages which every nation was believed to go through sequentially: (a) ancient communal period; (b) slavery period; (c) feudalism; (d) capitalism; and (e) socialism and early stage of communism (Kaplan *et al.* 1999). Thus, Soviet history promoted socialism as the advent of the final stage of human development, ending all exploitative systems (Manusevich *et al.* 1990: 5). Deviation from these positions was declared to be anti-Marxist and anti-scientific (Shamatov 2005).

Soviet history courses were principally based on Russian history. The histories of non-Russian republics were analysed only in relation to Russian history (Niyozov 2001), and were taught as an integrated part of Soviet history primarily after their incorporation into the Russian Empire and the Soviet Union (Medlin 1976). In reality, local histories were neglected and deliberately downplayed (Szekely 1987). A history teacher from Byelorus observed that "historical memory begins with the school textbook, so it is not at all surprising that the majority of the population of Byelorussia have, to put it mildly, an indistinct concept about the past of their native region" (Davies 1989: 181). History teachers had to decide whether to pay attention to local history or not, and time spent doing so took away from the core all-union curriculum (Seinenskii 1973: 57). Local history was not only diminished in official curricula; the Kyrgyz tradition of describing and tracing one's ancestry and genealogy (*sanjyra*), a process which essentially linked the individual to their family and clan history, was proscribed and restricted by the KGB and other state organs during Soviet times (Attokurov 1995).

Soviet textbook writers were selected experts who got a licence to work on textbooks directly from Moscow. A uniform textbook from Moscow, which stressed the common features of the Russian Empire and Soviet power, would have slightly varied versions for use in the different Soviet republics. Kyrgyz history was shaped to fit the five-stage paradigm of Soviet history, and only those aspects of Kyrgyz history that had direct connections with Russian history were studied. Kyrgyz rebels who fought against Russians before and after the October revolution were declared merely obstacles to the creation of a socialist state. The Soviets promoted the belief that Kyrgyzstan's people, along with other Central Asians, benefited from the socialist revolution, and that being part of the USSR enabled them to proceed from the feudal stage directly into the socialist phase, passing over the capitalist stage (Bekmakhanov and Bekmakhanova 1979; Brudnyi *et al.* 1988; Kolbin 1960; Tabyshaliev 1979). Many Kyrgyz historians, such as Belek Soltonoev, who did not conform to the Marxist-Leninist paradigm, were condemned as reactionary and were persecuted and their work banned (Megoran 2002). Soltonoev, was arrested and then killed during Stalin's repression, and his work, including his book *Kyzyl Kyrgyz tarykhy* (The History of Red Kyrgyz), was banned (Ibraimov 2001).

Perestroika and *glasnost* in the mid-1980s brought many changes to the teaching of history in the USSR. Mikhail Gorbachev, then General Secretary of the Communist Party, made his famous declaration that "there should not be any blank pages in either our history or our literature" (cited in Davies 1989: 130). A correspondent of *Izvestiya* wrote that history teaching had "deluded generation after generation, poisoning their minds and souls with lies" (I. Ovchinnikova, *Izvestiya*, 10 June 1988). Historians started openly criticizing misdeeds and distortions that had taken place in the USSR. Many grey areas of Soviet history were opened and publicly scrutinized; previous bans and censorship of works that criticized Soviet rule were lifted. Newspapers and television carried documentary stories of the Stalin-era acts of repression, mass killings in prison camps, and mass graves. Examination of the "blank pages" or "grey areas" in Soviet history occurred in literary journals, which were filled with long-suppressed works (Davies 1989). Many previously banned historical documents, accounts of events and novels were now published. However, all these changes still took place within the framework of Marxism-Leninism and textbooks were still produced centrally (Lisovskaya and Karpov 1999). Most debates and information about the "blank pages" of Soviet history were shared via the mass media, especially television, radio and press.

History teachers found themselves in really difficult situations, because they had to revisit many concepts that they had believed and promoted among their pupils. They faced challenges from pupils who got access to new historical information and concepts, which contradicted what was taught at school. The increasing gap between history curricula and the emerging history that pupils learned from the mass media and their families left many young people confused and distrustful (Davies 1989: 183). History teachers adapted to these challenges in different ways; some incorporated the new knowledge into their teaching despite the old syllabus; others were confused and struggled between new and old concepts, and some continued teaching what was in textbooks as they believed that the changes were temporary (Davies 1989).

Major changes in history teaching took place after the break-up of the USSR in 1991. Teaching national history became a high priority in ex-republics of the USSR, and the history of Kyrgyzstan, become a separate, compulsory subject in the curriculum. The Marxist-Leninist dogma with its five-phase approach to history was abolished from the curriculum[13] which now includes the study of concepts of democracy, liberty and the market economy (Kaplan *et al.* 1999; Lisovskaya and Karpov 1999; Niyozov 2001).

However, in the early post-Soviet years, history teaching was full of contradictions and inconsistencies, combining ideological symbols of nationalism, Westernization, capitalism and reinterpreted Communism (Lisovskaya and Karpov 1999). History teachers found it extremely difficult to deal with all these changes (Niyozov 2001).

In Kyrgyzstan, abolishing Marxist-Leninist dogma created a perceived ideological vacuum. Many people felt the need for a sense of security and a unifying political identity. In response, historians began searching for the pre-Soviet history of the Kyrgyz. Many scholars emphasized the sophistication of the "Great Kyrgyz Empire" which replaced the collapsed Uighur Kaganat in 840 CE (Ibraimov 2001) as a means to fill the ideological vacuum and promote the legitimacy of contemporary Kyrgyzstan as a state (Abazov 2004; Ibraimov 2001; Megoran 2002; Osmonov 2002). Preserving national cultural traditions and questions of nation building became a priority for both government and academics (Government of the Kyrgyz Republic 2000, cited in Dukenbaev 2004:16;

Megoran 2002: 117). History teaching provided an important means to promote an emerging national ideology with concepts such as nation building, construction of identity, and protecting and strengthening the country's independence (Ibraimov 2001).

Post-Soviet accounts of the 1916 anti-Tsarist uprising, previously explained through the Marxist interpretative framework of class struggle (Osmonov and Myrzakmatova 2000), are now presented through a national-liberation approach (Jusupov 1993; Megoran 2002; Omurbekov and Chorotegin 1998; Rashid 2003; Usenbaev 1997), and some original documents from the period have been reprinted (see Kazybaev 1996). The revised 11th grade history textbook, published in 2000, refers to the 1916 events as "the struggle for gaining full control of the land which was inherited by Kyrgyz people's ancestors, struggle for freedom, struggle for equality is valued as the most significant page of Kyrgyzstan history" (Osmonov and Myrzakmatova 2000: 38).

The reworking of Kyrgyzstan's history in the post-Soviet era thus necessitated designing and publishing new textbooks. However, due to the lack of finances and qualified specialists, it was difficult to publish new textbooks immediately after independence in 1991. New history textbooks were first introduced in universities in 1995; new school history textbooks only appeared in the early 2000s. Thus, schools in post-Soviet Kyrgyzstan struggled with teaching new history without new textbooks for almost a decade. In many cases, teachers taught without textbooks or continued to use Soviet textbooks. Soviet-trained teachers relied heavily on textbooks while teaching their subjects and it was difficult for many teachers to teach without textbooks (Heyneman 1995). History teachers had to design their teaching materials from sources that were sent from the educational authorities and also from their university notes, and other sources such as literature, newspapers or magazines. As in other former Soviet Republics, many experienced history teachers in Kyrgyzstan faced severe challenges as the worldview they had espoused and taught was completely discredited. One history teacher in neighbouring Tajikistan

> suffered from the intense post-Soviet emotional turbulence.... She felt guilty, betrayed, and hurt by the Soviet historians and politicians who had provided a one-sided and distorted version of reality....
>
> She was denigrated as one of those who had promised the students that socialism and communism were inevitable, that capitalism was behind all the problems in the developing countries, and that the USA was an enemy. As a teacher and a propagandist, she had apparently cursed capitalism and the market economy, fought religion, and promoted the cause of socialism and atheism.
>
> (Niyozov 2001: 317–318)

The story of a young teacher in Kyrgyzstan

Schooling and university

Kanybek (pseudonym) is a young history teacher who was born, raised and educated in a village Otuz-Adyr, not far from the city of Osh in southern Kyrgyzstan. The village has a history, which reflects the socio-political and economic changes of the broader society. The village was established as a collective farm in the late 1940s and early 1950s with the building of the Otuz-Adyr canal from the Kurshab River in Osh province (then district). A veteran worker from the village briefly narrated the history of the village:

> These areas were bare dry land before. Only insects and reptiles, such as black spiders, scorpions and snakes inhabited these territories until then. In 1940, the Ministry of Agriculture issued a decree to build a canal to establish a collective farm specializing in cotton growing. The canal construction started in early 1941. People worked on canal construction with their bare hands because there was no technology at that time. The construction stopped abruptly when the Great Patriotic War[14] broke out in 1941. The construction re-started after the war was over, and finally "the water of the canal came" in 1951. After that, the life of the people in the village got better.

With the arrival of water to the dry areas, people started growing various plants and vegetables. The main crop of the collective farm was cotton. The farm also had vast gardens where grapes, peaches, apples and apricots were grown. Kanybek's grandparents were among the first settlers in the village, and his father was an active member of the collective farm. From the beginning, the village was multinational, made up of Kyrgyz, Russians, Tatars and Uzbeks. Initially, there was no school in the village. The first primary school opened in 1954 and teachers were invited from Osh. Those teachers were provided with accommodation when they arrived. Eventually, the population of the village grew and there was a need for a bigger school. In 1956, the construction of a new school began and by 1961 the school was functioning. The school had classes in Russian, Uzbek and Kyrgyz. As the village was situated in a convenient place to reach the provincial and district centres, a boarding school was opened on the school premises for gifted and orphaned children from remote areas. As a result, the village school grew very large, with over 100 teachers and 1,000 students. In 1983, Kanybek was sent to school. He was sent to a Russian class by his parents who felt he could get a better education in it.[15] Being fluent in Russian was a requirement for successful upward career mobility.

After the break-up of the USSR, the situation in the village changed. Many villagers became unemployed when a poultry factory closed. Kanybek was a student of Class 8 in 1991. As with other schools across the country, his faced rapid changes. The school lost a lot of good teachers, who joined other professions or simply left for Russia and Kazakhstan to go into commerce. Many

Russian-speaking teachers migrated[16] to Russia and the status of the Russian language started rapidly diminishing. The number of Russian language and literature classes at schools was reduced dramatically and many Russian schools were closed. Kanybek's school also experienced a great shortage of teaching resources including textbooks, notebooks, chalk and furniture. The school curriculum was plunged into a state of transition, as the Soviet curriculum was to be replaced by the new Kyrgyz national alternative. Social subjects, such as history and literature, encountered the most changes. However, new textbooks and other materials were yet to be produced and many teachers continued using the old materials.

In 1999, a new school opened not far from the original school, due to the growing number of school-age children in the village and the need to move the location of the school away from the new, heavily trafficked Osh–Bishkek highway which went through the village.[17]

Kanybek graduated from the school in 1994 and applied to Osh State University, where he entered the Faculty of History. Kanybek said that he studied simply for the sake of getting a diploma and never thought that he would end up becoming a teacher. He graduated five years later, in the summer of 1999. He recalled,

> I did not want to become a teacher. I wanted to become a lawyer or a policeman.[18] They are considered to be a more masculine profession. I could also make more money there. But I did not have connections or appropriate documents. I did not have my military card. My parents did not want me to go to the army, because the situation at that time was getting worse due to border incidents in Batken.[19]

Kanybek joins the teaching profession

Kanybek returned to his village at his parents' insistence in 1999, and he joined his school as a teacher. At that time there were 75 teachers and over 800 pupils at the school. The school operated in two shifts due to limited space.[20] Secondary and higher secondary classes studied in the morning shift, and primary classes in the afternoon. After a couple of months, Kanybek took on another teaching job at a newly opened second village school, on a part-time basis. Working in two places, he could earn more since teachers are paid only sporadically and their salaries in real terms have fallen steeply. As a first-year teacher, Kanybek earned only 490 *som*[21] per month. Kanybek's willingness to persevere in the profession is atypical. An older teacher explains,

> Only *Cholponbays*[22] are left at schools nowadays. Many teachers left for business, because life is demanding it. But our hearts are in this school. I cannot imagine my life without this school and without these kids. I will continue teaching here irrespective whether my salary is delayed or I get a small salary.

Kanybek could hardly manage his time, working in two schools. He often hardly had time to plan his lessons for the next day. Like his students, Kanybek also had to help his parents with farming. They grew wheat on land they got after privatization. It was often difficult to grow wheat because they needed to find tractors and fuel at their own expense. Kanybek thought his heavy schedule inhibited his professional development. Besides, in the village area he did not see many opportunities for his professional growth and he wanted to go to town to work at the university.

> When I am teaching, I have to think about the weather, my crop, my cattle, and many other things that may affect my life. If I do not go today to collect my wheat, tomorrow it may rain and half of my grain will go underground. Sometimes I am teaching in my classroom, but my thoughts are in the farms, and my eyes are looking at the sky through the windows to see if it is going to rain. How can I concentrate on teaching then?

In addition to these economic realities, teachers now face reduced status. Previously, teachers were well respected and teaching was considered a noble profession. Many people wanted to become teachers. However, teachers' status and roles have been greatly diminished due to the socio-political and economic changes in Kyrgyzstan. Kanybek explains,

> Nowadays teachers are viewed as beggars. We often do not have money even to buy everyday products. Then we borrow money from the villagers. For example, some pupils' parents have small shops in their houses, and we go there and purchase everyday products. When we do not have money, we take products with the promise of paying as soon as we get our salary. They write our names in the debt books and let us take products.

Teachers spend most of their time inside their classrooms, the most immediate context of teaching and learning. Kanybek was assigned to teach history in classes 8 to 11 because of his university diploma in history. Most of his classes were Russian-medium, because he himself had graduated from a Russian class, and there were no other history teachers fluent in Russian.

Teaching approaches

New teachers spend a great deal of time planning, conducting and evaluating lessons. Their teaching practices are commonly based on personal practical knowledge, which they develop over a period of time by observing their teachers, reading literature, and attending formal teacher training at the university. However, most new teachers in Kyrgyzstan feel that their pre-service education was not as effective as they would have liked. Kanybek said,

> I never wanted to be a teacher; therefore I really did not pay attention to learning about teaching at the university. I am now reading those notes and

finding some of them really useful. It is difficult to bridge between theory and practice. I learned teaching by teaching.

Kanybek's initial years of teaching greatly influenced his teaching practices. He improved his practices while teaching and planning his lessons. He felt he made huge improvements in his personal and professional life by working at the school, however, he was also dissatisfied with the lack of opportunities and limited access to professional development in a rural school: "If I worked in a town, I would develop both career-wise and also professionally."

Kanybek's teaching approaches follow the Soviet-era pattern. He enters the classroom, greets pupils, then writes a date and a new theme title on the board. He stands or sits at the front of the room and checks the register. He checks homework, asking random or sequential questions of the pupils. Sometimes he goes through the pupils' notebooks to see that everyone has done their homework. Then he imparts knowledge to pupils by lecturing, retelling, asking the whole class and individual questions, responding to questions and explaining again if he finds out that the pupils do not comprehend the material.

Kanybek felt that he had faced a serious challenge in preparing a lesson plan for his history lessons. When he started teaching, there were no new history textbooks yet;[23] teachers still used Soviet textbooks. But the district education office would regularly send instructions that the teachers had to develop a new syllabus and lesson plans according to post-Soviet requirements. Therefore, Kanybek and his colleagues struggled to find relevant materials from news media and other sources. There was only one old history textbook for Kanybek's entire class. His pupils needed reading materials to study on their own after class, so Kanybek brought his conspectus and notes and had his pupils copy them so that they could study at home and prepare for the examinations. Thus, he mostly lectured in his lessons.

Kanybek also faced challenges with assessment. It was difficult for him to gauge the level of his pupils' academic performance. He often used to lower his standards of marking and give higher marks to his pupils than they probably deserved. He compared his village pupils with the pupils of the town school, whom he had observed while he was doing his practicum at the university, and came to the conclusion that village pupils were far behind. But he justified this on the grounds that the village pupils were getting only limited access to resources, including libraries and information technology, and they had to regularly help their parents in farming and cattle breeding, and missed school or did not have time for homework.

Kanybek assessed his pupils regularly in his lessons, and then used their average marks for quarterly evaluation. He recalled how one of his university professors was very demanding and strict with marking. It was very difficult for students to get marks in his courses. At the same time the professor was a competent teacher. Every winter and summer examination terms, he could easily figure out which of his students had and had not studied well for examinations, and he would send those that needed it back to study more. He would fail students who did not study well, and they would have to retake his examinations several times before they could pass. He had a reputation of being non-negotiable in terms of "doing favours for money". However, when the students finally passed the examination they would realize how much they learned from his course.

Kanybek wanted to be like that professor, strict and demanding. He wanted his pupils to study hard and learn concepts well. Some parents came to the school to meet Kanybek during the examination period, and wanted him to increase their children's marks: they wanted their children's attestation documents[24] filled with good grades, because that would help them later when they applied to universities. He acted firmly and did not compromise.

Kanybek as a class teacher

Apart from history teaching responsibilities, Kanybek was also assigned to be a *klass jetekchi* (class or homeroom teacher) for Russian class 10B. Previously, new teachers were generally not assigned class teacher responsibilities until they had three to five years experience, because it was a huge responsibility to work as a class teacher. The class teacher is responsible for the overall academic achievement and *tarbiya* (moral and value development) of the class pupils. The class teacher also organizes extracurricular and civics activities with the class pupils. Nowadays, however, many experienced teachers are reluctant to work as class teachers, because of the burden and the decreased incentives. At the same time, there is an increasing population of teachers with little or no teaching experience. In fact, more and more part-time university students are being hired to teaching positions due to the shortage of teachers, especially in rural areas. Consequently, many new teachers are also given class teacher responsibilities from the very beginning of their careers. This poses additional challenges, while they are still learning to become teachers themselves.

Assigning class teachers is a convenient way for the school administration to keep teachers accountable. Teachers' evaluations often depend on their performance as class teachers. The class teachers therefore take their job very seriously and work very closely with their pupils. They organize various events and class teacher sessions with their pupils. One such activity is compulsory and puts beginning class teachers under a lot of pressure: each class teacher is required to organize an open lesson on *tarbia* (upbringing) with their class. The open class is prepared and conducted around a certain theme, such as "respecting elders", "treating everyone equally", "helping the weak and poor". These lessons differ from ordinary subject classes and are more oriented to "show to inspectors" (school administration or local and regional educational board members) how well the pupils' social, moral and value development is being fostered. The school administration and education board members attend these open lessons to evaluate the class teacher's performance.

In Soviet times, class teachers organized their activities and lessons to promote the ideas and ideals of Soviet socialism and educate their pupils in the spirit of communism, providing political moral, social and patriotic input based on Marxism-Leninism. Pupils would be taught to become "good Soviet citizens" who fight for the freedom of all workers and fight against injustice and inequality. The class teachers emphasized values, such as helping poor people, collectivism, altruism and social-orientation of children. Egoism, individualism and greed were condemned as qualities characteristic of capitalist society. Nowadays, class teachers do not use anything related to "socialism". Rather, as another young teacher stated, "we are just preparing our pupils to be good human beings, to do good things for others, and to respect others' rights."

Classroom management issues cause great concern for a new teacher. Almost all new teachers' initial experiences are coupled with periods of stress and interpersonal conflicts with their pupils. These interactions are fundamental in making or breaking a new teacher's career in teaching. Addressing classroom management issues takes up the bulk of new teachers' work time. New teachers attempt to establish a certain degree of control over their pupils and at the same time gain the pupils' affection. They struggle to identify with their roles as effective teachers, on the one hand; on the other hand, they want to be respected, liked and cared for. The tension between these expectations of distance and closeness creates a fundamental ambiguity in the teacher's role. Kanybek decided that, like his mentor at university, he should be firm with his pupils from the beginning:

At the university I read a text on Makarenko's[25] pedagogy. He was against both authoritarian and "free" education and said that "strict punishment develops students into slaves and absence of punishment prepares hooligans." Therefore, I am not going to punish them (pupils) unnecessarily, but I will demand from them to study well.

One of the biggest challenges Kanybek faced was his pupils' lack of motivation. Many regularly missed classes. Kanybek would call and bring his pupils from the schoolyard or streets to attend classes. He expressed his frustration with these pupils and their rationale: "How can you punish them? If you do anything, they say, 'I don't need to study. What is this education going to give me? I would rather become a businessman and make a lot of money.'"

Kanybek established a formal teacher-pupil relationship, because he felt that otherwise the pupils "would sit on your heads". Some of his colleagues had problematic incidents. One young woman teacher decided to be very strict, but resentment mounted among her pupils and the principal had to come to address the conflict. Another young teacher, who taught junior secondary classes, faced an issue related to discipline. Her pupils came into class about 20 minutes late, because they kept playing soccer after the lesson started despite her calls. As a punishment, she made them stand in the corner holding school chairs over their heads. The boys were all exhausted, and one fainted. His parents complained and demanded that the teacher be fired. But the school administration and the teachers supported her.

Working in a school setting

The school principal, who is the chief administrative officer, is generally expected to provide leadership, advice and supervision, and conduct evaluations. Kanybek's principal hired him quickly because there were not enough history teachers (and especially male teachers) at the school when he returned to his village. The principal was a serious woman who expected hard work, punctuality and conformity to school rules from her staff members. She was a biology teacher herself, and had taught Kanybek when he was a pupil. Although she was very strict with school rules and logistics, the principal did not interfere much in what happened in classrooms. Kanybek was pleased, because he got more freedom in making his own decisions about curriculum and instruction, unlike his practice teaching experience at a town school where he was regularly observed and was required to follow strict instructions from his university professor and the schoolteacher.

Although teachers at a school work in the same building, their classroom structure and heavy weekly schedule make it very difficult to spend much time working and learning together. Teachers spend most of their time alone in their own classrooms. Typically, teachers have few opportunities to observe each other or to talk with one another about their work. This physical isolation conveys the message to beginning teachers that they ought to cope with their problems on their own, and thus reinforces the norm of individualism. Kanybek was hesitant to ask for help from other teachers. Instead he addressed his challenges in classroom management and instructional strategies on his own. He thought that if he asked for help from other teachers they would think that he did not know anything and "would become sceptical whether he learned anything at the university during five years of courses."

Kanybek also noted that most of his colleagues in the village schools were pessimistic and not very motivated to work. These teachers seemed more interested in completing their teaching service, and getting their pensions. Hence, Kanybek felt that in most cases, experienced teachers were not models for him. In the case of his fellow history teachers, Kanybek thought that even the experienced teachers were in the same situation he was in, because they too had to adjust to the new content of history after the break-up of the USSR. He stated:

> We are now teaching different history. Therefore, experienced teachers are also learning. Even colleagues who teach other subjects often ask us questions such as "What kind of history are you teaching nowadays?" I explain to them that we are teaching "our history", because those teachers studied only the "Soviet version" of history when they were at school.

Beyond the school context

New teachers interact closely with their pupils' parents. These interactions vary from formal meetings at school to informal meetings outside the school. The first formal encounter between teachers and parents takes place at the beginning of the academic year at a parent-teacher conference held for them to get to know each other and to elect the class parents' council. Regular class parent-teacher conferences are held at least once a quarter. Each homeroom class has its own parents' council, which works as a bridge between the school and parents of that class. The council also assists the class teacher with organizing extracurricular activities or in collecting money from parents for school expenses. Kanybek regularly met with parents at school or in the village streets, and he discussed their children's progress and any problems they had. At the same time, Kanybek was very reticent while communicating with parents, because he was young and he thought that parents had their own rich experiences raising their children.

Many parents complained that teachers were not working as hard as they used to and that their children were not getting a good education. One village parent observed, "Teachers only collect money and indulge in petty talks in the staff room. Therefore, sometimes I ask my children to stay at home and help us with farming rather than wasting time at the school." Many parents are busy with their everyday tasks, working from morning till evening in their fields. During harvest-time, they need their children to work with them on the farm. Some parents did not believe that their children would be able to get enrolled at a university due to corruption and nepotism. Even if their children could get enrolled, the parents feared they would not be able to find money for their children's study fees and other expenses. One parent observed,

> Even if I pay money and have my son get educated from the university, what is the use of that? What are the hundreds of the people who have university diplomas doing nowadays? They are working in *bazaars*. I guess it is the market economy.

Conclusion

This chapter has described the experiences of a young history teacher from a village school in Kyrgyzstan who is struggling in his work against all sorts of odds. Some of the challenges he faces are typical for beginning teachers from any part of the world, but these challenges are compounded by the socio-political and economic changes that Kyrgyzstan has faced since the break-up of the USSR. Kanybek's life story is similar to many other new teachers who received their school and university education when the USSR was breaking up. In addition to all the usual challenges faced by a new teacher (including adjusting to new schools, working with pupils with individual differences, learning how to plan, teach and evaluate, and working with older colleagues and pupils' parents), new teachers encountered challenges uniquely related to the break-up of the USSR. Kanybek struggled to teach his pupils who were often unmotivated to learn, while working in two schools and on his farm to make a living. He struggled to interact with pupils' parents who developed low opinions of schooling and needed their children to help them with their farm work. Still, Kanybek, like his mentor at university, holds idealistic notions and resists the temptations of accepting bribes for higher marks. Kanybek attempts to make his life and work meaningful, and he continues teaching despite all sorts of challenges.

Kanybek's initial frustrating experiences of working as a new teacher at a village school included interacting with the school administrators, his colleagues and community members. He also faced working in harsh climatic and poor economic conditions, teaching with limited resources, having poor content and pedagogical knowledge, addressing discipline and classroom management issues, and getting a low salary. He worried about teachers' low status. He attempted to improve his financial and material conditions by working at two schools, teaching more hours, and doing additional work, including working on his farm. All of this, in turn, negatively affected his teaching and professional development.

Kanybek's deep concerns were connected with teachers' deteriorating roles and status in the village setting; many villagers looked down on the teachers. Villagers observed the kind of life that teachers had, what salaries they got, what they wore and what they ate. Observing teachers' poor lifestyle reinforced their already low opinions of teachers. In addition, the parents resented the teachers' collecting money. All these challenges made Kanybek's life and work very difficult. He was often frustrated and often thought of leaving his job.

Kanybek's work become a constant negotiation between various challenges, and made his already tense life and work even harder. He was caught in different dilemmas and paradoxes: not wanting to become a teacher, yet working in a village school; complaining about hardships and working overtime for extra pay, yet teaching his pupils that not everything was about money; encouraging his pupils to have their own voices and discouraging memorization, yet heavily using the lecture method and dictating that his pupils learn concepts from the textbook (or his conspectus); loving teaching, yet contemplating a better job; caring for his villagers and their children's future, yet wanting to leave for town to find a job there; wanting to teach only those who wanted to learn, yet thinking about equity and access issues. Kanybek encouraged his pupils to have their own views, but nevertheless maintained that his views were final. He also did not want to admit that he did not know some history concepts, because he feared for his professional image. Because he had little time for his lesson planning or his own professional development, he did not always teach as well as he would have liked. He knew that his pupils suffered because of this.

At the end of the fieldwork, Kanybek was still working at two schools, helping his family on their farm, worrying about his pupils' future and struggling with his personal life challenges. He continued teaching and was gaining the respect of the administrators and his colleagues; at the same time, he was not sure if he would remain in teaching for long. This is a complex picture of a young man who is trying to make sense of his personal and professional life. Kanybek's awareness of the conflicting realities of his profession may help him deal with them. However, ultimately, one beginner teacher cannot continue to work and address these contradictions in isolation. The realities beginner teachers face are simply a reflection of the crisis of education in Kyrgyzstan. Listening to the stories and dilemmas of young teachers in Kyrgyzstan is an important step towards improving their lives, enhancing support for their professional development, and ultimately improving the quality of education in Kyrgyzstan.

Notes

1 Though Soviet education espoused equality and uniformity, many scholars argue that, contrary to official doctrine, Soviet schooling was never really monolithic or egalitarian. Besides clear disparities between Russian- and Kyrgyz-medium schools, obvious status differences also existed between urban and rural schools (Niyozov 2001; Sutherland 1999).

2 Despite high learning standards and an egalitarian approach, success in the Soviet Union was closely related to speaking and acting Russian, resulting in a neglect of, and even distain for, Kyrgyz language, identity and culture (Korth and Schulter 2003).

3 The concept of *internat* (boarding school) was a Soviet construct that enabled orphaned and half-orphaned children, as well as children from remote areas, to gain access to room, board and schooling. The pupils lived in the boarding school as a collective during the week, and visited their families on holidays.

4 Overall pre-school enrolment in Central Asia was only 14 per cent in 1999 (OSI 2002). Significant declines in enrolment in pre-school institutions across Central Asia are related to the increased costs of education, reduced state subsidies for transport and food, and lower family incomes.

5 *Ail okmotus* are the local self-government bodies of the Kyrgyz administrative system. They are appointed by the *raion* (district) administration. They administer governmental funds allocated to them from the *raion* administration, as well as local taxes generated in the village. Clusters of one to four villages form an *okmotu*, with representatives of the *ail okmotus* in each village (*ail bashy*).

6 *Som* is the Kyrgyz national currency introduced on 10 May 1993.

7 After continuous complaints from parents, the Ministry of Education issued a decree that permits schools to collect money from parents only once a year in the amount of an average monthly salary, estimated at 160 *som*.

8 Korth and Schulter (2003) observe that the Kyrgyz schools usually have a reputation for providing education of a poorer quality. The Russian schools continue to enjoy high prestige and are attended by children of different linguistic backgrounds, while the Kyrgyz schools are attended by exclusively Kyrgyz children (Korth and Schulter 2003).

9 In fact, challenges with rural schools are not an entirely post-Soviet phenomenon. The Soviets also realized that the rural and mountainous areas of the USSR, similar to Kyrgyzstan, had considerable difficulties in terms of education. The rural schools lagged behind urban schools, and they lacked "equipment for rooms devoted to various subjects in the curriculum, visual aids, technical teaching devices, education literature, and fiction" (Morozov and Ptitsyn 1975: 65). Rural schools experienced severe teacher shortages, because many young specialists failed to report to their job assignments (Anisimov 1989). Teachers also worked in harsh conditions. Pupils were overloaded with subjects (Mazhenova and Ospanov 1991) and had poorer knowledge than pupils from urban schools (Semykin 1971). The Soviets therefore attempted to improve the education system by investing more on rural education, establishing boarding schools, and using political organisations such as the Komsomol to promote better education in rural settings (Morozov and Ptitsyn 1975). The Soviets also provided young teacher education graduates with incentives, such as housing, to encourage them to go to rural schools, and also involved collective and state farms in sponsoring young people from villages to get teacher training to their villages (Semykin 1971).

10 See Dunstan (1978) on the history and purposes of Olympiads in the former USSR.

11 To address the issue of teacher shortages the Ministry of Education issued a decree 1993 which obliges the graduates from the state-funded "budget" programmes to be placed in a school to teach two years before they are awarded their teaching certificate (*diplom*).

12 As a Soviet legacy, teachers are awarded with qualificational categories as "zero", "two", "one" and "high". "High", the highest category, offers the highest salary. Professional retraining and teaching experience serve as a prerequisite to confirm or upgrade a teacher's category. This category is a standard base for determining a teacher's salary.

13 In fact, it was the first president of Kyrgyzstan, Askar Akaev, who played a major role in dismantling the Marxist-Leninist ideology at the end of the Soviet period and at the beginning of an independence created by the disintegration of the centre. From the outset he eliminated Marxist-Leninist dogma from schools. No other initial post-Soviet leader did it so decisively; his background as a physicist in the Academy of Sciences contributed to its rapid dismantling in the education system.

14 Soviet citizens refer to the period of 1941–1945 during the Second World War, after Fascist Germany attacked the territory of the USSR, as the "Great Patriotic War".

15 A system of education with both Kyrgyz- and Russian-medium schools was introduced in Kyrgyzstan early in the Soviet rule, and after the late 1950s, parents had a choice in the language of instruction for their children. However, socio-economic and ideological pressure to send children to Russian-speaking schools was intense (Korth and Schulter 2003), and in fact there were also some discriminatory differences between schooling in Russian and schooling in the local languages (Landau and Kellner-Heinkele 2001; Lewis 1973; Niyozov 2001). Education in the rural and predominantly Kyrgyz-speaking regions was marginalized and neglected, and pupils in Kyrgyz schools were disadvantaged and underprivileged (Korth 2001a). Kyrgyz and Russian schools divided people along linguistic lines, whereby Russian speakers occupied the higher positions (Korth 2001b). As a result, many people including elite Kyrgyz families, preferred Russian school education.

16 For more on migration in Kyrgyzstan, see Allen (2003).

17 The traffic has become extremely heavy during last few years. Uzbekistan, a neighbouring state, strengthened its borders due to increasing threats from religious militants. That led to stiff regulations at the borders between Kyrgyzstan and Uzbekistan, and several enclaves of each country were left on the wrong sides of the border checks and barbed wires. As a result, well established routes with modern highways could no longer be utilized. The Kyrgyz authorities built new highways that connected Osh and Bishkek without entering the enclaves of Uzbekistan. Building and improving these highways cost the government additional money. Since the highway started functioning, safety issues arose in several villages because of heavy and fast traffic. Over a short period, several traffic accidents involving school children were reported. The community members raised these concerns and got permission from the district education authorities to open a new school, so that pupils whose families lived on the other side of the highway would not have to cross it.

18 He knew that he needed to get a university diploma in order to find a job as a policeman or a lawyer.

19 There were border incursions by the religious militants in 1999.

20 Schools commonly use double and, in some cases, triple shifts.

21 Data from 2002. Currently, US$1 is approximately equal to 46 Kyrgyz *som*.

22 Cholponbay Tuleberdiev was a Kyrgyz soldier who gave his life in the Great Patriotic War. His name is often used nowadays to denote selfless people who sacrifice themselves or suffer for the common good.

23 New textbooks on the history of Kyrgyzstan for classes 10 and 11 were published in 2000 and 2002 respectively. The school still did not have those textbooks during data collection.

24 School leavers in Kyrgyzstan are awarded an *attestat* (diploma) for completing school with grades indicating their overall school performance.
25 Anton Semenovych Makarenko (1888–1939), a prominent Soviet educator. His works were influential in the development of Soviet pedagogy.

References

Abazov, R. (2004) *Historical Dictionary of Kyrgyzstan*, Maryland: Lanham.

Allen, J.B. (2003) "Ethnicity and Inequality among Migrants in the Kyrgyz Republic", *Central Eurasian Studies Review*, 2/1: 7–10.

Anisimov, V.V. (1989) "The Training of Teacher Cadres under *Perestroika*", (*Sovietskaya pedagogika*, 1989, no. 6), *Soviet Education*, 33/3: 6–14.

Attokurov, S. (1995) *Kyrgyz sanjyrasy* [The Kyrgyz genealogy], Bishkek: Kyrgyzstan.

Attokurov, S. (1996) *Kyrgyz etnografiasynyn tarykhnaamasy* [Historiography of Kyrgyz Ethnography], Bishkek: Ilim.

Ball, S.J. (1993) "Self-doubt and Soft Data: Social and Technical Trajectories in Ethnographic Fieldwork", in M. Hammersley (ed.) *Educational Research: Current Issues*, London: Open University Press: 32–48.

Bekbolotov, T.B. (2000) "Aktualnye voprosy obnovleniya shkol'nogo obrazovaniya [Issues of changing school education]", in *Proceedings of the International Scientific-Practical Conference "Problemy obnovleniya shkol'nogo obrazovaniya"* [Problems of School Education Reform], Bishkek: Kirgizskii Institut Obrazovaniya: 3–6.

Bekmakhanov, E. and Bekmakhanova, N. (1979) *Istoriya Kazakhskoi SSR* [History of the Kazakh SSR], Textbook for the 9–10th grades, 17th edn, Alma-Ata: Mektep.

Bogdan, R.C. and Biklen, S.K. (1998) *Qualitative Research in Education*, 3rd edn, Boston: Allyn and Bacon.

Brudnyi, A.A., Kadrakunov, J.K. and Amanov, S.A. (1988) *Kritika burzhuaznykh falsifikatsii sovremennoi deistvitelnosti Sovetskogo Kirgizstana* [Critique of bourgeois falsifications of the modern realities of Soviet Kyrgyzstan], Frunze: Ilim Academy of Science of Kirghiz Republic, Institute of Philosophy and Rights.

Charles, C. (1995) *Introduction to Educational Research*, New York: Longman.

Cohen, L. and Manion, L. (1997) *Research Methods in Education*, 4th edn, London: Routledge.

Cohen, L., Manion, L. and Morrison, K. (2000) *Research Methods in Education*, 5th edn, New York: Routledge Falmer.

Davies, R. (1989) *Soviet History in the Gorbachev Revolution*, Bloomington: Indiana University Press.

DeYoung, A. (2001) *West Meets East in Central Asia: Competing Discourses on Education Reform in the Kyrgyz Republic*, unpublished manuscript.

DeYoung, A. (2004) "On the Current Demise of the 'Action Plan' for Kyrgyz Education Reform: A Case Study", in S.P. Heyneman and A. DeYoung (eds) *The Challenges of Education in Central Asia*, Greenwich, Connecticut: Information Age Publishing: 199–224.

DeYoung, A., Reeves, M. and Valyaeva, G.K. (2006) *Surviving the Transition? Case Studies of Schools and Schooling in the Kyrgyz Republic since Independence*, Greenwich, CT: Information Age Publishing.

DeYoung, A. and Santos, C. (2004) "Central Asian Educational Issues and Problems", in S.P. Heyneman and A. DeYoung (eds) *The Challenges of Education in Central Asia*, Greenwich, Connecticut: Information Age Publishing: 65–80.

Dukenbaev, A. (2004) "Politics and Public Policy in Post-Soviet Central Asia: The Case of Higher Education Reform in Kyrgyzstan", *Central Eurasian Studies Review*, 3/2: 16–18.

Dunstan, J. (1978) *Paths to Excellence and the Soviet school*, Windsor, Berks: NFEP Publishing Company.

EFA (Education for All) (2000) *The EFA 2000 Assessment – Country Report: Kyrgyzstan*. Online. Available: www2.unesco.org/wef/countryreports/kyrgyz/contents.html (accessed on 19 March 2004).

Eversmann, E. (2000) "Dropping out: Schools Attendance in the Kyrgyz Republic", *PRAXIS, The Fletcher Journal of Development Studies*. Online. Available: http://fletcher.tufts.edu/praxis/xvi/Eversman.pdf (accessed on 22 February 2004).

Feiman-Nemser, S. and Remillard, J. (1996) "Perspectives on Learning to Teach", in F. Murray (ed.) *The Teacher Educator's Handbook: Building a Knowledge Base for the Preparation of Teachers*, San Francisco: Jossey-Bass: 63–91.

Glesne, C. (1999) *Becoming Qualitative Researchers: An Introduction*, 2nd edn, New York: Longman.

Hammersley, M. (ed.) (1993) *Educational Research: Current Issues*, London: Paul Chapman.

Haugen, A. (2004) *The Establishment of National Republics in Central Asia*, UK: Palgrave Macmillan.

Heyneman, S.P. (1995) "Obrazovanie v strankakh Vostochnoi Evropy i Srednei Azii: Politika reform [Education in Eastern Europe and Central Asia: Politics of Reform]", *Pedagogika*, 1, Moskva: Pedagogika: 20–29.

Heyneman, S.P. (2000) "From the Party/State To Multiethnic Democracy: Education and Social Cohesion in Europe and Central Asia", *Educational Evaluation and Policy Analysis*, 22(2): 173–191.

Holmes, B., Read, G.H. and Voskresenskaya, N. (1995) *Russian Education: Tradition and Transition*, New York: Garland Publishing.

Ibraimov, O. (2001) *Kyrgyzstan: Encyclopaedia*, Bishkek: Centre of National Language and Encyclopaedia.

Jusupov, K. (1993) *Ürkün: 1916 – Taryhyi-darektuu ocherkter* [Urkun: 1916 – Historical-documentary narratives], Bishkek: Ala-Too.

Kabylov, T. (2003) "Issues of Government-Based In-Service Teacher Education Programmes in Kyrgyzstan: What is Needed for Improvement?" Paper presented at CESS 4th Annual Conference at Harvard University, MA.

Kaplan, V., Agmon, P. and Ermolaeva, L. (1999) *The Teaching of History in Contemporary Russia: Trends and Perspectives*, Tel-Aviv: Cumming Centre for Russian and East European Studies.

Kanimetova, A. (2005) "Vvedenie 'Depozita molodogo uchitel'ya' ne reshit polnost'iu problemu nekhvatki uchitelei v shkolah Kyrgyzstana [The Introduction of 'Deposit for Young Teachers' won't completely resolve the problem of the shortage of teachers in Kyrgyzstan schools]", *Kabar News*, 16 February.

Karym Kyzy, G. (2003) "Problems of Secondary School Education in Kyrgyzstan", *Central Asia – Caucasus Analyst*, 26 February.

Kazybaev, P.K. (1996) *1916-jylky Kyrgyzstandagy kotorulush: L.V. Lesnaya tarabynan jyinalgan dokumentter, materialdar* [Revolts of 1916 in Kyrgyzstan: documents and materials collected by L.V. Lesnaya], Bishkek: Kyrgyzstan.

Kolbin, L.M. (1960) *Kirgizskaya SSR* [Kyrgyz SSR], Moscow: Publishing House under Central Committee of CPSU.

Korth, B. (2001a) *Analyzing Language Biographies*. Online. Available: www.ca-research-net.org/pdf/Korth-Language_biographies.pdf (accessed on 14 January 2002).

Korth, B. (2001b) "Bilingual Education in Kyrgyzstan: Pros and Cons", *Bilingual education and Conflict Prevention Conference Proceedings*, CIMERA, Bishkek, 141–150.

Korth, B. (2004) "Education and Linguistic Division in Kyrgyzstan", in S.P. Heyneman and A. DeYoung (eds) *The Challenges of Education in Central Asia*, Greenwich, Connecticut: Information Age Publishing: 97–112.

Korth, B. and Schulter, B. (2003) *Multilingual Education for Increased Interethnic Understanding in Kyrgyzstan*. Online. Available: www.cimera.ch/files/biling/en/MLG_Text1.pdf (accessed on 28 February 2003).

Kreusler, A. (1976) *Contemporary Education and Moral Upbringing in the Soviet Union*, Ann Arbor: University Microfilms International.

Landau, J.M. and Kellner-Heinkele, B. (2001) *Politics of Language in the Ex-Soviet Muslim States*, London: Hurst.

Lewis, E.G. (1973) *Multilingualism in the Soviet Union: Aspects of Language Policy and its Implementation*, The Hague: Mouton Publishers.

Lisovskaya, E. and Karpov, V. (1999) "New Ideologies in Post-Communist Russian Textbooks", *Comparative Education Review*, 43/4: 522–543.

Mazhenova, A.B. and Ospanov, T.K. (1991) "The Content of Education in Kazakh Schools", *Soviet Education*, 33/2: 71–77.

Maksimov, G. (1974) "The Educational Level of the Population of the USSR", *Soviet Education*, September/October: 47–59. Originally published in Russian in *Vestnik statistiki*, 1972, No. 6.

Manusevich, A.Y., Orlov, V.A., Stetskevich, S.M., Furayev, V.K and Kheyfets, A.N. (1990) *Latest New History: 1917–1939*, School textbook for 10th grade, trans. B. Urstanbekov, Frunze: Mektep.

McMillan, J. and Schumacher, S. (1997) *Research in Education*, 4th edn, New York: Longman.

Medlin, W.K. (1976) "The teaching of History in Soviet schools: A Study in Methods", in G.Z. Bereday and J. Pennar (eds) *The Politics of Soviet Education*, Westport, Connecticut: Greenwood Press: 100–116.

Medlin, W.K., Cavem, W.M. and Carpenter, F. (1971) *Education and Development in Central Asia: A Case Study on Social Change in Uzbekistan*, Leiden: E.J. Brill.

Megoran, N. (2002) *The Borders of Eternal Friendship? The Politics and Pain of Nationalism and Identity along the Uzbekistan–Kyrgyzstan Ferghana Valley Boundary, 1999–2000*, unpublished thesis, Sidney Sussex College, Cambridge.

Merriam, S. (1998) *Qualitative Research and Case Study Applications in Education*, San Francisco: Jossey Bass.

Miles, M. and Huberman, M. (1994) *Qualitative Data Analysis: An Expanded Sourcebook*, Thousand Oaks: Sage.

Morgan, G. and Smircich, L. (1980) "The Case for Qualitative Research", *Academy of Management Review*, 5/4: 491–500.

Morozov, F. and Ptitsyn, G. (1975) "From the *Komsomol* to the Rural School", *Soviet Education*, 17/5: 63–70 [from *Vospitanie shkol'nikov*, 1973, No. 5].

Naumkin, V. (ed.) (1993) *State, Religion and Society in Central Asia: A Post-Soviet Critique*, Reading: Ithaca Press.

Nersesova, A.I. (1973) "The Pupils' Interest in History is the Index of the Teacher's Skill", *Soviet Education*, 15/10: 68–78.

Niyozov, S. (2001) "Understanding Teaching in Post-Soviet, Rural, Mountainous

Tajikistan: Case Studies of Teachers' Life and Work", unpublished thesis, University of Toronto.

Niyozov, S. and Shamatov, D. (2006) "Trading or Teaching: Dilemmas of Everyday Life Economy in Central Asia", *Inner Asia*, 8: 229–262.

Olson, M.R. and Osborne, J.W. (1991) "Learning to Teach: The First Year", *Teaching and Teacher Education*, 7/4: 331–343.

Omurbekov, T.H. and Chorotegin, T.K. (1998) *Kyrgyzdar jana Kyrgyzstandyn tarykhy* [The Kyrgyz and History of Kyrgyzstan], 3, Bishkek: Kyrgyzstan.

OSI-ESP (Open Society Institute – Education Support Program) (2002) *Education Development in Kyrgyzstan, Tajikistan and Uzbekistan: Challenges and Ways Forward*. Online. Available: www.osi-edu.net/esp/events/materials/final.doc (accessed on 10 May 2003).

Osmonov, Ö.J. (2002) *History of Kyrgyzstan: Main Epochs from Ancient Times to Mid XIX Century*, Textbook for 10th grade of secondary schools, Bishkek: Technology.

Osmonov, Ö.J. and Myrzakmatova, A.S. (2000) *Kyrgyzstan History: Transitional Periods from Middle of 19th to 21st Century*, Textbook for 11th grade, Bishkek: Pedagogika.

Rashid, A. (2003) *Jihad: The Rise of Militant Islam in Central Asia*, US: Penguin.

Reeves, M. (2003) *Markets, "Missions" and Languages of Higher Education Reform in Kyrgyzstan*, Paper Presented to the CESS 4th Annual Conference, Cambridge, MA, 4 October 2003.

Seinenskii, A.E. (1973) "From the Experience of Teachers in Kazakh SSR", *Soviet Education*, 15/10: 56–78. [from *Prepodavanie istorii v shkole*, July/August 1972: 4].

Semykin, N. (1971) "Some Problems Confronting the Rural School", *Soviet Education*, March/April, 13(5–6): 35–47.

Shahrani, N.M. (2002) *The Kirghiz and Wakhi of Afghanistan: Adaptation to Closed Frontiers and War*, Seattle: University of Washington Press.

Shamatov, D.A. (2005) *Beginning Teachers' Professional Socialization in Post-Soviet Kyrgyzstan: Challenges and Coping Strategies*, unpublished doctoral dissertation, Ontario Institute for Studies in Education of the University of Toronto.

Shamatov, D.A. (2012) "Impact of Standardized Tests on Equity Issues in Kyrgyzstan", in A. DeYoung and T. Drummond (eds) *New Educational Assessment Regimes in Eurasia: Impacts, Issues and Implications* (special issue of *European Education*).

Shamatov, D. and Sainazarov, K. (2010) "The Impact of Standardized Tests on Education Quality in Kyrgyzstan: A Case of PISA 2006", in A. Wiseman (ed.) *The Impact of International Achievement Studies on National Education Policymaking*, International Perspectives on Education and Society Series, Vol. 13, Emerald Publishing.

Silova, I. and Steiner-Khamsi, G. (eds) (2009) *How NGOs React: Globalization and Education Reform in the Caucasus, Central Asia and Mongolia*, Bloomfield, CT: Kumarian.

Soktoev, I. (1981) *Formirovanie i razvitie Sovetskoi intelligentsii Kirgizstana* [Formation and development of the Soviet intelligentsia in Kyrgyzstan], Frunze: Ilim.

Steiner-Khamsi, G. (2009) *The Impact of Teacher Shortages on the Quality of Education in Kyrgyzstan*, Public Lecture presentation at University of Central Asia, 14 September.

Steiner-Khamsi, G., Mossayeb, S. and Ridge, N. (2007) *Curriculum and Student Assessment, Pre-Service Teacher Training: An assessment in Tajikistan and Kyrgyzstan*, New York: Teachers' College, Columbia University.

Sutherland, J. (1992) "Perestroika in the Soviet General School: From Innovation to Independence?" in J. Dunstan (ed.) *Soviet Education under Perestroika*, London and New York: Routledge: 14–29.

Sutherland, J. (1999) *Schooling in the New Russia: Innovation and Change, 1984–95*. London: Macmillan and St. Martin Press.

Szekely, B.B. (1987) "The New Soviet Secondary School History Course and the Social Studies Curriculum", *Soviet Education*, 29/11–12: 3–7.

Tabyshaliev (ed.) (1979) *Torzhestvo idei velikogo oktyabrya v Kirgizii* [Victory of the ideas of Great October in Kyrgyzstan], Frunze: Ilim.

UNDP (United Nations Development Programme in Kyrgyzstan) (2000–2001) Online. Available: www.undp.kg/english/publications/global_conf/chapter_3.htm (accessed on 23 March 2004).

UNDP (United Nations Development Programme in Kyrgyzstan) (2003) *UNDP: The Kyrgyz Republic. Millennium Development Goals: Progress Report*, Bishkek. Online. Available: www.undp.kg/english/publications/2003/mdgpr2003.pdf (accessed on 20 March 2004).

Usenbaev, K. (1997) *1916: Geroicheskie i tragicheskie stranitsy* (1916: Heroic and tragic pages), Bishkek: Izdatelstvo Sham.

Yin, R. (1989) *Case Study Research: Design and Methods*, Beverly Hills, London: Sage.

8 Redefining students and universities in the Kyrgyz Republic

Alan J. DeYoung

Among the most visible changes brought about by educational reforms in Kyrgyzstan since independence has been a continuing expansion of the higher education sector. Higher Education Institutes (*vuzy*) have increased from fewer than 10 to about 50; and enrolment from approximately 10 per cent of secondary school graduates to more than 40 per cent. These days, almost every other secondary school graduate becomes a university student, even though students must now pay tuition for their studies, and diplomas are no longer specifically linked to actual jobs as they once were.

Discussions of national higher education policy – or lack of same – are ongoing in Kyrgyzstan, and they invariably involve announcements about reorganizing the entire higher education system. University rectors meanwhile continue unabashedly to give speeches and issue press releases extolling the quality and innovativeness of their particular institutions in an effort to attract students. Most students, though, rarely see the sorts of higher education learning environments promised, or the sorts of innovations they hear about. If one wants to actually witness and understand the daily lives of teachers and students in a Kyrgyz university (like any other), the situation has to be experienced from the ground rather from pro-announcements of the education ministry or a university rector.

This chapter seeks to explore and explain the seeming contradictions in the higher education sector from "inside" perspectives: those of students, their parents, teachers and university administrators. How does a state university in the current era grow and operate in a national climate of both economic and educational decline and leadership confusion? How and why do increasingly impoverished parents send their children to the university when there is no guarantee that what their children will learn can lead to a job, even as these institutions proclaim their reformed specializations and programmes are market driven? And do students and parents actually perceive quality differences among the various state, inter-governmental and private universities in the country? These are the primary questions pursued in this chapter.

The larger project upon which this analysis is based comes from the author's decade-long fieldwork in half a dozen Bishkek universities that provide substantial humanities-oriented specializations. The data include student surveys, participant observation and ethnographic interviews completed between 2007 and

2009. Local newspaper and national media sources on higher education issues, as well as journalistic coverage on education and higher education concerns, were also collected and analysed. In several cases, the universities themselves provide important information via their websites. What emerges from all these sources is an image of a higher education system in flux, where academic quality is low, but appreciation for a variety of services not advertised is visible. At the same time, hunger for quality and higher standards still draws many students, which they appear to seek outside of state higher education institutions when they can.

Education opportunities before and after independence

By the late Soviet period, formal secondary education was virtually universal in Kyrgyzstan, while post-secondary education opportunities were limited and mostly connected to industrial and agricultural specializations involved in the Soviet economy, or to professional occupations in education and medicine (Holmes *et al.* 1995). A very small percentage of school graduates went into specific higher educational institutes for training to become teachers, engineers, veterinarians, agronomists or doctors – or to the only State University, which awarded the more prestigious higher education diploma. A larger percentage of students went into secondary professional (specialized) education; either to a *tekhnikum* to become mechanics and technicians; to a pedagogical *uchilishcha* to become elementary teachers; or a medical *uchilishcha* to become nurses.

Some students would leave secondary school with only an "incomplete" (*nepolnoe*) secondary education at approximately age 15, having received an *attestat* after the eighth or ninth grade. Since 15-year-olds were still not eligible to work, those uninterested in academic instruction often went to the professional technical *uchilishcha* (*PTU*) to undertake vocational training and to complete secondary education at the same time: then to join the labour force. Other students who could have stayed and finished their complete (*polnoe*) secondary education, but decided they would not be admitted to higher education or decided they wanted to prepare for their future professions sooner, could choose to finish both their final two years of secondary education, as well as gain applied or technical training, in the *tekhnikum*. In both the *uchilishcha* and the *tekhnikum* students were able to receive some stipend for study and/or minimal payments for their labours during professional practice.

Admission to higher education institutions was controlled under the Soviet command system, where manpower needs estimated by various government ministries determined the number of available spaces for allocating higher education opportunities. Admission to higher education study was highly competitive, since most occupations available through universities and institutes were considered prestigious: they meant joining the ranks of the intelligentsia (Dobson 1977). Education was free to those who were admitted; and students also received a living stipend. Graduates were assigned to their first jobs by the government in different locations across the USSR. They were legally obligated to stay there for two to three years – to work out their diploma (*otrabotat diplom*).

Compulsory secondary education, as well as the various forms of higher education, also had a moral and philosophical emphasis: *vospitanie*, or social upbringing. Since the aims of the state were to bring about world socialism, schools and post-secondary educational institutions were considered the training centres to create human and ideological capital required for a productive economic and social life: it was part of their educational mission (DeYoung 2007). Like factory and agricultural collectives, they were also organized into political collectives.

Due to the collapse of the Kyrgyz economy, education spending in Kyrgyzstan dropped precipitously from about 10 per cent of GDP during the 1980s to about 4 per cent in the mid-1990s. This has rebounded to almost 6 per cent now, but the government has not rededicated the financial resources that it would take to rebuild, remodel and equip schools in the fashion they were in under Soviet power (Mertaugh 2004; UNESCO 2002). In 2003, there were 2,051 schools where 74,000 teachers educated 1.2 million students. One hundred schools were reported in a "wrecked condition" for lack of resources, even as parents and international donors rather than the state have assumed substantial responsibilities for school operations (Karym kyzy 2003).

Resource deficiencies have been compounded by the demise of a centralized planning and distribution apparatus formerly implemented by Moscow. National and local governments in Kyrgyzstan today suffer from a "capacity gap", where few policy developers and implementers have had specific training in governance and budgeting matters (Gleason 1997, 2003; Olcott 2005). In public education, few office-holders in the education administration at any level have training or experience in such areas as education finance, curriculum theory and alignment, or measuring learning outcomes, since such matters were all previously orchestrated from Moscow. And the professionals with some experience and better qualifications in these areas have often left – like the teachers – for more lucrative private sector opportunities.

A news story in the Central Asia Caucasus Institute (CACI) *Analyst*, using education ministry data, described in 2003 the impact of over a decade of decline in the Kyrgyz education system.

One of the sharpest problems of secondary education in Kyrgyzstan is a lack of qualified teachers and specialists. According to information provided by the Ministry of Education and Culture of the Kyrgyz Republic, there is a shortage of 2,863 teachers in the schools. This problem is especially acute in rural areas. There are cases where people without proper qualification have been teaching some subjects. As a result, the quality of secondary education is suffering greatly. Part of the reason is that because of low salaries, many teachers and graduates of higher educational institutions with pedagogical degrees do not work based on their specialization but are engaged in private business or work in bazaars (markets). Some, especially teachers of English and Russian, have left for Kazakhstan and Russia, where the situation is believed to be comparatively better (Karym kyzy 2003). Soviet and Kyrgyz secondary and higher education pedagogy was highly text-dependent, with virtually all teaching materials and texts coming from Moscow. The primary instructional mode was to lecture from these texts and have students repeat or recall information. Although this teaching methodology has been severely criticized since independence in Kyrgyzstan and throughout the former Soviet Union (OSI 2003; Soros Foundation 2008), even under-qualified teachers might be effective if they had recent teaching materials and information to use in their classrooms. Unfortunately, the texts and materials supplied by the USSR are no longer an option. To make matters more complicated, education policy in Kyrgyzstan promises students to be able to study in the language of their choice, which was during the 1990s increasingly Kyrgyz (Korth 2004). But, again, there are no funds for developing new texts in Kyrgyz. The CACI account continues (Karym kyzy 2003):

> Prior to 1994 all the school materials both for students and teachers of Russian-language schools were received from the Russian publishing house *Prosveshcheniye*, but as the state ceased to provide books due to the lack of financial resources, the Russian supply also stopped. As a result, the school library funds of most of the schools became old. But the situation in Kyrgyz schools is even worse, especially for those located in rural areas. Most people do not have access to books and even if they do, not all of them can afford to buy them. Although the Kyrgyz government recognizes the seriousness of the issue, the lack of resources does not allow it to address the problem effectively, which forces it to turn to foreign assistance. In 2001, the government of the Russian Federation gave to the Russian-language schools in Kyrgyzstan 102,000 copies of textbooks ... (and) the Asian Development Bank gave US$2 million for publishing and purchase of books.

Using the schools and universities for national identity purposes or for building social cohesion in the post-Soviet era is also proving problematic. The Kyrgyz government has thus far been unable to replace the official moral teachings of Soviet times with a useable new citizenship strategy; and this problem also plagues the other Central Asian states. As Roy (2000) explains:

> The problem of the newly independent states of Central Asia is at once simple and insoluble. As we have seen, they were born during the Soviet period. But their independence was created in opposition to that period. One cannot imagine Kyrgyzstan making Stalin the father of its nation. Furthermore, they are not able to refer back to the period preceding Sovietization or Russian colonization in the way that can be done among the Georgians or in the Baltic countries, because what existed in that period, the emirates and the tribal confederations, does not fit with the ethnic-national legitimacy which they are building today.
>
> (Roy 2000: 161)

Even without a cohesive national ideology to focus upon, schools and universities are still required to provide a guided, morally appropriate socialization process for students. This is a holdover from Soviet times that, like many other practices in Kyrgyzstan, goes poorly attended to. For example, about a third of Kyrgyzstanis are not ethnically Kyrgyz, so the unwritten history of the Kyrgyz people cannot suffice as the moral centre. In a nation with large ethnic Uzbek and Russian and other minority populations, few non-Kyrgyz have been convinced that the epic Kyrgyz heroes (like Manas) are theirs as well. Islam, which is increasingly practiced by most of the population, is also still not allowed to be taught in state schools.

Meanwhile, debates over language policy and the status of Kyrgyz, Russian and Uzbek remain. Russian is still the lingua franca in most of the capital and often preferred among the political elites (Korth 2004). In many secondary schools (especially urban) and most national universities, instruction remains in Russian; and of course, the Russian Federation is an important trading and political partner in an era when it is re-exerting its influence throughout Central Asia. Demand for Russian language and good relations with the Russian Federation are also important these days since so many Kyrgyz have migrated north to engage in agricultural and construction. Remittances from such work have been important components of the Kyrgyz economy for almost a decade. At the same time, Turkey also claims strong cultural ties with Kyrgyzstan (as well as several other Central Asian republics) and has put great effort into strengthening such ties through education and the teaching of Turkish in the schools they support (Aypay 2004; Keles and Zakirova 2008; Marat 2007).

Even in the face of these myriad issues and problems, demand for education has remained extremely high, and the government yet proclaims secondary education is a right of each citizen and a high priority of the state (Akaev 2003; UNESCO 2000). But the *provision* of educational services has continued to slide. Accordingly, the government has increasingly looked to international donors for assistance. The European Union, Asian Bank of Development, USAID, the World Bank, the Soros Foundation, and the Russian and Turkish governments – among many others – all play substantial roles in aiding or propping up the delivery of secondary and higher education services in the Kyrgyz Republic today (DeYoung *et al.* 2006; Mertaugh 2004; Weidman *et al.* 2004).

Even with stabilizing resources and large-scale international assistance, current statistics on educational outcomes in Kyrgyzstan are dismal; corruption of the system is well recognized; and complaints about the capacity of the education ministry and the government in general to plan a way forward are rampant. Anvar Rahmetov outlined these issues in a journalistic essay for the Central Asia–Caucasus *Analyst* in April 2009:

> Kyrgyz school education is in a catastrophic situation. The reading skills of 74 percent of fifteen-year old Kyrgyzstanis are below basic ("pass") level. Math and science results are even worse – failing students constitute 84 percent and 82 percent respectively. Such were the shocking findings of an

independent national survey administered in 2008. Earlier in 2006, Kyrgyzstan recorded the lowest score among the 57 countries that participated in the Program for International Student Assessment (PISA).... Another factor is corruption in the educational sphere.... Petty corruption includes both school corruption with children or their parents bribing teachers in exchange for good grades, as well as corruption in college admissions which de-motivate vigorous knowledge acquisition, since high school students know they can buy their way into college. A third factor that contributed to the eventual failure of a once-progressive educational system is the lack of strategic vision and the absence of a single strategy for education reform. After the break-up of the USSR, the Soviet school system could not be sustained, nor was it relevant to contemporary social and economic needs. The consequent reform attempts have been piecemeal, inconsistent and half-hearted. Moreover, programmatic papers drafted by education specialists were often left unimplemented. Frequent ministerial reshuffles also contributed: with an average education minister in office for slightly more than a year, consistency talk is totally irrelevant.

(Rahmetov 2009)

State universities: reorganizing and joining international educational space

Since higher education no longer guarantees or leads to specific jobs in a depressed economy, since secondary school graduates score very poorly on most objective academic outcome measures, and since higher education is increasingly expensive in Kyrgyzstan, it seems paradoxical that both the number of universities and enrolments have exploded there over the past 15 years. Eager to join the world higher education market and to attract higher education donors and sponsors, many public or state universities in the capital city of Bishkek have formal working relationships with universities in other countries. The Kyrgyz Ministry of Education and Culture, too, works with a number of organizations like the EU's Tempus programme, the Soros Foundation and USAID. Tempus is conceptualized as a "modernization" effort designed to create an "area of cooperation" in and around Europe. Using Kyrgyz government data, it profiles the higher education landscape in Kyrgyzstan in 2005 thus:

Today the HE system of the Kyrgyz Republic is represented by 51 higher education institutions, 5 of which are not recognized by the Ministry of Education of the Kyrgyz Republic. Thirty six universities are public, the rest are private. Most of the HE institutions operate a set of substructures such as branches, institutes, education centers, etc. A total of 207,000 students attend universities. 92 percent of them attend public universities. Academic faculty and staff is represented by 10,500 teachers. According to the Law on Education of the Kyrgyz Republic, the Ministry of Education is the main agency responsible for quality of education and management of the education system.... In addition, 7 universities are intergovernmental and their activities are overseen by Ministries of Education of relevant states.

(Tempus 2005)

The various international donors and advisors working in the Kyrgyz higher education sector have all come to find that the systemic decline in financial support for state universities has significantly undermined their quality, even as enrolments have mushroomed. There is serious deterioration in faculty quality, few material resources, crumbling state university buildings, minimal student support services – and publicly acknowledged corruption. Yet, Kyrgyz education ministry officials remind all international advisors and collaborators about their intention to "preserve all positive experience in education that has been acquired during the Soviet period" while simultaneously striving for "innovations at all levels" (Tempus 2005).

Higher education reform in point of fact is not considered a high priority even among most international donor organizations, since a university degree is not compulsory and theoretically should be driven by market demand and user fees (Musabaeva 2008). But almost all major universities in the country claim to want to internationalize their programmes and reputations in the quest for increasing their marketability to students. Diplomas in almost anything "international" (e.g. international law, business, economics and journalism) are in high demand. This has led to accepting – rhetorically at least – proposals by international organizations to help them enter or align with international standards.

Although the Kyrgyz education ministry and most university officials exert considerable effort proclaiming their inheritance from the prestigious Soviet university, those higher education institutions that existed from before independence are but a shadow of their former selves in terms of faculty and student quality; and neither have they the resources to be as innovative as advertised. Universities that have been invented since 1991 have an even harder time resting underneath the Soviet higher education mantle. How Kyrgyz state universities can even be called state universities stretches the imagination, since the government actually only contributes about 10–15 per cent of their current annual costs. Most now charge tuition fees for services and have become semi-private by creating new institutes or branch campuses under their organizational rubric (Musabaeva 2008; Reeves 2004). The state does approve and control the curricular offerings of such universities, as they do with all other universities in the country which give the state diploma.

The higher education capacity gap earlier suggested is illustrated by the conflicting initiatives visible in the country today. One day the government proclaims it wants to compel or facilitate all statute universities to enter world education space by (for example) joining the European Union's Bologna Process (see Chapter 9, this volume). The next day spokespersons for the government say elimination of funding of state universities needs to occur, so that market forces can drive efficiency and innovation among them. The contradiction between announcing that the government is interested both in "aligning" universities with

Bologna while at the same time proclaiming an interest in getting out of the higher education business by allowing them to privatize further underscores the lack of coherence in national higher education policy. Musabaeva outlines the sorts of policy and leadership problems the Kyrgyz government appears to have when they talk about higher education reform:

> It is interesting to note that plans for privatization of universities were provided in the law "On Education" in 2003. According to this law, university privatization should have started in 2005. But because of March events (the national revolution that year), it was postponed for an indefinite period. Nevertheless, in 2006 and 2007, this idea was announced several times by the senior leadership of the country, including high officials of the Ministry of Education and Science.... The topic is still privately discussed (but) there is no plan of privatization that clearly sets forth the state's priorities for university reforms as well as its principles for regulating the reorganized universities' activities. There are difficulties in developing concrete mechanisms and a corresponding normative basis; there is no serious financial-economic analysis of universities.... A public dialogue that considers the opinions of experts, professors, students, and the wider public is absent. Therefore, there are well-grounded concerns that embarking on the process unprepared may simply result in a veiled redistribution of property and provide a method of realizing the interests of state and private officials, creating an opportunity for corruption.
>
> (Musabaeva 2008: 80)

Many of the innovations which international advisors and advocates would likely introduce – in order to attract more students – contradict essential Soviet pedagogical aims and structures. Tempus, among others, argues for strengthening measures to introduce academic freedom and academic honesty; improve transparency of the decision-making processes; improve the level of skills of teaching and administrative staff; increase the wages of teachers and introduce merit-based salary scales; increase efficiency in university management; move toward financial and administrative decentralization; develop and expand distance learning opportunities; introduce a credit system compatible with the European Credit and Transfer System; and so on (Tempus 2005; Weidman *et al.* 2004).

However, most international groups that suggest systemic reform of the higher education system in the country have a problem, since the Kyrgyz education ministry (even the title of the education ministry has changed several times since independence) has little history of developing and implementing on their own systematic academic improvement plans, and has yet to comprehend that educational outcomes rather than curricular inspection needs to be the focus of academic quality (DeYoung 2004; Musabaeva 2008; Rahmetov 2009). According to Tempus, "Quality has depreciated in many universities", and even though the ministry has created a "Quality Assurance Division" and universities are to be obliged to introduce QA departments, a strategy on improving quality of education does not yet exist" (Tempus 2005: 7).

Then and now: views about quality from senior university administrators

This research project started from the premise that the Soviet university was once respected and hard to enter, and studying there was an intense experience. My interviews and observations were undertaken mostly in the Spring semester of 2008 and 2009 within several foreign language faculties in several of the nation's largest universities. Humanities and "Exact Sciences" were the two main directions in the former Soviet higher education system. Today, exact sciences have seen a serious decline in popularity, while institutions which primarily taught humanitarian subjects (history, foreign languages, political science and geography) have become the most prestigious. All humanities higher education institutions have often retained and added to their international language focus – Chinese, for example, is a widely popular subject – while also attempting to add new and previously unheard of specializations in international business, law, tourism, etc. These new specializations invariably require extensive foreign language training, and every one now requires several years of English or German or French or Chinese (or some combination) for graduation.

Foreign language departments or faculties are thus excellent locations to study dynamics of higher education reform here, since they are myriad and intertwined with most other desirable specializations now. In 2009, there were 17 specific international language programmes and faculties in Kyrgyzstan, while many other specializations also included language training as part of their required curriculum. My research involved several faculties involved with international languages, although it was centred in one particular university. I begin here by considering the views about higher education from two key informants who first were students in Soviet schools and the university, and later university teachers and administrators. They reported big changes in how the system runs and what constitutes appropriate study today.

One local university educator who experienced the past 20 years of education reform in Kyrgyzstan at multiple levels in the system and who attempted several types of pedagogical as well as structural reforms here was ironic about the evolution of higher education in her country in my interview with her. Janat – not her real name – was able to be outspoken perhaps because she is no longer working within the system:

> After independence – under the slogan of Perestroika – we "people" decided to enter the market economy, (and) we decided what type of institution (the university) should be. And the reforms which were started then were probably not well thought out. There was no principled strategic view of how we were to transform – to (transform) the higher education of Soviet times – to move to a more liberal education. And every year the curriculum for higher

education institutions was changing. And then a new minister would come and again something else was changing. (Before), all this stuff was coming from Moscow and all the basic documents (governing) schools and for higher education was coming from Moscow. (Meanwhile) here the Minister of Education was responsible basically (only) for implementing. (S/he) had no designing or developing function. When we decided to be independent from Moscow, we (thought we) needed something new, something national. And then the problem arrived, because there were no people – no qualified professionally trained people – who could develop curricula at the national level and with high quality. And then what would happen is that we would again and again return back to Russian standards, to the Russian curriculum, trying to copy it. And then maybe we would introduce some (small) change.

Janat had attended the only state-level (academic) university in the 1970s (now renamed Kyrgyz National University or KNU). Earlier, she and seven of her classmates graduated from one of Bishkek's best known secondary schools, and been among the fewer than 10 per cent of such graduates nationwide able to continue in the university. All seven of these young women ended up in the same state university in the same department, learning how to teach English. There, they received the state curriculum and prepared to teach in schools, which was then a high prestige job and was well paid. But after *perestroika*, chaos descended:

> ...(and) then private institutions appeared; and, the Minister of Education at the beginning lost its controlling functions (in the government); then – maybe in 3–5 years – it regained (its authority) again. But the problems had started already, there was some ministry dysfunction and some universities refused (to be controlled).... At present, the Minister tries somehow to make all these universities meet some standards, but again there is freedom of the university, and there is the question of (how) private higher education institutions (should be monitored): how it should be done. What are the requirements; what are the responsibilities of the privatized universities? A lot of questions have appeared.

Janat talked about the problem of creating new specializations and courses within the old university structures and using new teachers who were the only ones who could afford to work in the university. She described the situation of her (newly renamed) university this way:

> In the beginning we had a highly centralized type of administration and management (and) the education ministry controlled our curriculum. After perestroika we were allowed elective courses, and the ministry allowed us up to 20 per cent (later 30 per cent) to be defined by ourselves.... But the problem is that the universities are not developing any new courses ... the teachers (were often asked) to work hard to develop a programme. (But), all

the time teachers were saying, "Oh we need freedom, we want to be able to have elective courses – like in the west", but when it came to submitting (their) developed courses, it was a problem; because teachers did not know about resources or the internet, even. And again, it is (both) a time problem and all these teachers should be interested somehow; and the administration of the university should be interested in real reforms (and) updating courses. But no one is interested; everyone says they are interested in reforms, but no one wants to do the work.

Although talk of reform and education reform were all the rage in earlier years after independence – and even today – there remains lots of talk but with little action:

> If we want really to go into the world, we have to try somehow to be competitive with other international universities and educational institutions.... And what happens? All we have are old textbooks; and developing publication (or) teaching materials? No, each university basically survives by itself.... Then they use students' money. From the government, it's nothing except for salary: no renovation, there is no money for books; there is no money for anything; no money for development – nothing: only salaries and building utility payments. And now, does our parliament listen to the universities? (Does) it support secondary schools? But of course not – someone else somewhere is more important.

Rather than reforming in any rationally consistent manner, Janat argued that individual universities have been the driving force of change, with university rectors grabbing power and installing friends and relatives within newly privatized sub-structures of the organization. She claimed that student tuition rather than academic quality now drives most university decisions. To be named a university rector means also that you have a political connection to those at the top of the government who allow rogue universities to operate; possibly for a share of the tuition money:

> Under one rector, an institute was established, and a personal friend (of the rector) was named director. Then, another rector was nominated, and he wants to bring his people. The only way he can do this ... is to reorganize (the institute). And when you reorganize, there is a law that (only by) improving the concept of the institute is this possible. Like, an Institute of World languages (is created): the same department (for example) changes its name to the Institute of Lingustics or Informatics, but otherwise nothing (except the director and his staff) changes. The same department; the same curriculum; the same teachers.

Janat understood, however, that many parents in Kyrgyzstan find themselves between a rock and a hard place for their children, and see no alternatives for their children after secondary school:

In Soviet times, vocational schools were very functional because there was a demand at (for example) the Lenin plant, which was producing some military stuff; it was one of the biggest plants in Soviet times. And there was an agricultural plant; there were a few other very big and nice plants and factories in light industry – I mean, like a sewing and textile factory; and one for producing shoes,... and for them the country needed specialists; and there were well developed vocational schools. And it was really "if I get this training I go to work in this Lenin plant" – or whatever plant; "I get a nice salary, I have a permanent job;" I mean basically, it worked for everyone.... But then, after perestroika, the plants were closed, everything was closed; nothing is working now. What is working is the Dordoi Bazaar, where all people are selling and buying something, but the country is not producing anything at the moment. For what do we need vocational schools? And that is why they are closed.

Janat agreed that depending upon whose numbers are to be believed, between 35 and 50 per cent of secondary school graduates go into higher education, even when the local economy has no room for most of them:

The situation in the country is very paradoxical, if I can use that word.... (Parents) have a very primitive idea of what to do. Your kid finishes high school, but there is no job for this kid. He is 17 or 18 years old and has no qualification and (there are) no (attractive) vocational schools. There are no places where your kid can work maybe a couple of years before he is mature, so (parents) have to decide what to do and how to do it. Your kid cannot just travel, because you have no money just to have your kid explore the world. So, the easiest way is just enter the university, or the institute – with a hope that after he graduates from the university he will get a job somewhere – in the international organization or whatever. That is why it is a problem.... Especially several years ago, the most popular departments were English language departments, because a lot of people were connecting their future with international organizations, or to get a scholarship or internship, but basically, we have no plants; we have no factories, we have no high technology; agriculture is basically at a low level. You do not need as many specialists in agriculture (anymore) either.... And there are no real alternatives ... except for education; our government does not offer anything except higher education institutions.

I had another extended interview with a senior faculty member who now is a university institute director where multiple foreign languages are core subjects. I was able to pursue the question of differences between higher education in Soviet times and the current era. When Kanikei was a student, for example, she focused so extensively upon her studies that she rarely had time to leave her classrooms or her dormitory. Her students today are currently distracted, she claims, by other pursuits, and many of them do not attend their classes daily. Yet she is sympathetic to their situations and she and her teachers do the best they can:

> I genuinely think that we have (some) hard working students, but there are some lazybones. You see, when everything depends on money – (students) can go to another university who will adopt them. That is why we try to keep our own students and to do all our best to give them knowledge. But it depends on them, too; how the students will behave in classes. For example when I studied here – at the National University (for three years), I did not go anywhere. I did not even know that there was a *TSUM* [the main shopping building in every major Soviet city].... I was busy with my studies all the time, you see. I knew the way to the library and to this university building; that's it; I did not go anywhere ... (but) students are different now. The main demand for us (when she was a student) was to perform "home reading", (where) we read one hundred pages of American and British writers; and the process of retelling (these stories) gave a lot of knowledge. You realized where your mistakes were, and then the teacher would help you to find this and that. And there was a laboratory in the main building; a very good language laboratory and we worked there till 11 o'clock at night.

Language learning should be better now, according to Kanikei, since the world has opened up to allow Kyrgyz students access to foreign native language speakers. Still she claims that while some students are taking advantage of this possibility, most do not study seriously outside of class; neither do they have as much daily contact with their teachers. But Kanikei also fails to mention that there is no language laboratory in her institute; and most of the books in their library are seriously out of date:

> (Language labs) were a great experience for the teachers (and) for the students (before). Now it is good we can go and communicate with different people who know English well, and we can visit them sometimes. But some (students) are just lazybones.... You see, we were hard working people at that time. But now young people do not want to work too hard. They demand to receive the results right now – without any hard work. This is the psychology of the students nowadays. (Meanwhile), relations between teachers and students are quite different now. The teachers are working in different places; they run from one university to another because of their salary: it is impossible. (In Soviet times), I received 55 roubles. It was the highest stipend for that time; and that was enough for me. I even sent something for my parents. (Sometimes) I bought them some clothes here, and I sent them money. See, I was full of money at that time.

Kanikei seemingly agreed with her colleague above that the lack of prestigious job prospects after graduation may explain some of the reasons standards have slipped in state universities. State universities themselves do not have placement centres or services, and students are on their own to find somewhere to use any skills they might acquire. Kanikei's students – theoretically eligible to become secondary school teachers – are thus expected and encouraged to miss their classes if they have better things to do: like making an occupational connection. They usually do not get formal credit for interning or work-study. Rather, teachers and administrators look the other way when the mandatory classes students are expected to take are in essence not attended:

> Before, we had a special list from Ministry of Education, and your name is there, and it is written where you go to work for two years. It was compulsory, and your salary was there; the house was there, waiting for you. (And) your salary was more than the usual ones. There were (also) so many privileges for (rural) school teachers; there was (extra) money for Young Specialists – the beginners; so many privileges. And when I worked at school after graduation – in the village – I conducted a lot of classes because there was no teacher before me in the school, and I received a house and 400 rubles because (I taught) so many classes; you see. But now, we do not guarantee our students that we will find them a job. That is why we appreciate it when students work (often without pay) for international organizations. They work with their English speciality. We agree to that, and we allow them to work.

(Rural) parents' and teachers' views on university quality

I completed over 30 ethnographic interviews with students, parents, teachers and administrators in several universities over the two years of this study. The primary site of my fieldwork was Bishkek New University (BNU) – a pseudonym. No interviewee there believed teaching was better now than before, and no one suggested that current students are as serious in their academic work as during Soviet times. But, for many parents and students, this was less an issue than it was for the long-term faculty remaining in the system. For parents, sending their children to the university was the best current option from among possible choices; and for some it gave their children opportunities "to study" which they had not been able to experience in Soviet times.

Kunduz left her rural village in the north to attend the national pedagogical university with the full support of her parents. Now a university teacher herself, she argued that sending most or all of their children to the university is the aim of every Kyrgyz family, which usually involves everyone in the extended family. Contributions and donations from uncles, aunts, cousins and grandparents are collected, since going now to the university is virtually a rite of passage to adulthood, and no other options are seen as pleasant or desirable. Families often want to send their children/nieces/nephews/grandchildren to university not because they have necessarily been great students, but because there are no other decent career choices, and they do not want their young relatives working in agriculture or in the bazaar. According to Kunduz:

Every parent wants their children to be happy and to live in good conditions, and that is why they send their children to the university, because you know, if you do not have a diploma or specialization, you can live (only) in the country or in the village, working with animals.... In the village you cannot have any progress in your career, you know, but in the city, there are a lot of chances to be progressive.... If I were in the village, by this time I would be married, and maybe have several children. I know some young women who are my age: they have already two or three children, and they live in villages, and you know their mentality is very different. They think (only) about their family, and not about their future. They think (only) about their children and what will happen tomorrow.

Aika, a ten-year veteran teacher from the south, took Kunduz's argument one step further, explaining that sending your children to the university is often seen as a moral duty, even if many parents understand the university was no longer the same kind of place as before; and even if the character of those who now "study" has drastically changed:

Sending children to the university is a family thing. This is interesting, since only 13 per cent or 15 per cent used to attend.... Now it is true that parents consider that it is their holy duty (to send them); if they do not give them education or provide them education, they think themselves guilty. And therefore, they make their children study, even though they are not capable to study; if they are not interested.... Before, university students were very intellectual; and it appeared in everybody's mind, "Oh, he is a university student." Of course, then there was only one university, and everybody could say (a graduate) was a highly educated, well educated (person). He was very literate and highly qualified. But (now), you can find students who cannot write correctly and the university lost its quality. When our parents studied – even if not at the universities – at technical schools – they were literate!... At present, there is no difference between the man who is working in the market and the one who is coming from the university – there is no difference!!!

Another Kyrgyz teacher with an international academic degree claimed that going to the university now is understood by parents as only partly about academics; there are more serious maturational issues involved. Omurbek said:

So the thing is, (higher) education has (become) a priority for each family; ... those parents who might have been working (themselves) after high school, now they know that they can send their son to (the) university ... it is probably true that (parents) really don't expect from their kids (some academic) tradition, but they do expect that their children will learn some specialty so they can live with that major, with that background (of) education for their entire life. The education (may) give a stable income, (and) may give a stable – psychology. So, if you have stability, it's a huge thing. (Parents understand) the situation of the university: its high corruption and (its) poor quality. That may be, but still (they) tend to think that at the university kids learn something that will help in their future lives and plus they while getting a major at least they can figure out what their interests are.

Omirbek further believed that entrance standards and a proven academic history in secondary school ought not be prerequisites for entering a university; village schools were weak, and it might take more time for young men and women to find themselves and become mature. Universities were just the place for this to happen:

> Yes, there (might be) some changes when you send your son to (the university) who was doing badly in high school. They (might) really succeed at the university.... Sending a kid for four or five years to university, I think, will make them think about their lives in the future. Parents want to push students to think what they want from this life; their current expectations, and their general view of life.

For some parents, access to the university is conflated with the idea of independence and freedom of choice not possible during the Soviet power. Nurbek was one of the best students in his faculty at BNU when I was doing my fieldwork there. I interviewed his parents one day about their satisfaction with his university and course of study. Rather than talk about teacher and resource issues, however, they wanted only to talk about the general freedom to travel and have economic opportunities nationally and internationally now, compared to before.

Nurbek's parents had been compelled to remain at their collective farm with few entrepreneurial opportunities. Nurbek's ability to enter a Bishkek university was thus considered yet another opportunity for the entire family to enter a new and bigger world. In point of fact, very few of the students and parents I interviewed had ever been in a university in the city centre before, and had found BNU either by word of mouth or by roaming the city streets looking for any university to enrol in. They were mostly from the village and had little comparative information upon which to make any higher education choices. They only knew that BNU was registered with the state; that it proclaimed to be new and innovative; and that it promised international connections. Both of the later claims were actually inflated. But neither Nurbek nor his parents could have known this:

> In the Soviet Union, there were few universities; and there were also colleges (*tekhnikumy*), (but) they only took a predetermined or assigned number of students. But now higher education is getting better; now we are on top of good education; now it is better than before.... In the Soviet Union there was free education, but (people) earned only a little salary: and they did not have a chance to make their own business. Now we can make

any business we like…. I sent my son to the university to have education, higher education and to see other countries, to learn other cultures, and also to know the world and (about) new technologies.

Concerns about academic quality at BNU

Nurbek's father was quite pleased with his son's progress at the university, since it did in fact expose him to a variety of international visitors and experiences. And teacher quality and university resources were not criticized by him. He actually knew little about what went on curricularly at BNU, and he calculated he could afford some occasional corruption there if the need arose. What he did not like and what he did complain about were some of the other students who studied with his son at BNU who he thought had no business being there:

> Some parents, they (send) their son to the university even if they know that they cannot study; they haven't done well in their (earlier) studies. They want to get them diplomas, but they cannot study. Some of them (parents) they give money for diplomas; we know some (of these parents). Parents should (actually) see how (their children) studied at school, and the child's ability…. I cannot see the students who buy a diploma for money (ending) in a good place. They should never work as a leader or be in politics. They won't be good persons for our Kyrgyz future.

Nurbek's university specialization was in Western Studies (WS), one of three specializations in the Faculty of Foreign Languages (FFL). Kanikei, whose opinions about "then and now" we heard earlier, was the dean of this faculty which enrolled almost 400 students and 16 student cohorts in that faculty's three specializations. My fieldwork over about five months, however, revealed a pattern of frequently missed classes by students; absences of teachers for days and even weeks at a time due to illness or other family matters; inadequate equipment for the teaching of languages; poorly trained faculty; grades often negotiated independently of announced standards; etc. (DeYoung 2011). Students also freely admitted that entrance standards into the university were much more relaxed than advertised, and that it was very difficult to actually be expelled from the university for poor marks. Many admitted students also lacked basic language skills, which were a formal requirement for university entrance. And many would go on to graduate as interpreters or translators of English or German or French with marginal language skills, in my opinion.

A number of explanations for poor student performance were acknowledged to me by teachers and administrators. Both groups confided that the physical condition of classroom facilities were old and equipment outdated or broken. None of my informants, though, understood how and why the higher officials in the university let this occur, considering that students were paying a hefty sum (by local standards) to be in the FFL. For many students – perhaps a third – the lack of academic possibilities at the university was not that critical. They were happy to be comparatively independent and out of the immediate supervision of parents. Sometimes they went to class; sometimes they walked around the city instead with their friends. Then they would have to scramble at the end of the term when exams were about to occur. Some students actually came to the university with serious academic or career purpose on their minds. For them, much of the university experience at BNU led to frustration and despair.

Nazgul had entered BNU in 2007 but transferred her second year to an intergovernmental university for a variety of reasons. She reported that the infrastructure of BNU was poor; the teachers uninvolved; and many students unmotivated. She also made some comparisons to the university where she is now:

> There were terrible conditions (at BNU) – there were bad chairs, bad chalk boards, and (few) computers, while here we have a computer for an hour and thirty minutes (every day); it's good, I like it. And here, if you have problems all teachers can help you – can explain to you – and they are glad if you are interested in their topics; but if you asked some questions at BNU ... it was difficult. Maybe because of their salary, teachers did not want to work there; maybe because of that.... There were (also some) very, very smart girls there, but there were some girls who for one year did not speak English (at all). I just do not know what they were doing in the university. They did not get knowledge; why were they interested in the university? I do not know why. I think they did not want to look like lazy girls, or so poor that they could not (afford) the university. And (to impress their friends) is why they entered. But they didn't come to get education; they did not get any knowledge.

Kyrgyzstan has experienced great internal as well as external migration during the past 15 years. Like Nurbek, many families (and teachers) at BNU are recently arrived in Bishkek from the village or from regional centres and towns. The less prestigious universities in the city appear to recruit heavily from newcomers who are not familiar with the higher education landscape they find themselves in. Nazgul's family was from the south, which led in her opinion to mistreatment by fellow students and teachers who thought themselves more cosmopolitan and held low expectations for girls like her. One teacher seemed incredulous that Nazgul actually undertook a non-required evening class to improve her computer skills:

> I can give you one example, while I was studying in BNU, I took an (extra) computer class (in the evenings), and one teacher was sort of like "you are crazy." I explained I did not have this experience at (secondary) school, which is why I wanted go to this class. This was interesting for me – first of all. Secondly, I know now some (computer) programmes that last year I did not know. My (BNU) teacher could not explain things well to me; and she also said things like "you are from the south;" that "you are village girls." She always said that; and it was not to me only. I even wanted to cry,

because I am from the south.... It made me so sad, and after that, I did not come to her classes; but in the end of the year, she gave me a "3" (passing grade) anyway.

Students who actually had academic or professional expectations and goals that they thought the university could help them develop were often frustrated at BNU. Some, like Nazgul, were able to escape and enter other institutions. Others were not as successful. Galina and Svetlana felt trapped at BNU for lack of other options. Neither of them believed they were learning what they needed, but neither of them had the resources to transfer. So, they did the best they could to pick up skills outside of the university while they also waited out the five years required to get a diploma. They complained sarcastically about the undereducated and overwhelmed teachers they had:

> We have many teachers here who just graduated from our (own) university, (which means) they have only five years preparation, (which) is not enough. I think that they must (continue) their education, and only after that come back to teach other people.... One of our teachers sometimes tries to teach (English grammar) in Russian – but he cannot (help us) because he does not know Russian. He (appears) to know Kyrgyz well, but we do not know Kyrgyz. He tries to teach in English, but if somebody does not understand, he cannot explain it (well enough) to us.... So for one year (in this class) we studied for nothing.... Often in other classes when we are present at our lessons, we are left alone doing our exercises, or we are asked to read something, but (halfway through) the class she (our teacher) will leave the room, and we are on our own.... And, we have plenty of teachers who (show up) later than they (are) supposed to. I think that teachers have small salary and they don't want to work for this salary and they try to do nothing and that is why they take money for marks.... (But) besides our classes, we try to learn on our own. We work with different visual materials and with disks, and cassettes. I have computer at home, and I buy a disk, and I listen at home.

Kunduz, the young teacher from the village discussed previously, routinely had a 20–30 per cent absentee rate in her courses; and she was perhaps the most popular teacher in the FFL! I teased her about this and asked why she held class at all and did not just work with all students independently. But she seemed sympathetic to their typical sorts of explanations for non-attendance and instead of demanding better, implored them to come since they were paying for her services. Yet she recognized that many of her students were not only "lazy", but were also here just to get a diploma:

> You know, not all the students work (like to study). We have some students who want to study; and who want to get some education and some knowledge. That is why I explain to my students (that) "you have to come to my class because I am getting my salary; you pay for your education." And at

the beginning of the semester I explain (that) "you have to require (things) from me, like, for example you pay me, and I have to – to teach you.... You know, I explain it this way. But sometimes – they just want to have their diploma.... This is one of the main problems in Kyrgyzstan, because some students – some of the young generation – they just want to have a diploma in five years or four years – because they want to work in good places; and of course, if they do not have diploma, they will not work in a good place, but if they have diploma ... (Some) kind of students who have much money – their parents have high status – they think "I will get my diploma in 5 years and my father or my mother will help me to find a job."

Family connections are understood to be important in finding work as in securing many other benefits in Kyrgyzstan. Kunduz went on to describe the importance of connections, family and "tribe" among the Kyrgyz and even within organizations in the country, including her university:

Usually it happens that parents find jobs for their children, but sometimes if some students are good in their language – in their specialty – they will find a job (in) international organizations. (But), we have – how to say – tribalism in government structures; the ministry of education, or (in some) international affairs (offices). So, in these structures we need to have some people there who our parents know.... How does tribalism work? Like, for example, if I work in a high job – like in the ministry of education – I will have – like – relatives and they will come and say "ooh-ooh, you are working here!" And "I have a daughter or son, and can you hire him or can you find him a job?" So, of course I will say yes! And this will be one relative, and then the other will come and so ... it continues kind of *tsepochka* (like a chain). It continues.

Omurbek, a previously mentioned part-time BNU teacher whose major responsibility was in the university administration, was the model of patience with his students. He kept working with them even when they were obviously bored or not interested. I audited his class on comparative politics in the Spring of 2009 and wondered why he tolerated the absences, tardiness and interruptions he endured, and why he worked so hard to teach when his students seemed so uninterested in his efforts. Omurbek actually had an interesting and complicated explanation and rationale for how and why he taught the way he did. He connected his pedagogy to larger cultural and social problems of the country – which were correctable but would take years and years to remedy:

I have been working on those issues of higher education, and I have realized that education has started changing; but it is not one day change, you cannot make it change in one day. It needs time, but I cannot say how much time it needs. I have been in a state university, and I've been in a private (university) plus an American (university): and it is a huge difference between them. The first thing is this university and (my) Osh university are totally different. For instance, teachers come (there) and most teaching is based on mere theories. So we had students to write class papers (from) books based on theories which worked before during the Soviet times. So (students) are (still) writing and listening to old stories. But, we cannot blame this on our state, or because of our university or because of persons that teach. We cannot blame anybody; because (the issues) are complex. Teachers come to the class and tell all the old theories and (use) old reading materials which might be not relevant today, especially to modern standards, international standards.

Meanwhile, Omurbek also opined that instructional styles and strategies used in international universities, like the one he had spent a year in, were far superior to those to be seen in Kyrgyz state universities like BNU:

In the United States, they come, and, it is a different environment. There the professor comes and asks questions about (material) students are reading. They profit from the professor. It's huge; it is very different. (American) professors focus more on topics these days. So we talk about today's issues and try to make things relevant with the international, too.... And, in Kyrgyzstan, it is another culture, we could say. It is a method of teaching (still) based on the Soviet type where instructor dictated information (just) to repeat and remember. But we cannot work on our own ideas; our own way of conversation; and this delays us from understanding the subject, I think.

Omirbek also believes that teacher expectations for Kyrgyz students need to be sensitive to their cultural and psychological differences, since many come from poor and/or rural backgrounds:

Oh, the situation is complex and the students are different; and the first thing is you need to understand students' psychology; their needs – what they need. And (my) course is really hard for them as a subject. But I try to make international affairs (helpful) to understand the world that the students live in ... what happens in the country, in the region, and in the world. They need to understand what is going on. Plus, (there is) a student problem I was facing, (some) are interested, but they live in not very good economic conditions – about 30 per cent, I would say.... I realized that the students did not have such an experience before, and they did not have a writing course. I went to their curriculum; they now have a writing course, but students cannot write ... I looked at the subjects they are taught and they do not coincide these days with (academic) needs. We just do not have "essays" in Kyrgyzstan, (we) call it "*sochinenie*" (composition), and they say just write (from memory). Plus, when they use facts, they misinterpret. This is a big problem: the majority of students cannot write (due to) lack of (school) experience.

I was curious how Omirbek turned his empathy for previously uneducated or undereducated students in my Western Studies group into a teaching strategy. Not surprisingly, he not only held (by my estimation) low standards for performance, but even then allowed for negotiations to happen when the low standards were not met. I pursued this question with reference to a mid-term exam he gave. The multiple-choice test included 25 questions and a short essay. Each part was to be worth 50 points, with a total possible of 100. Omirbek claimed that such an objective test was rarely given among the faculty in the FFL; on the other hand, students were allowed to use notes and copied articles in class even to answer the multiple choice questions; and a total of 30 out of 100 would enable a student to pass the exam.

Fewer than half of the students actually completed the essay for the exam in the 80 or 90 minutes given for the test. They were allowed to finish the essay and turn it in later in the week. None of these essays was theoretically more than two pages in length, and those who did not finish were allowed to turn them in even later. The "25" multiple choice questions asked actually numbered only 22, so students got three free points there. When grades were announced weeks later, everyone had passed, and three students out of 15 received a "5" on the test for scoring above 65 points out of 100. Two other students on the official class list did not take the test nor even appear in class during the six weeks I was there. They had to negotiate a grade with Omirbek on the side.

Omurbek explained that a main objective of his in giving the exam was to find out if students were actually reading the take-home sheets he had duplicated for them, and if they were taking notes at all in class. He argued that the primary problem for many students was that they could only articulate their own opinion on political affairs, and were not able to see two sides of an argument. In an early course exam given to these third-year students, he found that they usually gave only their own opinions about the issues they had heard him talk about, and/or to turn to other students for their views. He wanted them to instead locate competing arguments in their notes or from his handouts. He actually did not mind if they shared information as long as it came from his presentations and readings rather than only from previous uninformed opinions.

Omurbek carefully explained the logic of the course and the protocols he would use in evaluating student performance. Having learned about a syllabus from his international universities experiences, he had incorporated some formal objectives and evaluation languages into a syllabus, which was rarely presented to students in FFL classes. Although Omirbek did stick with his announced topics during the semester, in the end he did not use those announced protocols to actually award grades, which was also typical in the several other courses I participated in. His grades were based mostly on student attitude and value added dimensions rather than on absolute or even relative objective performance. They were based upon relationships:

> Before the students begin their class, I always inform that there will be a midterm. I wrote it in the syllabus what would happen. "First, for the

midterm I expect some performance. Then I will let you write bonus papers, but these bonus papers will be essays. The (midterm) questions will derive from the (assigned) literature." I use the first experience – multiple-choice – in the formulation to set up the papers; maybe two or three papers. It depends on the student. But at the moment, I am pushing them to submit the papers, and now about 80 per cent have submitted the (first) papers, (but) only 80 per cent (have been) submitted. And (only) half of them have started to be able to explain another side (of an issue or dispute). They still do not correctly know how to use citations. But still, I think it's a good performance.

For Omurbek, at the end of the day, students who passed or did well received their grades as much (or more) for developing good rapport with him outside of class. What they did in class – or if they did not even come to class – could be negotiated later. He would "push" students to write papers that he would carefully guide so that they could see the other side of issues he already tried to present during his assigned lecturing hours. Unfortunately, most teachers at the FFL did not have the kind of time or office space to mentor students as Omurbek did. Although he believed in Western standards and expectations, he did not think they could really be used in the current Kyrgyz context. Meanwhile, he was critical of other teachers who did not work daily and weekly with students and only negotiated with them at the end of the semester:

> But if I graded (now), I would give grades today only for participation and performance in class; plus how often they talk to me in my office hours. (See), if students are coming now (after performing poorly on his test and assignments), and we have very good – quite normal relations, I never (demand) a deadline. If they come, I will try to push them to write some papers. Seventy percent (of students) are working these days in Kyrgyzstan, (so) even if (we) used a syllabus in the education system – for another class maybe different method will be approached – but for this class I will be using this grading system. Why? Because I do not see any advantage of a system (like ours) where you will come (to teachers) at the end of the year (where teachers) will ask some (new) questions before they give you a mark in their journal. I want to grade students according to what they have been doing and how much progress they have made.

Kanikei, the FFL Dean – who earlier described the academically challenging life she had as a student – has had to amend her understanding of the university today and who her students are. She believes there are basically three sorts of students in her university now; perhaps only one third of whom would have qualified to be in the university 20 years ago. By education ministry stipulations, to be a full-time student at a state university requires full-time attendance. This is rarely the actual case at BNU now, where many are working part-time instead of coming to the university, usually performing jobs unrelated to their declared specializations. Other students have come to understand that class attendance is not necessary, since they either have connections to important people in the university or can pay for passing grades or both. They know the university cannot afford to flunk them out. Negotiating assignments and grades after-the-fact are basic student strategies for both of these two groups; although some switch into a distance education format, where their actual performance is even harder to document. According to Kanikei:

> You know students – not only at our university – now are working everywhere (like restaurants); or they work some other places. Of course it is very difficult to combine everything.... And they are too tired to come to the classes. That was the reason for our opening of distance education; so if they cannot study as day-time students (and be in) day-time courses, they can get a distance education – by email.... But (another group) of our students are lazy. Pedagogues started dividing (university students) into three groups: the first – students who are really good students who are willing to know and who never miss classes: they work hard. Maybe they even graduated from the village (school); from the country. And after some years, their level of knowledge (equals) our best students who graduate from specialized (city) schools. And the next group is the students that know that they will receive a diploma anyway, because they are from a city. They know Russian well, and may not or cannot come to their classes. But, anyway they receive their diploma. They know a "three" is (only) "satisfactory", but it does not matter for them; the diploma is (all that) is important.... Then, there are the working students...

Kanikei concluded one interview with me that underscores just how far her institution and most of the other state universities have strayed from an emphasis on academic rigour and standards, no matter what the Ministry of Education says. Instead of providing and certifying academic or professional learning and progress through the system, BNU and most of the others have become a place of refuge for many young people awaiting another opportunity – professional or social. Kanikei related with partial admiration the tenacity of one student who did not speak English when she was admitted to her faculty and did not speak English when she graduated from her faculty, but who spent five years in an English language focused programme:

> We had a girl – I forget her name; Dasha? She studied here for five years; and as a student, she was not bright, but she was very diligent. She did not miss any classes, and when (a foreign visitor) came, they spent all their time together. When I asked her, "Dasha, why are spending so much time here; where will you end up working?" And she said "in Dordoi". And then I asked her: "for Dordoi you spent five years here; to sit in that market?" "No", she said. "After I collect some money, I will go to the US and then I'll learn (English) there." You see, she found some work (in America) and

she (got) an invitation letter. And she is there now, without any English skills. I hope that she will learn there; but anyway, she has a diploma.

Where to go for a more predictable academic or professional higher education

The education ministry and the Kyrgyz government have been arguing for over a decade about how to reform higher education, even as they receive international assistance and proclaim interest in joining Western international higher education space (Dukenbaev 2004; Merrill 2006). They have instituted policy changes allowing for the expansion of programmes and institutions, but virtually nothing focusing upon academic outcomes (as opposed to courses of study), or job placement success of the universities. And they have sometimes resisted policy implementations designed to objectively assess quality in the education system (Drummond and DeYoung 2004). This has allowed state university rectors with good political connections to grow their own institutions with little attention to quality or utility. Rectors know that holding students accountable for academic performance is either irrelevant or counterproductive to growing their enrolments; and growing enrolments mean more tuition dollars.

Universities here thrive on parents being able to tolerate the fact that higher education may not be what it used to be, but that the other options appear even worse. Likewise, many students are content to enrol at university just to obtain a diploma – which can frequently be bought without benefit of serious study. At BNU, most students are drawn from the village, and also many now from India and Pakistan where higher educational opportunities are greatly restricted. Academic or professional quality indicators are little demanded; only access and the promise of a diploma at the end of four or five years.

It must be true that there are pockets of excellence in state universities. How one would locate them among the heaps of misleading institutional proclamations would be difficult, however, since these would likely be attached to particularly good and committed teachers able to rise above (or remain hidden) within institutional smokescreens. Finding sound and legitimate programmes thus remains a problem for that significant percentage of university students – from the north and from the south, and from the city and from the village – who are like Nazgul or Galina and Svetlana, all of whose voices were heard earlier in this chapter. They and many others sought or seek what they cannot find in the state universities: either sound academic programmes or professional training that is linked to employment.

Sensing that some universities were better at delivering upon academic quality and career focus than others in the country, I constructed a 38-item open-ended survey to assess student perceptions on such matters in the spring of 2008. The 204 students who responded came from five different Bishkek universities, including two state universities – Arabaev Pedagogical University and International University of Kyrgyzstan (MUK); one inter-governmental university – Kyrgyz Russian Slavic University (KRSU); and two private universities with heavy international backing – American University of Central Asia (AUCA) and the International Atatürk-Alatoo University (IAAU).

For purposes of this chapter, I wanted to consider the answers to several questions in my survey. One question (No. 23) asked students to rank-order the three best universities in the country regardless of cost. They were also asked to explain their choices in an open-ended format. Not every student gave three choices, and not every student explained their choices. In fact, the response rate and sophistication of answers suggests a qualitative difference between students within different university types, a topic we do not have time to address here. The clear "winners" of the admittedly unrepresentative sample from among students was AUCA and KRSU, even though the survey included only 31 students from AUCA and 16 from KRSU. None of the state universities ranked in the top four overall, which is revealing since most of the students in the sample were enrolled in state universities. One hundred and five students named AUCA as first choice, while another 38 students listed it as their second or third choice. KRSU garnered 29 first place votes, and 62 additional students ranked it second or third. Falling just behind AUCA and KRSU in terms of perceived quality, but ahead of the Kyrgyz state universities, were the two Turkish universities operating in Bishkek: IAAU and Turkish-Manas University.

Trailing in the rankings were the three better known state universities in the city. These theoretically should have had (and perhaps once did have) a popular head start, since two of the three were institutions of higher learning from Soviet days (Kyrgyz National University; Arabaev). Students apparently felt unconvinced that any of these places is now as prestigious or as internationally recognized as their rectors proclaim.

Rankings and reasons given for them corresponded closely with an earlier survey question (No. 19) regarding reasons students chose their institutions of study in the first place. In my sample, university prestige, quality of foreign language instruction and international connections/opportunities were the typical responses given by students as to why they had initially chosen their place of study. Such features were also identified as reasons for ranking of the top universities on question No. 23. Lack of corruption was also cited frequently as a reason for ranking one or another university high on a student's list. Respondents from one of the two state universities in this survey also suggested that their high ranking of other universities was due to the better facilities and resources they perceived in universities other than their own.

The inconvenient facts are that most inter-governmental and private universities in Kyrgyzstan that teach humanitarian subjects these days are understood as the better and more prestigious institutions in the country. Their prestige appears to be based upon their use of more objective entrance exams to screen potential students; that their foreign language teaching as well as most other courses are based upon international standards and is assessed using international examinations; that many provide merit-based scholarships based on transparent criteria; that faculty are paid higher and facilities are newer or in better repair; that most of them provide formal internships or scholarships to work or study overseas;

and that student services and opportunities are budgeted and provided for, rather than depending on student initiative alone.

Another inconvenient fact – perhaps – is that most of the inter-governmental and private universities heavily market their services toward what they consider are the moral and/or social needs of students which they imply are no longer the focus of state universities; and they also claim geopolitical attachments unlike those of the state institutions. KRSU, for instance, defines its mission as continuing to connect Kyrgyzstan to its Russian culture and heritage by focusing upon "job training of youth of Kyrgyzstan and Russia in humanities, science, economics and law as well as satisfaction of language and cultural needs of (the) Russian-speaking population in Kyrgyzstan". On the KRSU homepage, they also target "close bilateral collaboration of both states", as well as facilitating "participation of outstanding scientists and teachers of Russia in educational activity of the country", in an effort to "render their assistance to the development of scientific and technical potential of Kyrgyzstan, creative contacts and mutual enrichment of both Kyrgyz and Russian cultures" (KRSU website).

Turkish Manas University as well as IAAU both serve intentionally as channels to connect and strengthen ties between Turkey and Kyrgyzstan (Aypay 2004; Marat 2007). Both universities teach primarily in English or in Turkish, implicitly to counter any remaining Russian regional hegemony. As well, both institutions create formal internships to Turkish businesses either in Turkey or within Kyrgyzstan as part of their instructional and occupational missions. The Turkish-Manas website also suggests its organizational model presents the sort of transparency not visible elsewhere in Kyrgyz higher education:

> The mission of the university is to secure an education, in community for the Kyrgyz and Turkish young people as well as for the young in other Turkic Republics and communities, along with helping them develop (a) common approach and cooperation. It is believed that in this way the university will contribute to contemporary scientific developments and will support the renaissance of Turkic civilization. In this frame the goals of the university are: To serve as a model for the higher education system of Kyrgyzstan, and in this way to play a leading role in global integration.
>
> (Kyrgyzstan–Turkey Manas University website)

IAAU, meanwhile, portrays itself as another Turkish option that is both democratic and focused upon Turkic renaissance in Central Asia. Inspired by Gulen, IAAU has a liberal Islamic orientation which is perceived as necessary to counteract what they believe was a moral vacuum created by the former USSR. Rather than direct teaching of Islam in the curriculum, IAAU is described as an institution where morality is couched in more humanistic terms and occurs in face-to-face relations between teachers and students during the day and in mentoring and academic support offered in residential dormitories where most students are expected to live (Agai 2002; Keles 2007; IAAU website).

The first choice universities in my survey samples – which was of course biased since most students were interested in and were studying English or other subjects in English – was the American University of Central Asia. Unlike both of the Turkish universities which target many able but less affluent students throughout the country, AUCA states that its mission is to prepare students who have already demonstrated superior academic achievement for leadership positions in both the private and public sectors throughout Central Asia. Like Manas, IAAU and to some extent KRSU, its faculty and student body are more international than the supposedly international state universities; teachers are better paid; student services and resources are better; and the university has a career centre and finds international academic scholarships for its best graduates. And many students know about such things, as we heard earlier from Nazgul.

As Reeves (2004, 2005) argues, AUCA claims unabashedly to be about inserting a foreign presence into Kyrgyzstan. It proclaims to follow an American liberal arts format (while also providing a Kyrgyz diploma), while using a critical thinking approach pedagogical to teaching and learning as sponsored by the Open Society Institute (OSI 2003). AUCA argues that it also serves as a research university where students and faculty research policy issues related to the needs of Central Asia:

> (We are) an international, multi-disciplinary learning community in the American liberal arts tradition that develops enlightened and impassioned leaders for the democratic transformation of Central Asia … (we are) honest, self-critical, and respectful, (cherishing) critical inquiry and investigative learning both for their own sake, and for the development of an open, diverse and just society that suits the region in which we learn and serve. We will become the best teaching and research university in Central Asia, distinctive for our emphasis on critical thinking and on faculty and student research. We will make the results of our cutting-edge research available for the use and benefit of the citizens of Central Asia.
>
> (AUCA website)

Conclusion

There is a serious disconnect between expressed aims for higher education in Kyrgyzstan at the level of both the education ministry and university presidents and rectors compared to what is actually happening. Official proclamations embrace a call to improve academic quality and prepare students for the world of professional practice. The reality at state universities is that academic outcomes and training for professional practice have come to take a back seat to other agendas. Many parents hope that something good will happen for their children once they are allowed to enter the university, but too many first-year students come unprepared to study; attendance is obligatory but not enforced; teachers are overwhelmed and not up to date in many of their specializations; and grades are negotiated rather than earned. Access rather than excellence has become the focus of state universities. Those students who earnestly hope for and work toward gaining academic quality in state universities have a hard time; but for those able to enrol and study in several of the alternatives – intergovernmental and private higher education institutions, the possibilities remain and are improving. The directions all of this will take are unclear at the present time, regardless of continuing rhetoric about joining the international higher education community.

Acknowledgements

Much of the fieldwork upon which this research was based was supported by US State Department Funding under the Title VIII Programme, as administered in this case by IREX and ACCELS. In addition, thanks are extended to Galina Valyayeva and Todd Drummond who read and critiqued earlier drafts of this manuscript. And of course I want to express my sincere appreciation to the many students and educators whose voices and insights are presented and considered here.

References

Agai, B. (2002) "Fethullah Gulen and his Movement's Islamic Ethic of Education", *Middle East Critique*, 11/1: 27–47.

Aidakyeva, A. (2007) "Distance Education Projects in Kyrgyzstan", *Journal of Space Communication*, 12. Online. Available: http://satjournal.tcom.ohiou.edu/Issue12/aidakyeva.html (accessed on 20 November 2008).

Akaev, A. (2003) *Education for All: A Resource for Social Transition in Kyrgyzstan*, Bishkek: Innovation Center "ARCHI".

AUCA (American University of Central Asia) website. Online. Available: www.auca.kg/en/about_auca/NMission (accessed on 10 November 2009).

Aypay, A. (2004) "Turkish Higher Education Initiatives towards Central Asia", in S. Heyneman and A. DeYoung (eds) *Challenges for Education in Central Asia*, Greenwich, CT: Information Age Publishers: 81–96.

Briller, V. and Isakova, S. (2004) "University Ranking in Central Asia: The Experience of Kazakhstan", in S. Heyneman and A. DeYoung (eds) *Challenges for Education in Central Asia*, Greenwich, CT: Information Age Publishers: 257–274.

DeYoung, A. (2004) "On the Demise of the Action Plan for Kyrgyz Educational Reform: A Case Study", in S. Heyneman and A. DeYoung (eds) *Challenges for Education in Central Asia*, Greenwich, CT: Information Age Publishers: 199–224.

DeYoung, A. (2006) "Problems and Trends in Education in Central Asia since 1990: The Case of General Secondary Education in Kyrgyzstan", *Central Asian Survey*, 25/4: 499–514.

DeYoung, A. (2007) "The erosion of *vospitanie* (social upbringing) in post-Soviet Kyrgyzstan", *Communist and Post Communist Studies*, 40/2, 239–256.

DeYoung, A. (2011) *Lost in Transition: Redefining Students and Universities in the Contemporary Kyrgyz Republic*, Greenwich, CT: Information Age Publishing.

DeYoung, A., Reeves, M. and Valyayeva, G.K. (2006) *Surviving the Transition? Schools and Schooling in the Kyrgyz Republic since Independence*, Greenwich, CT: Information Age Publishing.

Dobson, R. (1977) "Social Status and Inequality of Access to Higher Education in the USSR", in J. Karabel and A. Halsey (eds) *Power and Ideology in Education*, New York: Oxford University Press: 232–253.

Drummond, T. and DeYoung, A. (2004) "Perspectives and Problems in Education Reform in Kyrgyzstan: The Case of National Scholarship Testing", in S. Heyneman and A. DeYoung (eds) *Challenges for Education in Central Asia*, Greenwich, CT: Information Age Publishers: 225–242.

Dukenbaev, A. (2004) "Politics and Public Policy in Post-Soviet Central Asia: The Case of Higher Education Reform in Kyrgyzstan", *Central Eurasian Studies Review*, 3/2: 16–18.

Dzhaparova, R. (2006) "On whether Kyrgyzstan should Join the Bologna Process", *Russian Education and Society*, 48/10, 92–98.

European Commission (2007) *Implementation of the Implications of the Bologna Process in Kyrgyzstan*. Online. Available: http://ec.europa.eu/education/programs/tempus/countries/higher/Kyrgyzstan.pdf (accessed on 20 January 2010).

Gleason, G. (1997) *The Central Asian States*, Boulder, CO: Westview Press.

Gleason, G. (2003) *Markets and Politics: Structural Reform and Political Change in Central Asia*, London: Routledge.

Heyneman, S. (1998) "The Transition from Party/State to Open Democracy: The Role of Education", *International Journal of Educational Development*, 1: 21–40.

Heyneman, S. (2004) "Education and Corruption", *International Journal of Educational Development*, 4/6: 638–648.

Holmes, B., Read, G., and Voskresenskaya, N. (1995) *Russian Education: Tradition and Transition*, New York: Garland Publishing.

IAAU (International Atatürk-Alatoo University) website. Online. Available: www.iaau.edu.kg/index.php?lang=en.

IWPR (Institute for War and Peace Reporting) (2007) *Kyrgyz Universities up their Game*, Online. Available: http://iwpr.net/?p=bkg&s=b&o=337777&ape_state=henbbkgdate2007 (accessed on 10 October 2009).

Karym Kyzy, G. (2003) "Problems of Secondary School Education in Kyrgyzstan", *Central Asia – Caucasus Institute*, 26 February. Online. Available: www.cacianalyst.org/?q=node/344 (accessed on 23 June 2009).

Keles, I. (2007) *Contributions of the Gulen Schools in Kyrgyzstan*. Online. Available: http://en.fgulen.com/conference-papers/contributions-of-the-gulen-movement/2467-contributions-of-the-gulen-schools-in-kyrgyzstan.html (accessed on 10 October 2010).

Keles, I. and Zakirova, M. (2008) "Foreign Higher Education Institutes in Kyrgyzstan", *American University of Central Asia Academic Review*, Bishkek. Online. Available: http://elibrary.auca.kg:8080/dspace/bitstream/123456789/250/1/Keles_Zakirova_2008_1.pdf (accessed on 10 January, 2009).

Korth, B. (2004) "Education and Linguistic Division in Kyrgyzstan", in S. Heyneman and A. DeYoung (eds) *Challenges for Education in Central Asia*, Greenwich, CT: Information Age Publishers: 97–111.

Kuehnast, K. and Dudwick, N. (2004) *Better a Hundred Friends than a Hundred Roubles? Social Networks in Transition: The Kyrgyz Republic*, Washington, DC: World Bank.

KRSU (Kyrgyz-Russian Slavic University) website. Online. Available: www.krsu.edu.kg/Eng/about.html (accessed 15 December 2010).

Kyrgyzstan-Turkey Manas University website. Online. Available: www.manas.kg/alt.php?id=1 (accessed 17 January 2010).

Marat, E. (2007) "Turkey's Economic and Cultural Presence Grows in Kyrgyzstan", *Eurasia Daily Monitor*, 4/145. Online. Available: www.jamestown.org/single/?no_cache=1&tx_ttnews[tt_news]=32896 (accessed on 20 January 2010).

Merrill, M. (2006) "Internationalization of Higher Education in Kyrgyzstan: Three Potential Problems", *Central Eurasian Studies Review*, 5/2, 34–40.

Mertaugh, M. (2004) "Education in Central Asia, with Particular Reference to the Kyrgyz Republic", in S. Heyneman and A. DeYoung (eds) *Challenges for Education in Central Asia*, Greenwich, CT: Information Age Publishers: 153–180.

Musabaeva, A. (2008) "Higher Education in Kyrgyzstan: Is it a Public Good or a Private Good?" *Institute for Public Policy*, 2/1: 77–83. Online. Available: http://se1.isn.ch/serviceengine/FileContent?serviceID=ISN&fileid=22529CED-2B6A-594D-1EFA-1B837F4D7268&lng=en (accessed on 12 September 2009).

Natsionalnyi Statistichekii Komitet Kirgizskoi Respubliki [National Statistical Committee of the Kyrgyz Republic] (2000) *Social Development of the Kyrgyz Republic, 1995–1999*, Bishkek.

Olcott, M. (2005) *Central Asia's Second Chance*, Washington, D.C.: Carnegie Endowment for International Peace.

OSI (Open Society Institute) (2003) *Educational Development in Kyrgyzstan, Tajikistan and Uzbekistan: Challenges and Ways Forward*. Online. Available: www.osi-edu.net/esp (accessed on 20 January 2010).

Rahmetov, A. (2009) "Scary Statistics: The State of Schools in Kyrgyzstan", *Central Asia-Caucasus Institute*, 22 April. Online. Available: www.cacianalyst.org/?q=node/5087 (accessed on 25 October 2009).

Reeves, M. (2004) "Cultivating 'Citizens of a New Type': The Politics and Practice of Educational Reform at the American University of Kyrgyzstan", in S. Heyneman and A. DeYoung (eds) *Challenges for Education in Central Asia*, Greenwich, CT: Information Age Publishers, 365–386.

Reeves, M. (2005) "*Kontrakty* and Critical Thinking: Encountering 'Market Reforms' in Kyrgyzstani Higher Education", *European Educational Research Journal*, 4, 5–21.

Roy, O. (2000) *The New Central Asia: The Creation of Nations*, London: Tauris.

Slaughter, R. (2002) "Poor Kyrgyzstan", in M. Goldman, *Global Studies: Russia, the Eurasian Republics and Central/Eastern Europe*, 11th edn, New York: McGraw-Hill: 231–236.

Soros Foundation, Kyrgyzstan (2008) Information. Online. Available: www.soros.kg/index.php?option=com_content&view=article&id=48&Itemid=132&lang=en (accessed on 25 November 2009).

Tempus (2005) Modernisation of Higher Education in countries surrounding the EU. Online. Available: http://ec.europa.eu/education/external-relation-programmes/doc70_en.htm (accessed on 10 December 2010).

UNDP (United Nations Development Programme) (2000) *Corruption in Kyrgyzstan*, Bishkek: Center of Public Opinion Studies and Forecasts.

UNDP (United Nations Development Programme) (2005) "The Influence of Civil Society on the Human Development Process in Kyrgyzstan", *National Human Development Report (NHDR)*, Bishkek: UNDP.

UNESCO (United Nations Educational, Scientific and Cultural Organization) (2000) *"Educational for All": Country Report on Kyrgyzstan*. Online. Available: http://www2.unesco.org/wef/countryreports/kyrgyz/contents.html (accessed on 10 December 2010).

UNESCO (United Nations Educational, Scientific and Cultural Organization) (2002) *National Report on Higher Education in the Republic of Kyrgyzstan: Current Status and Prospects*, Paris: UNESCO. Online. Available: www.unesco.org/fileadmin/MUL-TIMEDIA/INSTITUTES/UIL/confintea/pdf/National_Reports/Asia%20-%20Pacific/Kyrgyzstan.pdf (accessed on 18 January 2010).

USAID (United States Agency for International Development) (2003) *The National Scholarship Test of the Kyrgyz Republic, 2003: First Look. National Scholarship Test.* Online. Available: www.testing.kg/en/testing (accessed on 15 February 2010).

Weidman, J., Chapman, D., Cohen, M. and Lelei, M. (2004) "Access to Education in Five Newly Independent States of Central Asia and Mongolia", in S. Heyneman and A. DeYoung (eds) *Challenges for Education in Central Asia*, Greenwich, CT: Information Age Publishers: 181–197.

9 Higher education in Kyrgyzstan

The inevitability of international actors

Martha C. Merrill

The internationalization of higher education in the twenty-first century is both unavoidable and problematic. As Kyrgyzstan's former Minister of Education, Ishengul Boldjurova rather poetically put it:

> [The] process of globalization of various political, social and economic spheres of life has many negative effects (among all, loss of national identity), but it also has a very positive outcome. I see it as a fantastic opportunity of creating a global educational space, of universal access to a magnificent ocean of knowledge which has been accumulated by humanity throughout its long history.
>
> (Boldjurova 2007: 1)

Yet, as Nurgul Djanaeva (2001: 1), the former Vice President for International Affairs and Planning at the International University in Kyrgyzstan recognizes, internationalization in transition nations has dimensions not found in many other countries: linkages are formed not simply for networking, but also for "reshaping our internal higher education structure".

Nevertheless, Djanaeva (2001: 2–3) sees many benefits to internationalization, including quality improvement, external recognition of qualifications, and adjustment of Kyrgyzstani higher education to new, post-socialist conditions.

Yet, as Dukenbaev warns, in Kyrgyzstan the choices are not those of educators alone:

> [A] characteristic of the policy process in higher education is its high degree of centralization restricted to interactions mainly among the four institutions: 1) Presidential Administration, 2) Ministry of Education, 3) Parliament, and 4) major universities.
>
> (Dukenbaev 2004: 18)

Given this complexity, for a dozen different reasons, in the field of higher education, Kyrgyzstan cannot isolate itself from the demands, priorities and pressures of international actors. Each of these reasons will be discussed below. Three of these reasons are beyond Kyrgyzstan's control: its geographic location, its history and heritages, and the small size of its population. Six are factors over which it has limited control. These include the languages in which academic materials are produced; the fact that the country's poverty means it often must accept donor-funded reforms (and thus donor priorities); the realities of labour migration and "brain circulation"; the existence of international rankings and the globalization of quality assessment standards; the fact that its membership in the WTO requires it to participate in the General Agreement on Trade in Services (GATS); and the rapid development of the "world-class university" movement. Three are factors which Kyrgyzstan could do something about if it wished to assert priorities different from those of international actors or, alternatively, if it decided that greater integration with selected international systems was to its advantage. Those three are degree structures, the level of Ministry of Education control of many aspects of higher education, and corruption.

Higher education institutions around the world are being influenced by forces that are international (between nations) and global (worldwide, not controlled by nations). Some commentators believe that this will lead to the homogenization of higher education, as ranking systems like Shanghai Jiao Tong (now Academic Ranking of World Universities) compare institutions internationally and accreditors such as the agencies listed in the European Quality Assurance Register evaluate institutions outside their home countries. Yet global and international forces affect different countries and different institutions in very different ways. The purpose of this study is to look at the role of international actors in one country, pointing out the ways in which a specific context and specific confluence of factors create a unique situation. The presence and influence of international actors are inevitable in Kyrgyzstan's higher education system, yet, as this analysis will show, that does not mean that higher education in Kyrgyzstan will lose its contextual characteristics and become simply a duplicate of other systems. Similar forces play out differently in different places.

Factors Kyrgyzstan cannot control

The three factors that Kyrgyzstan cannot control are its geographic location, its history and heritages, and the small size of its population. Each of these three factors is important on its own, and the factors also interact with each other. For example, Kyrgyzstan's location near China and Russia would be important in any case, but the fact that Kyrgyzstan has a population of 5.4 million (*CIA World Factbook* 2009b), whereas China has an estimated population of more than one billion, 338 million (*CIA World Factbook* 2009a), and Russia has a population of 140 million (*CIA World Factbook* 2009c) clearly affects the power dynamics inherent in Kyrgyzstan's location.

Geographic location

Kyrgyzstan's geographic location may be thought of in four ways, each of which limits its ability to act independently, in higher education as well as in other fields. First, the concerns of its two large and powerful neighbours, China and Russia, always must be considered. Were a Kyrgyzstani university to start a programme in Uighur Studies or to form a partnership with a university in Taiwan, China would be displeased and could react with a variety of options, such as limiting trade or complicating visa regulations. Were the *UMO* (*Uchebno-metodicheskoe ob'edinenie*) or Curriculum Design Department (a group of subject matter experts for each academic field in Kyrgyzstan, based in higher education institutions, advisory to the Ministry of Education on curriculum content) responsible for the history curriculum used in Kyrgyzstani universities to design or approve a course of study that labelled Russia a colonial power that thwarted the development of what is now Kyrgyzstan during the Soviet era, repercussions certainly would follow. The concerns of powerful neighbours both subtly and directly limit academic freedom.

A second way that Kyrgyzstan's geographical location influences its ability to act independently is that it is surrounded by neighbours, such as Afghanistan, Pakistan and Iran, whose actions disquiet superpowers such as the US, not to mention Kyrgyzstan itself. Iran, additionally, is concerned about its own prestige and influence in the region. The interests of these nations affect Kyrgyzstani higher education in, among other factors, the provision of funding by the US for Afghani students to study in Kyrgyzstan, in Kyrgyzstan's agreements for educational exchanges with Iran (Jani 2009), and in the International University of Kyrgyzstan's medical school operating in English, so that South Asian students may study there.

Kyrgyzstan's Central Asian neighbours, particularly Uzbekistan, and their ethnic diasporas are a third aspect of its geographical location that affect higher education. Given Kyrgyzstan's intertwined borders with Uzbekistan in the Fergana Valley, plus its own Uzbek population, it is perhaps not surprising that one of the largest universities in Osh before the June 2010 violence was the Kyrgyz–Uzbek University.[1] Language of instruction issues are regularly discussed in Kyrgyzstan: to what extent should teaching be available in languages other than that of the titular nationality? To what extent should Russian, the "official" language, be used? What is the role of Uzbek, particularly in the south of the country?[2] Additionally, Kyrgyzstan, like Turkey, has a "Should headscarves be allowed on campus?" issue. The women wishing to wear headscarves traditionally are predominantly from the Uzbek population, and the issue would not be likely to have such prominence were it not for the repressive measures against many aspects of the practice of Islam in Uzbekistan, plus Uzbekistan's ability to cut off gas to Kyrgyzstan in the winter and to otherwise assert its power (Mamaraimov and Asanova 2008; "Headscarf Ban Lifted after Protests" 2009).

Fourth, Kyrgyzstan's location in Central Asia means that various international donors, including the European Union, often see it as part of a larger whole, rather than as distinct nation with specific needs in education and other sectors. As Merrill and Dukenbaev (2011) have argued:

> While many issues in education, including meeting the needs of rural populations, affect all of the countries of Central Asia, the lack of attention to the

differentiation of needs in either the [EU's] *Strategy* paper (2007) or in the *Joint Progress Report by the Council and the European Commission to the European Council on the Implementation of the EU Central Asia Strategy* (EC External Relations, 2008) suggests a lack of understanding of how the challenges of creating structures which lead to security and stability differ from one country to another.

(Merrill and Dukenbaev 2011: 125)

An additional problem with the regional focus, as Melvin and Boonstra (2008) point out, is that relevant connections to projects in nations outside the region may not be investigated.

History and heritage

Kyrgyzstan was part of the Soviet Union. The Kyrgyz people, as well as the Uzbeks, Kazakhs, Uighurs, Tatars, and others who live within its borders, are of Turkic descent. Ethnic Russians, Ukrainians, Germans and Tajiks also live in what the former president of Kyrgyzstan, Askar Akaev, called "our common home". The majority of the people in the Kyrgyz Republic are Muslims, although what exactly that means varies from individual to individual: for some, it simply means observing rituals at weddings and funerals; for others, it is involvement with Sufi orders; and for still others, it means, in part or in full, attending Friday prayers, going on the hajj, or wearing a headscarf. All of these factors mean that Kyrgyzstan is connected to people, places and educational practices beyond its borders.

Examples of the influence of history and heritage on Kyrgyzstan's higher education system are easy to find:

1   The structure of most of Kyrgyzstan's indigenous universities, as well as that of its Ministry of Education, is inherited from the Soviet Union, despite the limited inroads of reforms such as the Bologna Process, a European-originated system now encompassing 47 nations, including Kazakhstan, designed to encourage student and professional mobility between nations by promoting transparency and comparability regarding degrees and credits, quality assurance procedures, national qualifications frameworks and student learning outcomes (Official Bologna Process website 2010).

2   Kyrgyzstan has two Turkish universities, the government-supported Manas as well as the privately supported Ala-Too.

3   The student with the highest score on the nationwide university admissions test in 2009, who could go to any public university in Kyrgyzstan free of charge, instead is planning to attend Bosphorus University in Turkey, to which she also has a full scholarship (Benliyan 2009). She is a graduate of the Republican Anatolian Kyrgyz-Turkish Lycée, one of the 25 Turkish lycees (Najibullah 2009) in Kyrgyzstan.

4   The first university founded in the Commonwealth of Independent States (CIS) after the collapse of the Soviet Union was the Boris Yeltsin Kyrgyz-Russian Slavic University (KRSU website).
5   Kyrgyzstan now has an Islamic University as well, although it has not been licensed, reportedly for including too little secular content in its curricula (Bayram 2009; Commercio 2008; Namatbaeva 2008) plus a Kuwaiti university, now renamed the Mahmud Kashgari-Barskani Eastern University (Eastern University website).

While the presence of these universities within its borders, and the structure of the Ministry, are within Kyrgyzstan's control, the "mentalitet" of the current generation of higher education leadership and its experiential and educational base, were formed in Soviet times, and personal and professional connections link people in Kyrgyzstan with other former Soviet countries. It is not unusual for parents and children or brothers and sisters to be citizens of different former Soviet countries, given the vagaries of where someone was working or attending school in 1991, when the Soviet Union collapsed, as well as the convoluted borders of the Fergana Valley. These patterns of thought and personal relationships are impossible to erase and argue for Kyrgyzstan not being too far out of step with the educational practices of places to which its citizens are linked.

Population size

At a session preceding the 2009 UNESCO World Conference on Higher Education, Mark Bray, Director of UNESCO's International Institute for Educational Planning, said, "Small states are almost by definition outward looking and international" (Sharma 2009, Para. 7). This is indeed the case for Kyrgyzstan.

The small size of Kyrgyzstan's population, estimated to be 5.4 million in 2009, with two-thirds, or more than 3.5 million, scattered in rural areas, means that Kyrgyzstan cannot provide either the diversity of types of higher education institutions nor the full range of degrees and subjects that all of its citizens might need or want.[3] As Ishengul Boldjurova, the former Minister of Education in Kyrgyzstan, wrote in an article titled "Higher Education in the Kyrgyz Republic: Problems of Modernization and Internationalization", (2007: 2): "We believe that the main reason for studying abroad is a home country education system that is far from satisfying demands and necessity of getting a competitive education." This is particularly true at the graduate level. The situation is exacerbated by the fact that 32 per cent of Kyrgyzstan's population is between the ages of 15 and 25, and fully half the population is under 25 (UNDP Kyrgyzstan 2010: 2). This young population needs new subjects and new ways of teaching to meet the needs of a post-Soviet era, yet many professors in Kyrgyzstan were trained in the Soviet era, when subjects such as marketing did not exist and others, such as American literature or economics or religion, had very different underlying premises than they do now.

Responses to this dilemma have come in two forms. First, a growing number of students seek education abroad, either for an entire degree or on shorter-term programs, financed either by personal resources or by one of the international programmes operating in Kyrgyzstan, including Erasmus Mundus; DAAD, the German academic exchange organization; various US government programmes, such as the Muskie scholarship for Master's degree work in selected disciplines in the US; and a number of programmes supported by the Turkish government and other organizations in Turkey. Such programmes are not confined to the capital city or to a limited number of universities. Tourism students at Osh Technical University are studying marketing in California and Turkey (Uzenbayev 2009), the Head of the Department of Strategy and Analytical Work in the Ministry of Education is writing her *kandidat nauk* thesis on innovations in higher education in Kyrgyzstan under supervision from Moscow, and students and practitioners interested in the field of higher education administration study at the University of Michigan and at Kent State University. Even in the field of Central Asian Studies, graduate students and scholars from Kyrgyzstan trek to Indiana, to Harvard, to universities in the UK, and elsewhere.

Second, to a degree greater than any of its Central Asian neighbours, and likely to a degree greater than many countries anywhere, Kyrgyzstan has invited or accepted the presence of universities with various kinds of international support, funding, teaching staffs and influence. As noted above, the higher education institutions in the country include the Kyrgyz–Russian Slavic University, the Kyrgyz–Turkish Manas University, the privately sponsored Turkish Ala-Too University, the Kuwaiti-sponsored East University and, prior to June 2010, the Kyrgyz–Uzbek University. In addition, Kyrgyzstan is home to the American University in Central Asia; the Kyrgyz–European *Fakultet* at the National University; a campus of the University of Central Asia, sponsored by the Aga Khan (University of Central Asia website) and branch campuses of at least six Russian universities (Jamasheva 2000; Erasmus Mundus External Cooperation Window website 2009).

The international universities operating in Kyrgyzstan include two founded on the basis of government-to-government contracts. One is the Kyrgyz–Russian Slavic University, founded on 9 September 1993 (KRSU website 2007b) as a result of an agreement between the Kyrgyz government, then led by President Askar Akaev, the former head of the Academy of Sciences, who had spent most of his own academic career in Leningrad, studying physics, specializing in optics, a field not developed in Kyrgyzstan, and the Russian government, then headed by Boris Yeltsin (KRSU website 2007a). KRSU has offered both Bachelor's degrees and the Soviet-style *diploms* since it opened (KRSU website 2007a). The second institution founded by government-to-government contract is the Kyrgyz–Turkish Manas University, founded in 1995 by an agreement between the Kyrgyz and Turkish governments (Kyrgyzstan–Turkey Manas University website 2009a). It offers Bachelor's and Master's degrees, and not the Soviet-style five year specialist degrees (Kyrgyzstan–Turkey Manas University website 2009b).

These two universities reflect different aspects of Kyrgyzstan's history and heritage, but the fact that universities from any country outside of Kyrgyzstan itself were invited in and established by government contract suggests that the Kyrgyz government understood that it could not, on its own, provide the higher education opportunities its citizens needed. Financial pressures, a desire to stem the exodus of ethnic Russian citizens in the early 1990s, and a wish to cement relations with Turkey all were likely factors in the establishment of these institutions, but the diversity of educational options they provide to Kyrgyzstan's small population is an additional bonus in a country which no longer has all of the institutions of the Soviet Union at its citizens' disposal.

Factors over which Kyrgyzstan has only minimal control

Language of academic materials and cultural assumptions

If a student in Kyrgyzstan is going to study certain fields in any depth – for example, higher education administration, intercultural communication, public relations, contemporary literary theory, comparative politics, or even the history and laws of Islam – he or she is going to use sources that not only were not originally written in Kyrgyz (or even in Russian), but also that do not make assumptions about politics, economics, the purposes of education, tax policy and a myriad of other subjects as those issues exist in Kyrgyzstan. The priorities of international actors may show themselves in many aspects of life in Kyrgyzstan, and assumptions in books and materials used in universities may not be the most blatant of these, but in some ways the daily exposure of students to those foreign assumptions may have more lasting effects than some of the more blatant pressures on Kyrgyzstan by outside actors. Of course, it may be argued that throughout the world, knowledge is no longer parochial: students of higher education administration in the United States, for example, read works of European authors in order to understand the Bologna reforms, and students in physics and other sciences study in fields where international collaboration in research and writing has become the norm. But the use of literature from elsewhere in classrooms in the US, in Western Europe, and probably in most non-transition countries, does not challenge fundamental assumptions about how life is lived at home in the way that it does in a transitioning country like Kyrgyzstan. In supporting the use of US texts at what was then the American University in Kyrgyzstan (now the American University in Central Asia), the university's founder, Camilla Sharshekeeva (c.1997–2001), regularly reminded faculty, "Remember, the Soviet Union was the country that flunked economics."[4]

The links between materials from abroad in non-local languages and change in both practice and perception are evident in two examples, both connected to the point which follows this, regarding donor-funded reforms in education. One instance of new language and new practice took place in the field of accounting. The Soviet Union had followed its own accounting standards; in order to engage in international commerce, Kyrgyzstan, along with other former Soviet countries, needed to adopt International Accounting Standards (IAS). The United States Agency for International Development (USAID) hired the CARANA

Corporation to provide the needed training in Central Asia, a process which went far beyond students' reading a text imported from abroad. Speaking of its work in Kyrgyzstan and Kazakhstan, the CARANA Corporation writes on its website:

> Over the life of the project, CARANA converted more than 2,000 companies from the former Soviet-style statutory accounting to new national standards based on IAS. We trained over 8,000 local accountants, auditors, and finance specialists in IAS, financial accounting, managerial accounting, tax accounting, financial management, and conversion methodology. In addition, CARANA helped establish the first ever self-regulatory system of professional accountancy in Kazakhstan and Kyrgyzstan.... In Kyrgyzstan, CARANA supported the formation of the Union of Accountants and Auditors and the Association of Accounting and Audit Teachers.

Students at the American University in Central Asia (then the American University in Kyrgyzstan (AUK)), as well as other universities, used the CARANA curriculum, and several of the AUK students subsequently travelled to Augusta, Maine, to take the Certified Public Accountant exam (Becker Professional Education 2009; Office of Licensing and Registration 2009).[5] Thus their exposure was not simply to a text in a different language, but rather to different assumptions about business practice, and eventually, to a different nation.

Similarly, in the field of anthropology, changes in teaching materials have implications that extend far beyond the use of a different language. Dyikanbaeva (n.d.:2) describes the Soviet-era emphases in what was then called "ethnography": "Most ethnographic work in Central Asia right up until the end of the Soviet Union had the character of 'salvage ethnography', with the purpose of describing traditions which were meant no longer to exist under the Soviet system".

In the post-Soviet era, due to economic constraints, according to Dyikanbaeva (n.d.), the situation did not improve, but rather deteriorated, as the newly independent nations had few resources to devote to higher education and to the support of younger scholars, who might have been most open to new methodologies. She adds:

> The links with Russian scholarship that sustained ethnography in Central Asia, such as it was, have also largely been broken. All in all, the result is that dissertations defended in the last 15 years have not even been up to the standards of Soviet times.
>
> (Dyikanbaeva n.d.: 2)

For Kyrgyzstani students and professors, therefore, studying anthropology with a Western text means not merely understanding a different language, but rather understanding a different worldview and a different set of underlying assumptions.

In the sciences, although the Medical Academy in Kyrgyzstan, founded during Soviet times, continues to teach in Russian, as does the medical school at the Kyrgyz–Russian Slavic University, the new medical school at the International University in Kyrgyzstan teaches entirely in English (WHO 2007). While the motives for opening this medical school may have been strategic and financial – the number of students from India and Pakistan interested in studying medicine is not inconsiderable, and the option of doing so in English of course draws them to IUK, rather than to the Medical Academy, which traditionally has had a South Asian contingent but which teaches those students in Russian – nevertheless, the focus on texts and research from the US and other English-speaking countries, with different assumptions about health care standards and availability than exist in Kyrgyzstan, likely affects the perceptions of Kyrgyzstani students who attend the medical school regarding what is needed and what is possible in health care at home.

In the language of instructional materials, and, more importantly, in the assumptions those materials carry, Kyrgyzstan thus cannot escape international influences – ones which lead it in directions not all local educational and political decision-makers might choose independently.

Kyrgyzstan's income level leads to donor-funded educational reforms

Kyrgyzstan is a poor country and one which is deeply in debt. According to the CIA World Factbook (2009b), Kyrgyzstan's estimated 2008 GDP per capita of $2,100 places it 184th in the world, of 229 countries, lower than the West Bank, Sudan and the Western Sahara. In 2007, when Kyrgyzstan's external debt was over US$2 billion, after protracted debate, it rejected the opportunity to write off half of that debt by accepting the designation of an HIPC (Heavily Indebted Poor Country) at least in part to avoid external controls on business activities. As Erica Marat (2007) writes, "The current system of large-scale corruption bridging the state and the business sector would be jeopardized if Kyrgyzstan allowed international involvement in the domestic economy." However, rejecting international involvement in one sector may mean accepting it in another. When this researcher was working in Kyrgyzstan in the late 1990s, she was told by reliable sources that the budget of the Soros Foundation in Kyrgyzstan was larger than that of the Ministry of Education. With an 18 per cent unemployment rate in 2004 and 40 per cent of the population living beneath the poverty line in 2007, and with a 22.5 per cent inflation rate in 2008, supplemented by the interesting statistic that Kyrgyzstan's 2008 revenues were US$1,170 billion, but its expenditures were $1,192 billion, Kyrgyzstan clearly is unable to make substantial investments in its higher education system. Thus, it must accept both the funds and the priorities of external donors and actors. Indeed, the mission of the Kyrgyzstan Turkish Manas University, established by a contract between the Turkish and Kyrgyz governments, includes as one objective internationalizing the educational system of the country which is its host: "To serve as a model for the higher education system of Kyrgyzstan, and in this way to play a leading role in global integration by making use of contemporary education standards and methods in a modern university administrative model" (Kyrgyzstan–Turkey Manas University website 2009b:

para. 3). However, as DeYoung (2005) discusses with regard to Kyrgyzstan and Steiner-Khamsi and Stolpe (2006) discuss with regard to Mongolia, educational borrowing is a complex affair that often leads to outcomes that, in whole or in part, may not be what the donor intended. Additionally, as Djanaeva (2001) points out, donor-driven reforms may not be sustainable:

> Internationalization of higher education exists on the framework of international donor assistance to the country's development. In many cases it includes visiting experts on various issues to the higher education sector for various reasons. I think that it is time to consider sustainability issues of the current directions in higher education and to spend funds and time to develop our own local corps of higher education experts, instead of always inviting foreign experts to do the job for us.
>
> (Djanaeva 2001: 3)

However, she also notes that universities' ability to attract donors in some ways increases their power and academic freedom:

> Colleges and universities have become independent from the state through the possibility of direct financing of institutional projects by donors, and setting up institutional linkages without approval from state authorities. This contributes to the future of decentralized system of management in higher education and to the development of the academic freedom through placing faculty in various academic settings abroad, via high valuing of the idea of academic freedom and the process of its implementation.
>
> (Djanaeva 2001: 3–4)

In some cases, the idea for a reform has originated in Kyrgyzstan and then external funding was sought. This was the case with the National Testing Program for university admission, which was conceived of by Camilla Sharshekeeva, when she was Minister of Education (2000–2002), as a way of avoiding the corruption then existing in the admissions processes in many universities in Kyrgyzstan. Initially, Minister Sharshekeeva invited educators based in Kyrgyzstan, both local and foreign, to work on the design of such a test. This author, who was a member of one of those early consulting groups, sought advice from the Educational Testing Service (ETS) in the US, since it was clear that creating a valid and reliable test to be given annually to thousands of students in several languages required both time and expertise beyond that possessed by the educators volunteering for periodic committee meetings at the Ministry. However, the cost of services from ETS far exceeded the Ministry's budget. Never one to shrink from a challenge, Minister Sharshekeeva pursued external funding options. As Drummond and DeYoung write, in a comprehensive analysis of this reform:

> In order to achieve her goals, Sharshekeeva sought technical and financial assistance from the United States, approaching the US Embassy in Bishkek

and the Coordinator for US Technical Assistance in Washington. American Councils received funding to carry out the testing component of the Ministry's larger education reform program through the US Agency for International Development funded Education Network program implemented by the CARANA Corporation.

(Drummond and DeYoung 2004: 227)

The National Testing Program, the brainchild of a Kyrgyzstani, continues to operate as its creators envisioned.[6] Other reforms, in their practical application, work out not quite as their international proponents may have planned. Reeves (2006) gives an example of a teacher in Batken, Kyrgyzstan's southernmost and poorest province, who very much enjoyed a UNESCO-sponsored workshop on active learning techniques, but thought of those techniques as "special occasion" techniques, partially because she and her school could not afford the continuous purchase of markers and poster paper. Similarly, a current initiative, the "Quality Learning Project", started on 30 September 2007 by a USAID contractor, Creative Associates International, cites as its goal, for selected schools not only in Kyrgyzstan, but also in Tajikistan and Turkmenistan: "With QLP, education in the three Central Asian Republics will move away from the tradition of rote learning and memorization to student-centred learning approaches that develop critical thinking skills" (Creative Associates International). Given the low salaries of teachers, particularly in rural areas, and the increasing class sizes assigned to them as many flee the profession for more lucrative work, plus the lack of a critical thinking emphasis in most teachers' own training, it is difficult to see how the Quality Learning Project will succeed, even in the relatively open society of Kyrgyzstan, to say nothing of the much more repressive Turkmenistan.[7]

In some cases, the donor has a solution and Kyrgyzstan is determined to be an appropriate recipient, even in the absence of a formal needs assessment. As Merrill and Dukenbaev (2011) show, the European Union, in the implementation of TEMPUS projects focused on Bologna Process reforms and Erasmus Mundus projects focused on exchanges, provides little evidence of having done formal educational needs assessments in Kyrgyzstan or in the other Central Asian republics. While the European Training Foundation (Asiurov *et al.* 2007; Grootings *et al.* 2007; Tasbulatova and Belosludtseva 2007), on the other hand, has indeed commissioned fairly nuanced vocational training needs assessments by local authors, the actual projects it has emphasized include implementing the Dublin Descriptors (ETF 2005) in redesigning tourism programmes – arguably not the highest priority for a country that is 184th in the world in terms of its GDP per capita.

Globalization: labour migration and "brain circulation"

Connected to the poor economy in Kyrgyzstan is the issue of labour migration. One usually hears about this in relation to the less educated who flock to Russia to work in construction or to Kazakhstan to work in oil fields, or regarding the "shuttle traders" who buy goods in bulk in China and bring them back to sell in bazaars in Kyrgyzstan, but the highly educated leave as well, and a higher education system that is "out-of-sync" with the systems of nations to which the highly skilled migrate benefits neither the migrants nor those who depend on them for remittances sent home, nor, by extension, the economy and thus the stability of Kyrgyzstan. Just as the Bologna Process itself was designed to facilitate labour mobility within Europe, by making degree requirements transparent and credits transferrable, so too, Kyrgyzstan with its poverty and lack of local opportunity, must facilitate labour mobility in order to achieve economic stability, and thus if its educational system is not integrated with those of recipient countries, migrants will have problems. Professionals will not be qualified for equivalent positions abroad, and if they stay in the host country long enough to obtain those qualifications, they will be unlikely to return to Kyrgyzstan, if their qualifications are not recognized at home. Thus, if Kyrgyzstan wishes to encourage what has come to be known as "brain circulation", rather than brain drain, it needs to consider how its educational system interacts with others. Saxenian, the originator of the term "brain circulation", describes the concept as it plays out in Silicon Valley in the US state of California:

> Far from simply replacing native workers, foreign-born engineers are starting new businesses and generating jobs and wealth at least as fast as their U.S. counterparts. And the dynamism of emerging regions in Asia and elsewhere now draws skilled immigrants homeward. Even when they choose not to return home, they are serving as middlemen linking businesses in the United States with those in distant regions.
>
> (Saxenian 2002, para. 3)

Of course, such "brain circulation" depends upon not only the synchronization of structures for professional preparation in Kyrgyzstan with those found elsewhere, but also the realities of practice: a system known for corruption, as Kyrgyzstan's unfortunately is (see below), will never be fully integrated into "the world educational space", regardless of what structures are created on its surface.

Ivakhnyuk, in her 2006 review of migration patterns in the CIS, written for a UN conference on migration, adds to the discussion of factors leading to permanent and to "circulatory" migration, citing "low wages" and "reduced prestige for intellectual labor" at home as factors that push researchers to leave (p. 6), and adding that some researchers who emigrate maintain contacts at home and others do not.

She elaborates on this theme:

> In many fields of science ... development within the frames of only one country is hardly possible now. Projects in these fields of highest priority need huge resources – human and financial. Besides, cooperation between

researchers from different scientific schools gives more effective results, and "brain exchange" is an important instrument of scientific progress and mutual enrichment of scholars. So, nowadays development of fundamental science needs global management...

Gradually, the most advanced CIS states are coming to a new understanding that in order to participate in a newly organized global scientific research process most effectively they should not only give their brains but also be ready to absorb produced innovations in their economy.

(Ivakhnyuk 2006: 6)

If Kyrgyzstan wishes to participate in such "circulation", rather than to simply lose talented people to positions abroad, then it needs to have a higher education system in which people can prepare for careers abroad and an employment system in which internationally recognized qualifications also are accepted by employers in Kyrgyzstan. Ishengul Boldjurova (2007), Kyrgyzstan's former Minister of Education, was not unaware of these issues:

One of the most powerful stimuli for curricula internationalization is increase of influence that world professional unions have on the process of education. Rapid growth of international trade in services and goods encourages specialists to re-organize their activity on international level by uniting in professional communities. These unions concentrate on issues of quality guarantee, minimization of standard requirements, criteria of professionalism, accreditation, etc. ... [that] are often worked out and implemented by international organizations.

(Boldjurova 2007: 5)

Since frequent destinations for Kyrgyz students – Russia, Turkey, Germany and the US – are all either in the Bologna Process or have another version of the "three-cycle" (Bachelor's, Master's, Doctorate) educational system, and Kazakhstan, a frequent destination for migrants, is on a self-proclaimed "Path to Europe" ("Path to Europe" 2008), it makes sense for Kyrgyzstan to adopt such a three-cycle higher education system. However, according to Rahat Bekboyeva, the Director of the National Bologna Process Center in Kyrgyzstan, in 2008, of all the degrees given in Kyrgyzstan, only 7 per cent were Bachelor's degrees, and only 3 per cent were Master's.[8] The remaining 90 per cent were the Soviet era "specialist" *diploms*, a degree not in use outside the former Soviet Union. Thus students who want to work abroad, at least temporarily, in countries that are accustomed to the BA-MA system, will find it easier to become qualified for such positions by studying abroad. However, that preparation abroad unfortunately makes it *less* likely that a student who would like to return can find employment in Kyrgyzstan. This is because, as this author was told repeatedly in interviews conducted with university educators in Bishkek and Osh in June and July 2009, employers in Kyrgyzstan, for the most part, do not understand what a graduate with a Bachelor's degree is qualified to do. This situation is exacerbated by the fact that *klassifikators* – the descriptions produced by the Ministry of Education to explain what positions a person with a particular degree is qualified for – exist only for specialist degrees. None have been written for Bachelor's or Master's degrees. Thus a student who obtains a degree in Germany or the US, upon returning to Kyrgyzstan, is likely to find employers who are unable to evaluate his or her credentials. Indeed, Uzakova (2009) reports an instance of a student who dropped out of the Kyrgyz-Turkish Manas University, arguably one of the best universities in Kyrgyzstan, when she realized that she would be receiving a Bachelor's degree.[9] She believed that degree would limit her employment possibilities. Such attitudes, unfortunately, encourage brain drain rather than brain circulation – to the detriment of Central Asia's economic and societal progress.

Globalization: international rankings of universities, attracting international faculty, and the globalization of quality assessment standards

Internationalization differs from globalization, according to most commentators, in that internationalization concerns the activities of nations and usually is under the control of nations, whereas globalization concerns non-state actors and usually is beyond the control of nations. Thus one might speak of an international treaty to control global warming, or of international police efforts to control the global narcotics trade. Higher education traditionally has been concerned with internationalization: students studying abroad, faculty from other countries lecturing for a semester, a professor teaching a course about another country, issues decided between nations and controlled by national laws, including visa regulations. Now, however, higher education is becoming globalized. Electronic communication systems allow researchers to discuss and share data and ideas without having to ask their governments for visas. Online programmes allow students to receive not only courses but even degrees from institutions in other countries without ever leaving home. Moreover, organizations such as the Academic Rankings of World Universities and QS World University Rankings are ranking universities across the globe – recognizing that both faculty and students are *internationally* mobile, but setting in motion processes of *global* quality assessment. EQAR, the European Quality Assessment Register, is an example of this: a quality assessment agency that has EQAR's imprimatur may, with the host country's agreement, evaluate universities outside of its own national borders. Similarly, almost all of the US regional accrediting agencies and a number of the specialized accrediting agencies now accredit internationally. Another example is OECD's AHELO project – the Assessment of Higher Education Learning Outcomes, designed from the start as an international project, involving nations as diverse as Norway and Mexico in the common assessment of higher education learning outcomes.

Kyrgyzstan is not immune to these trends. Nurgul Djanaeva in her article "The Internationalization of Higher Education in Kyrgyzstan", notes that:

Internationalization has become one of the key indicators of the organizational quality in our university system. Therefore, international participation is reported as an achievement, because it means recognition in the international arena.

(Djanaeva 2001: 2)

That recognition is no longer international, nation-to-nation. Even a micro-level activity – inviting a scholar from abroad to teach at a university in Kyrgyzstan – now has global implications. One reason, discussed below, is that under GATS, the World Trade Organization's General Agreement on Trade in Services, the so-called "movement of natural persons" is a choice not simply of one university or even of one government, but instead may come under the rules of a global agreement on trade in services. A second reason is that the internationalization of the faculty now is a criterion in the global ranking of universities.

Attracting faculty from abroad often is seen as both a source of excellence[10] and as a way to offer subjects that could not otherwise be taught, as well as offering instruction by native speakers of languages critical to Kyrgyzstan's needs, so integration with international systems of higher education becomes important. As the Bologna Process has shown, vibrant and sustainable exchanges depend upon comparable systems. Umland (2005) has written about the problems that European faculty encounter in teaching at post-Soviet institutions, including the institutions' heritages of isolation from contemporary debates in the social sciences and of social science disciplines being used for indoctrination rather than free inquiry, a situation reinforced by those universities that still use the contact hour system, generally based on faculty lectures and student re-iteration, rather than independent student reading and research. In addition, Umland discusses post-Soviet universities' financial problems and issues arising from the fact that, for students, not only are universities in transition, but also the secondary schools from which the students come and the labour market to which they are going also are in flux. Also, Umland emphasizes the degree to which corruption is so pervasive that many students do not realize that it is not the norm elsewhere. As long as such issues continue, the recognition that Kyrgyzstani universities desire in the broader "world educational space" will be difficult.

Yet, for the reasons discussed above, isolation is not an option. Subsuming essential Kyrgyz *content* in fields as diverse as agriculture, history and economics to global mandates, as could easily happen under GATS, could be detrimental to Kyrgyzstani higher education institutions, but adopting appropriate *processes*, such as individualized institutional missions, credit hours, elective courses, adequate salaries for professors, academic freedom and institutionally designed curricula, would be an advantage to Kyrgyzstan as its institutions seek international recognition.[11] Boldjurova elaborates on this tension:

Every national university faces the task of making its degrees transparent and recognizable not only for its students and employers, but also attractive for foreign citizens and organizations. This goal ... means mobility of students and teachers, internationalization of study programs and curricula, creation of international university networks and co-operation agreements, usage of international quality control models.

On the other hand, we witness the process of searching for a national education system that is better shaped to meet the needs of the civil society, needs of national identity in the global world.

(Boldjurova 2007: 6–7)

Djanaeva adds:

> What are the weak sides of internationalization? Strong dependence on foreign support, tremendous lack of internal resources for internationalization, lack of human capacity in the development of international ties. It can destroy the advantages of the previous higher educational system if implemented without careful analysis of the needs and mission of Kyrgyzstani higher education institutions.
>
> (Djanaeva 2001: 8)

Askat Dukenbaev, a political scientist, is more specific about these national identity needs and their sources:

> the country's educational policy is highly politicized, and has become an important tool in political mobilization, socialization, and state building. Since independence in 1991, promotion of the cultural values of the "titular" nationality – ethnic Kyrgyz – has become one of the major questions on the political agenda of Kyrgyzstan. The Ministry of Education plays a pivotal role in this process.
>
> (Dukenbaev 2004: 17)

Despite these concerns about national identity and the role of higher education in promoting it, given the globalization of quality assessment standards – the worldwide scramble to crack the ARWU 500 or to get on the QS list, the American University in Central Asia's awarding of dual degrees with Bard College in New York, the participation of 13 institutions in Kyrgyzstan in a two-year TEMPUS project to assess learning outcomes in 11 disciplines using methodologies designed in Europe under the Tuning Project – Kyrgyzstan cannot remain immune from global forces in quality evaluation, whether or not they are adapted to or in Kyrgyzstan's interests.

Djanaeva comments:

> The existing national institutional assessment system of higher education is working, but it seems not to be able to fulfill the demands and needs of the Kyrgyzstani citizens, as well as the needs of Kyrgyzstani higher education institutions to be recognized for equal opportunities abroad. We have to

convince foreign universities, companies, foundations, educators and various organizations that our degrees, diplomas, programs, colleges and universities are of good and high quality by means of international assessment, which is provided by accrediting agencies.

(Djanaeva 2001: 6)

One recent attempt at such convincing was a project carried out by the Ministry of Education of the Kyrgyz Republic, the Soros Foundation of Kyrgyzstan, and the Association "EdNet". They jointly produced a *Handbook for Organizing Systems of Guaranteeing Quality in Higher Education Institutions of the Kyrgyz Republic* (Bragina *et al.* 2007). The document reveals a reader's but not a practitioner's awareness of contemporary quality assessment practices. Perhaps because a number of the authors and members of the editorial board have business backgrounds, including positions at the Bishkek Academy of Finance and the newly renamed University of Economics, the models analysed, while all western in origin, are models of quality assessment in business. In both this volume and in Simbard's presentation to the TEMPUS-sponsored workshop on the Bologna Process held at the Edelveiss Resort in Barskoon, Kyrgyzstan, 19–21 June 2009, the European Foundation for Quality Management (http://ww1.efqm.org/en/) model is emphasized. Although the authors adapt this model to higher education, its underlying premises are quite different from contemporary quality assessment processes generally used in higher education, which tend to focus on learning outcomes. Integration into "the world education space" will require a different kind of quality assessment.

WTO membership means accepting GATS

Kyrgyzstan is even less able to remain immune from global standards, offerings, and pressures in education than are its Central Asian neighbours because of its membership in the World Trade Organization (WTO) (Pomfret 2007; Quigley 2004) which means that it is subject to GATS, the General Agreement on Trade in Services. GATS is a complex and controversial subject; the American Council on Education (ACE 2008) provides a useful primer on the topic. Education is one of the 12 service sectors included in the agreement. Kyrgyzstan could easily trade away access to its educational system to foreign providers (higher education is one of the five categories in education under GATS) in order to gain access to markets for its own services abroad, under pressure from other nations, or from its own wish to be open to foreign providers, perhaps without understanding all of the implications of such a move, some of which are discussed below. Alternatively, Kyrgyzstan could see the opening of its own higher education markets as an income-generating possibility.[12] The English-language medical school at the International University in Kyrgyzstan, designed at least in part to permit access to the South Asian student market, is one example of the opening of Kyrgyzstani higher education to international markets. Kyrgyzstan's former Minister of Education, Ishengul Boldjurova noted:

International education and education services market is becoming a rapidly developing sector of economics, central elements of which are international education institutions' market and purposeful admission of foreign students. In Kyrgyzstan, export of education services has only recently started to come into the focus of attention as an income opportunity.

(Boldjurova 2007: 4)

However, any educator who has observed the dramatic changes in another service sector in Kyrgyzstan, banking, since Kyrgyzstan joined the WTO in 1998 – Bishkek now rivals Manhattan in having a bank on every corner – will be forgiven for having a few qualms about what might happen were Kyrgyzstan's educational sector to be equally open.[13] One concern is that unregulated, non-academic, for-profit providers, ready to offer whatever education and training will make money, will flood into Kyrgyzstan. Boldjurova was not unaware of this danger:

Thus we find that internationalization carries great opportunities for Kyrgyzstan. At the same time, it exacerbates competition and generates tensions by creating new education services providers (training companies, telecommunication companies, distant learning centers and corporate bodies).

(Boldjurova 2007: 6)

As Jane Knight (2002), one of the more lucid and even-handed commentators on the topic of GATS in education, writes:

GATS is the first legal trade agreement that focuses exclusively on trade in services – as opposed to products. It is administered by the World Trade Organization, a powerful organization with 144 member countries. Education is one of the 12 service sectors covered by GATS. The purpose of GATS is progressively and systematically to promote freer trade in services by removing many of the existing barriers.

(Knight 2002: 5)

In a 2006 publication, she adds:

The purpose of GATS is to liberalize trade: that is, to reduce or eliminate restrictions and barriers in order to promote further trade. It is important to note that national policies and regulations that have been established by some countries in order to control the import of education and training services into their country are in fact sometimes seen by exporting countries as trade barriers that need to be removed.

(Knight 2006: 29)

The comprehensiveness of what could be considered barriers to trade in education, that is, elements that Kyrgyzstan (or any other WTO country that chooses to open access to its educational system – perhaps in return for getting access to trade another of its own services) could be forced to give up control of under GATS makes the list worth quoting in its entirety:

> A number of barriers are specific to higher education services. The more important ones that education and trade policy makers need to pay close attention to are listed below:

Mode 1: Cross-border supply
- Restriction on import of educational material
- Restriction on electronic transmission of course material
- Non-recognition of degrees obtained through distance mode

Mode 2: Consumption abroad
- Restriction on travel abroad based on discipline or area of study
- Restriction on export of currency and exchange
- Quota on the number of students proceeding to a county or institution
- Prescription of minimum standards or attainments

Mode 3: Commercial presence
- Insistence on a local partner
- Insistence that the provider be accredited in the home country
- Insistence on partner/collaborator being from the formal academic stream
- Insistence on equal academic participation by foreign and local partner
- Disapproval of franchise operations
- Restrictions on certain disciplines/areas/programs that are deemed to be against national interests
- Limitations on foreign direct investment by education providers
- Difficulty in approval of joint ventures

Mode 4: Presence of natural persons
- Visa and entry restrictions
- Restriction on basis of quota for countries and disciplines
- Nationality or residence requirements
- Restriction on repatriation of earnings

(Knight 2006: 33)

Thus Kyrgyzstan's membership in a trade organization may have substantial impact on the internationalization of its higher education system – and on the government's ability to control that system.

The "world class" university movement

As Philip Altbach and Jorge Balan (2007) have noted, in the last decade or so, the concept of a "world class" university has come into being. Having a national university that meets national needs is no longer the goal for many nations;

having a "world class" university is now the aim. Yet pouring resources into a large research university with more than simply adequate laboratories and libraries can seriously disfigure a national higher education system, leaving universities in places like Batken even more severely underfinanced and ignored than they are now. As Jacob Roope (2009) suggests, an analogy might be giving a bar of premium chocolate to one privileged student, versus providing bite-sized supermarket-brand chocolates to the whole class. And when a government disenfranchises elements of its own population, becoming unable to provide them with basic services, then groups like the Muslim Brotherhood move in, as happened in Egypt.[14] Attempting to meet "world class" standards can lead to losing the hearts and minds of the majority of the population at home, yet, in an era of global rankings of universities, student and faculty mobility, and instant worldwide communication, the temptation to pour resources into a university that will make a nation known always is present. However, as Salmi points out:

> the superior results of [world class universities] (highly sought graduates, leading-edge research, and technology transfer) can essentially be attributed to three complementary sets of factors at play in top universities: (a) a high concentration of talent (faculty and students), (b) abundant resources to offer a rich learning environment and to conduct advanced research, and (c) favorable governance features that encourage strategic vision, innovation, and flexibility and that enable institutions to make decisions without being encumbered by bureaucracy.
>
> (Salmi 2009: 6–7)

Kyrgyzstan is a nation with its share of talented students and faculty, but no-one could argue that it has either abundant resources or that its higher education institutions are able to innovate and make decisions unencumbered by bureaucracy. The fundamental requirements for a world class university thus are absent in Kyrgyzstan. Yet, in the twenty-first century, pressures to create such a university will remain, particularly in a small, resource-poor nation which needs to rely on the brains of its people and on "brain circulation" of its own citizens and others for economic, social and political survival.

Factors which are under Kyrgyzstan's control

Three factors – degree structures, the level of Ministry of Education control of many aspects of higher education, and corruption – as currently constituted work against Kyrgyzstan's desire for international recognition of its own institutions and instead give more power, authority and prestige to foreign institutions.

Degree structures

The authoritative Russian-English dictionary, compiled under the direction of A.I. Smirnitsky (1971) defines *kasha* not only as "porridge", but also in its informal meaning of "a jumble" or "a mess". This was the kind of *kasha* that at least four of this author's interviewees were referring to in June and July 2009, when they used the term to describe current degree structures in Kyrgyzstan.[15] Although the government of Kyrgyzstan has decreed that all higher education institutions in the country will adopt the Bachelor's – Master's and credit hour system for the 2012–2013 academic year (Merrill and Ryskulova, 2012), for now, a plethora of degree options exist. AUCA and Manas offer only Bachelor's and Master's degrees. The Slavic University, the University of Economics, the International University, Osh Technological University, the Kyrgyz State University of Construction, Transport and Architecture, and several others offer Bachelor's, Master's, and the five-year Specialist *diplom*. Other universities offer only the Specialist *diplom*. Soviet-era *kandidat nauk* and *doctor nauk* degrees are not awarded by individual higher education institutions, but rather by the Higher Attestation Committee of the Ministry of Education; following the Soviet pattern, neither one requires additional course work, but rather publications and a publicly defended thesis (Foley 2003). Depending on the subject, it is not unusual for the thesis to be defended before a committee in Russia and for the degree to be awarded there. The western-style Ph.D. is not available in Kyrgyzstan.

As noted above, switching to the Bachelor's – Master's system, or some other two-cycle system, would aid Kyrgyzstan in achieving greater labour mobility and "brain circulation" rather than "brain drain". However, these are not the most important reasons for changing degree structures. The Specialist degrees are based on an outmoded idea of what constitutes preparation for a career – even assuming that the sole purpose of higher education is preparation for a career, a debatable proposition. Specialist degrees prepare students for specialities, and very narrow specialities at that. A glance through websites of universities in Kyrgyzstan shows that student can earn *diploms* in fields with names such as Motor Transport, Hydrotechnic Construction, Trade Law, Food Products Technology and Power Plants. The idea of broad preparation in the liberal arts, except at the American University in Central Asia, is unknown, and in most universities, students have very limited or no opportunities to take electives; they still move through their degrees as a group of classmates, taking all classes together. In an era where not only technology but also management techniques, forms of education, modes of transportation, financial products, clothing designs, environmental concerns, forms of journalism, food products and political issues, to name only a few, change daily, such narrow and inflexible specialties, with every student in the country who specializes in a particular field having the exact same preparation, are dysfunctional, particularly for a country which, as noted, has few natural resources and must depend upon the creativity and brain power of its citizens for economic development and thus political stability.

Leaving behind the specialist degree means more than changing from a five-year degree to a three- or four-year degree, although, based on interviews this author conducted in June and July 2009, that fact seems to be little recognized. Concomitant with broad and flexible preparation for the twenty-first century is replacing the lecture-based contact-hour system with credit hours and student independent work. This, however, means changing the basis on which professors are paid, currently based on the number of hours they are in class, and also redefining what it means to be a full-time employee and to be eligible for benefits – also currently dependent upon the number of hours spent in class. Thus both the Ministry of Labour and the Ministry of Finance would need to be involved in shifting university teaching from a contact-hour system to a credit-hour system. Leaving behind the Specialist *diplom* also means permitting individualized programs, with student electives, and thus creating registrar's offices and new ways of scheduling classes and classrooms. It means educating employers about what Bachelor's and Master's students can do – but also abandoning the *klassifikator* system, which narrowly defines specific occupations graduates are qualified for. The *klassifikator* system worked in a Soviet-era command economy, but when success is defined as creating the prototype Apple computer in a garage or thinking up a lucrative application for smart phones, limited, inflexible and unchanging *klassifikators* are both irrelevant and dysfunctional.

Ministry of Education control

Implicit in the recommendations above is a shift in control of the curriculum from the Ministry of Education to individual higher education institutions.

Reeves (2004: para. 3) describes the current system and its implications:

> Kyrgyzstan, as many other post-Soviet educational systems, retains a high degree of ministerial control over the content and structure of university curricula. Ministerial plans dictate the precise number of hours that students of a given "speciality" are to dedicate to different subjects during the course of their five years of university education; these plans are typically displayed prominently in university corridors, and they regulate closely student and teacher course loads in any given term, the scope of particular disciplines, and the chronological order in which subjects are to be taught. A small percentage of courses can be nominated by faculty deans and departmental chairs (also subject to ministerial approval), and students are nominally entitled to one or two "optional courses" (kursy po vyboru) in their final years of study, although in practice these tend to be narrowly prescribed – often to a choice of just one. The standard teaching course load is 500 classroom hours per term, a figure that, week-by-week, would stagger many Western academics. Punishingly low rates of pay mean that it is not uncommon for teachers, especially younger teachers (who need more time for course preparation) to take on 1.5 and even double course loads in order to make ends meet.

Institutional control of curriculum development also means that the Ministry would have to change graduation requirements, as those now are based on checking off that the specific list of required courses all have been completed.

Additionally, in order to meet the requirements of the European Association of Quality Assurance in Higher Education (ENQA), important for gaining that international recognition of quality Kyrgyzstan desires, the Ministry would have to give up its authority over attestation of institutions and allow an independent accreditation body to function.[16] The idea of an independent accreditation body is being widely discussed in Kyrgyzstan at the present time. The author's interviewees frequently referred to the work of USAID in this regard; a USAID consultant, Amy Lezberg, spent a month researching the prospects for an independent accrediting agency in Kyrgyzstan and presented her findings to a group of Ministry staff and rectors in June 2008 (see Lezberg 2008). She strongly recommended the creation of such an independent agency.

Such changes would be both expensive and time-consuming, and, moreover, would require a change in the "mentalitet" of many educators, not just those at the Ministry. However, if one recalls that one of Salmi's (2009) criteria for a world class university was the ability to innovate, free from unnecessary bureaucracy, one sees the necessity of making such changes.

"Corruption" and academic integrity

As Reeves (2004) points out, it is simply impossible for Batken State University, isolated in the rural southern part of the country, in the nation's poorest oblast, to meet some existing nation-wide university requirements, designed by the Ministry of Education as if all entering students and all universities were homogenous. Instead, as Reeves describes, students from tiny, under-resourced village schools enter unable to follow first-year classes prescribed for universities nation-wide; texts and laboratory equipment and internet access – sometimes electricity itself – may simply be unavailable. Yet with a centralized curriculum, and centralized standards for attestation, professors either teach what students cannot understand, or teach something different and call it what the Ministry wants. Either way, academic integrity is impossible. This, in turn, leads to a culture in which, since following written rules and standards is impossible, everything becomes open to informal negotiation – including financial negotiation. Reeves (2004: para. 6) elaborates:

> Such a lack of correspondence leaves the door wide open for corruption. Obviously, teachers are far more likely to seek bribes, and students are far more likely to give them when it is nearly impossible to answer exam questions honestly for want of coverage of the relevant material. More insidiously, the constant – indeed institutionalized – lack of correspondence between what is claimed and what is delivered (and what can, in fact, be delivered), between the actual and the "certified", blurs the boundary between ethical and unethical. Acting "ethically" in academe becomes divorced from the idea of testing ability according to firm, transparent, and nonnegotiable standards of knowledge gained. With so much improvisation required by the system (the paradoxical consequence of ministerial over-control), the grade book is no longer an index of "knowledge gained" but

instead a statement of a personalized relationship between teacher and student.

As Reeves (2004: para. 9) further notes, the implications of addressing these issues are profound:

> To deal with the problem of corruption in higher education, therefore, it is not enough simply to ask, as is typically done in Kyrgyzstani public discourse, "how do we stop students from giving bribes, and teachers from taking them?" We must ask the much broader questions,... Answering these questions demands, more radically, that we think structurally and systematically about the relationship between the Ministry of Education, particular institutions, the student body, and the wider public.

Until the Ministry permits institutions to have individual missions and curricula which reflect those missions and local needs, then, as Reeves states, integrity often will be impossible, and international institutions, such as the American University in Central Asia and the Kyrgyz–Turkish Manas University, with greater curricular flexibility, more individualized programs, better salaries for professors, and, most importantly, a culture in which rules, standards and policies are both realistic and actually are implemented, rather than being open for negotiation – these universities, in the minds of both local and foreign observers, will be the ones associated with both excellence and integrity.

When Kyrgyzstan's own universities are disparaged by students and the public alike, and seen as places where it is impossible to escape deeply imbedded and widespread practices that undermine integrity, then foreign influence will persist – and, as with foreign teaching materials, this influence will seep deeply into a generation's consciousness.

Conclusion

This review of a dozen ways in which international actors inevitably have influence in higher education in Kyrgyzstan reveals the importance of its specific contexts – geographical, historical, demographic, political, cultural and economic. The poet Wallace Stevens (1972: 133) wrote, "Things as they are/are changed upon the blue guitar." Kyrgyzstan, like a blue guitar, is unique. Its context matters.

Djanaeva concludes her paper on the internationalization of the higher education system in Kyrgyzstan with the following reflection:

> Internationalization has many benefits for higher education in Kyrgyzstan during its transitional period, but it raises many questions as well.... We must not be too quick to discard everything about the old system, as parts of it were positive. We have to be wary of relying on external funding and of developing programs that are not sustainable. Overall, however, the benefits

of internationalization outweigh the questions, particularly since any funding that supports the capacity development of people is indeed sustainable – even if the funding ceases to exist, the ideas remain. And ideas are what higher education is all about, in Kyrgyzstan or abroad.

(Djanaeva 2001: 10)

Djanaeva's wariness about reliance on international assistance and the sustainability of reforms is well founded. Kyrgyzstan, like all nations, wishes to direct its own future. As noted above, Kyrgyzstan's ability to act in some realms is limited by factors such as its size, its geographic location, its economic situation, and the restrictions of GATS. Yet the spheres over which Kyrgyzstan does have control but is not acting are the ones which, arguably, are hurting it the most. The timidity with which Kyrgyzstan engages Bologna Reforms – allowing universities to receive TEMPUS grants, but not following through with the changes in laws or Ministry structures or evaluation procedures or the myriad of other issues which such reforms require – leads to a system which is, as the author's interviewees termed it, *kasha*. Additionally, it leads to greater prestige for institutions such as AUCA and Manas which have clearly defined missions and processes for achieving them. Moreover, the Soviet holdover of Ministerial control over curriculum, awarding diplomas, and attestation, with no flexibility for a changing society or local circumstances, is, as Reeves (2004) suggests, the foundation for destroying academic integrity, as well as for encouraging brain drain among some of the most talented members of Kyrgyzstan's population and inadequate preparation for Kyrgyzstan's changing needs at home. Paradoxically, Kyrgyzstan's attempt to maintain national control over what it can maintain control over undercuts its larger objectives of international recognition for its own universities and the quality of its students and faculty. As Salmi (2009) notes, quality in the twenty-first century requires flexibility and innovation. These characteristics, along with academic integrity, curricular independence, and transparency in operations are what Kyrgyzstan needs to strengthen its own universities. Centralizing and politicizing academic decision-making is a recipe for national weakness, not national strength.

Notes

1 According to the OSCE High Commissioner on National Minorities, in the autumn of 2010 the university reopened as Osh Social University. See Vollebaek 2010: 3. Students and administrators whom I interviewed in the summer of 2011 referred to the university as Osh State Social University, although that name had not been approved by the Ministry of Education. For a fuller discussion, see Merrill (2011).
2 See Carlson (2004), for some of the issues involved in these debates in Kyrgyzstan, and Weitz (2008), for a brief review of William Fierman's insights on these issues in Central Asia as a whole.
3 Calculated from the CIA World Factbook (2009b) and the International Fund for Agricultural Development (IFAD); see also Abdurakhmanov (2009) regarding problems with the 2009 census count.
4 Sharshekeeva, C. (*c.*1997–2001) Personal communication.

5 Maine is one of a number of states in the US that does not have a residency require-ment or a citizenship requirement for taking the CPA exam.
6 See Benliyan (2009) for a human interest story on the results of the current test.
7 On Turkmenistan, see Merrill (2009).
8 R. Bekboyeva (2009) Interview with the author, 9 July. On 23 August 2011, the gov-ernment of Kyrgyzstan decreed that by the 2012–2013 academic year, all higher education institutions in Kyrgyzstan, with a few exceptions, such as medical schools, would adopt the BA-MA and credit hour system. See Merrill and Ryskulova (2012).
9 S. Uzakova (2009) Personal communication, July.
10 It is one of the factors counted by international ranking systems – directly by the Times Higher Education (now QS World University Rankings), and indirectly by the Shanghai Jiao Tong system (now Academic Ranking of World Universities), which assigns fully 40 per cent of its points for evaluation to the number of citations faculty have in listed western scientific and social science indexes. See Ranking Forum of Swiss Universities (2009a, 2009b).
11 Kyrgyzstan is scheduled to implement accredit hour system in the fall of 2012. See Merrill and Ryskulova (2012).
12 See Merrill (2006), for further discussion of some of the concerns raised by the pos-sibility GATS in Kyrgyzstan's higher education system.
13 See the financial services section, of WTO, "Kyrgyz Republic – Trade Policies by Sector" (2005: 101–109) for a sense of how that services sector was reformed under WTO rules.
14 Munson (2001); see also McClinchey (2009), for a parallel situation in Kyrgyzstan.
15 For a more complete discussion of this issue, see Merrill (2012).
16 Licensure takes place when a *fakultet* is opened; attestation takes place when its first class is graduated. Both are repeated every five years.

References

Abdurakhmanov, A. (2009) "Kyrgyz Census Figures 'Overstated,'", *Institute for War and Peace Reporting (IWPR)*. Online. Available: http://iwpr.net/print/report-news/kyrgyz-census-figures-%E2%80%9Coverstated%E2%80%9D (accessed on 25 July 2009).

Altbach, P.G. and Balan, J. (2007) *World Class Worldwide: Transforming Research Universities in Asia and Latin America*, Baltimore: Johns Hopkins University Press.

ACE (American Council on Education) (2008) *An Overview of Higher Education and GATS*. Online. Available: www.acenet.edu/Content/NavigationMenu/ProgramsServices/cii/global/policy/Intl_GATS_overview.htm (accessed on 24 July 2009).

Asiurov, S., Babajanov, R. and Miraliev, K. (2007) *Skills Development and Poverty Reduction: Tajikistan*. Online. Available: www.etf.europa.eu/pubmgmt.nsf/(getAttach ment)/2C4F505914C1FCCBC125739B0056D8A7/$File/NOTE797LJD.pdf (accessed on 1 October 2009).

Bayram, M. (2009) "Kyrgyzstan: New Law to Introduce Sweeping Controls on Religious Education?" *Forum 18 News Service*, 9 September. Online. Available: www.forum18. org/Archive.php?article_id=1345&pdf=Y (accessed on 29 November 2009).

Becker Professional Education (2009) *CPA Exam Requirements*. Online. Available: www.becker.com/accounting/cpaexamreview/state/dsp_state_search_results.cfm (accessed on 29 November 2009).

Benliyan, A. (2009) "Luchshii ball: Yevgenia [The Best Score: Yevgenia]", *Vechernii Bishkek*, 27(9795), 10 July: 1–2.

Boldjurova, I.S. (2007) "Higher Education in the Kyrgyz Republic: Problems of Modern-ization and Internationalization", Online. Available: http://libw01.kokushikan.ac.jp/

data/1000763/0000/registfile/ajj_002_01.pdf and www.international.ac.uk/resources/ Higher%20Education%20in%20the%20Kyrgyz%20Republic%20-%20Problems.pdf (accessed on 26 July 2009).

Bragina, N.V., Djanaliev, A.F. and Simbard, S.R. (2007) *Rukovodstvo: Po Organizatsii Vnutrennei Sistemy Garantii Kachestva v Vysshih Uchebnyh Zavedeniyah Kirgizskoi Respubliki* [Tutorial: How to Organize the Internal System of Quality Assurance in Higher Education of Kyrgyz Republic], Bishkek: Foundation Soros-Kyrgyzstan.

Carana Corporation website. *Central Asian Accounting Reform.* Online. Available: www. ednetca.org/index.php?option=com_content&view=article&id=121&Itemid=61 (accessed on 24 July 2009).

Carlson, C. (2004) "Kyrgyzstan: Parliament Debating Controversial New Language Law", *Radio Free Europe/Radio Liberty*, 5 February. Online. Available: www.rferl. org/content/article/1051448.html (accessed on 27 July 2009).

CIA World Factbook (2009a) "China". Online. Available: www.cia.gov/library/publications/the-world-factbook/geos/ch.html (accessed on 23 July 2009).

CIA World Factbook (2009b) "Kyrgyzstan". Online. Available: www.cia.gov/library/publications/the-world-factbook/geos/kg.html (accessed on 25 July 2009).

CIA World Factbook (2009c) "Russia". Online. Available: www.cia.gov/library/publications/the-world-factbook/geos/rs.html (accessed on 23 July 2009).

Commercio, M. (2008) "Women's Proclivity towards Islamic Education in Kyrgyzstan and Tajikistan: A Backlash against Communist Gender Equality", *IREX Short Term Travel Grant Research Report.* Online. Available: www.irex.org/programs/stg/research/08/Commercio.pdf (accessed on 29 November 2009).

Creative Associates International. *Central Asian Republics (Kyrgyzstan, Tajikistan, Turkmenistan)/*Quality Learning Project. Online. Available: www.caii.com/ (accessed on 24 July 2009).

DeYoung, A. (2005) "Ownership of Education Reforms in the Kyrgyz Republic: Kto v dome hozyain?" *European Educational Research Journal*, 4/1: 36–49. Online. Available: www.wwwords.co.uk/pdf/freetoview.asp?j=eerj&vol=4&issue=1&year=2005&article=4_DeYoung_EERJ_4_1_web (accessed on 29 November 2009).

Djanaeva, N. (2001) "The Internationalization of Higher Education in Kyrgyzstan", Paper presented at the annual "Soyuz" conference. Bloomington, IN, April. Online. Available: http://condor.depaul.edu/~rrotenbe/aeer/v17n2/Djanaeva.pdf and www.international.ac.uk/country_profiles_and_news/kgz/library.cfm (accessed on 26 July 2009).

Drummond, T. and DeYoung, A.J. (2004) "Perspectives and Problems in Education Reform in Kyrgyzstan: The Case of National Scholarship Testing", in S. Heyneman and A.J. DeYoung (eds) *The Challenge of Education in Central Asia*, Greenwich, CT: Information Age Publishing: 225–242.

Dukenbaev, A. (2004) "Politics and Public Policy in Post-Soviet Central Asia: The Case of Higher Education Reform in Kyrgyzstan", *Central Eurasian Studies Review*, 3/2. Online. Available: www.cesr-cess.org/pdf/CESR_03_2.pdf (accessed on 29 November 2009).

Dyikanbaeva, A. (n.d.) *Application for Institutional Development Grant 2008*, Wenner-Gren Foundation for Anthropological Research. Online. Available: www.afpwebfolio. org/_files/9145_101.doc (accessed on 7 December 2009).

EACEA (Education, Audiovisual, and Culture Executive Agency of the European Commission). TEMPUS. *Update on State of Affairs in Higher Education in Kyrgyzstan.* Online. Available: http://eacea.ec.europa.eu/tempus/participating_countries/higher/kyrgyzstan.pdf (accessed on 29 November 2009).

Eastern University (Makhmuda Kashgari-Barskani) website. Online. Available: http:// eng.chygysh.kg/index.php?option=com_content&task=blogcategory&id=14&Itemi d=34 (accessed on 22 November 2009).

ENQA (European Network for Quality Assurance) (2009a) *Application for Membership, Criterion 5*. Online. Available: www.enqa.eu/becomeamember.lasso (accessed on 29 May 2009).

ENQA (European Network for Quality Assurance) (2009b) *Standards and Guidelines for Quality Assurance in the European Higher Education Area*. Section 3.6 (3e). Online. Available: www.enqa.eu/files/ESG_3edition%20(2).pdf (accessed on 29 November 2009).

Erasmus Mundus External Cooperation Window (2009) *List of Universities in Kyrgyzstan*. Online. Available: http://eacea.ec.europa.eu/extcoop/call/documents/kyrgyztan.pdf (accessed on 25 July 2009).

ETF (European Training Foundation) (2005) *Four Countries Sign Joint Declaration on Qualification Frameworks in Central Asia*, 9 December. Online. Available: www.etf. europa.eu/web.nsf/pages/526DC579E0DBFE70C12570D200595DD7_ EN?OpenDocument (accessed on 16 May 2009).

European Commission External Relations (2008) *Joint Progress Report by the Council and the Commission to the European Council on the Implementation of the EU Central Asia Strategy*. Online. Available: http://ec.europa.eu/external_relations/central_asia/ docs/progress_report_0608_en.pdf (accessed on 4 June 2008).

Foley, C. (2003) *The Educational System of Kyrgyzstan*, Washington, DC: AACRAO.

General Secretariat, Council of the European Union (2007) *European Union and Central Asia: Strategy for a New Partnership*, Brussels. Online. Available: http://ue.eu.int/ uedocs/cmsUpload/EU_CtrlAsia_EN-RU.pdf (accessed on 1 October 2007).

Grootings, P., Bakirova, A. and Beishembaeva, A. (2007) "Skills Development and Poverty Reduction in Kyrgyzstan", *European Training Foundation Working Paper*. Online. Available: www.etf.europa.eu/pubmgmt.nsf/(getAttachment)/AF58FE7EB0D3 66FFC125739B0052A5AE/$File/NOTE797KMN.pdf (accessed on 1 October 2009).

"Headscarf Ban Lifted after Protests", *Russia Today*, 11 March 2009. Online. Available: www.russiatoday.com/Top_News/2009-03-11/Headscarf_ban_lifted_after_protests. html (accessed on 25 July 2009).

IFAD (International Fund for Agricultural Development) "IFAD in the Kyrgyz Repub-lic", *Rural Poverty Portal*. Online. Available: www.ruralpovertyportal.org/web/guest/ country/home/tags/kyrgyzstan (accessed on 21 July 2009).

Ivakhnyuk, I. (2006) "Migration in the CIS Region: Common Problems and Mutual Ben-efits", paper presented at the International Symposium on International Migration and Development, UN Secretariat, Turin, Italy, 28 June. Online. Available: www.un.org/ esa/population/migration/turin/Symposium_Turin_files/P10_SYMP_Ivakhniouk.pdf (accessed on 22 July 2009).

Jamasheva, A. and Adresheva, S. (2000) "Fact Sheet: Kyrgyz Republic Higher Educa-tion". Online. Available: www.bibl.u-szeged.hu/oseas/kyrgyz_facts2.html (accessed on 14 December 2012).

Jani, F. (2009) "Relations between Iran and Central Asia (Synopsis)", *Fergana.ru*, 13 April. Online. Available: http://enews.Fergana.ru/article.php?id=2520 (accessed on 23 July 2009).

Knight, J. (2002) "Trade Creep: Implication of GATS for Higher Education Policy", *International Higher Education*, 28: 5–7. Online. Available: https://htmldbprod.bc.edu/ pls/htmldb/f?p=2290:4:2584675268137907::NO:RP,4:P0_CONTENT_ID:99884 (accessed on 17 January 2011).

Knight, J. (2006) "Higher Education Crossing Borders: A Guide to the Implications of the General Agreement on Trade in Services (GATS) for Cross-border Education", Report Prepared for the Commonwealth of Learning and UNESCO. Online. Available: www.col.org/GATS (accessed on 23 July 2009).

KRSU (Kyrgyz-Russian Slavic University) (2007a) "Chronika" [Russian version]. Online. Available: www.krsu.edu.kg/Rus/About.htm (accessed on 22 July 2009).

KRSU (Kyrgyz-Russian Slavic University) (2007b) "KRSU history" [English version], last updated 24 May 2007. Online. Available: www.krsu.edu.kg/Eng/about.html (accessed on 21 July 2009).

Kyrgyzstan-Turkey Manas University website (2009a) "University" [English version]. Online. Available: www.manas.kg/alt.php?id=1 (accessed on 21 July 2009).

Kyrgyzstan-Turkey Manas University website (2009b) "Our Mission". Online. Available: www.manas.kg/alt.php?tip=1&id=4 (accessed on 25 July 2009).

Lezberg, A.K. (2008) *Assessment of Issues and Opportunities in University Accreditation in Kyrgyz Republic*, USAID Kyrgyzstan.

Library of Congress, Federal Research Division (2007) "Country Profile: Kyrgyzstan". Online. Available: http://lcweb2.loc.gov/frd/cs/profiles/Kyrgyzstan.pdf (accessed on 22 July 2009).

Mamaraimov, A. and Asanova, S. (2008) "Headscarf Ban Remains Live Issue in Central Asia", *Institute for War and Peace Reporting (IWPR)*, RCA No. 556, 14 November. Online. Available: www.iwpr.net/?p=rca&s=f&o=347799&apc_state=henh (accessed on 25 July, 2009).

Marat, E. (2007) "With Kulov Gone, Bakiyev Dumps HIPC Initiative", *Eurasia Daily Monitor*, 4/38, 23 February. Online. Available: www.jamestown.org/single/?no_cache=1&tx_ttnews[tt_news]=32528 (accessed on 24 July 2009).

McClinchey, E. (2009) *Islamic Revivalism and State Failure in Kyrgyzstan*, Project Report for the National Council for Eurasian and East European Research (Seattle). Online. Available: www.ucis.pitt.edu/nceeer/2009_822-09g_McGlinchey.pdf (accessed on 29 November 2009).

Melvin, N. and Boonstra, J. (2008) "The EU Strategy for Central Asia: Year One", *EUCAM*, 1, October.

Merrill, M.C. (2006) "Internationalization of Higher Education in Kyrgyzstan: Three Potential Problems", *Central Eurasian Studies Review*, 5/2. Online. Available: www.cess.muohio.edu/cesr/pdf/CESR_05_2.pdf (accessed on 29 November 2009).

Merrill, M.C. (2009) "Turkmenistan: Fixing Decades of Damage", *International Higher Education*, 56. Online. Available: https://htmldbprod.bc.edu/pls/htmldb/f?p=2290:4:4086699645050802::NO:RP,4:P0_CONTENT_ID:101176 (accessed on 18 January 2010).

Merrill, M.C. (2011) *Higher Education in Osh: A Descriptive Analysis of Current Conditions*, IREX Scholar Research Brief. Online. Available: www.irex.org/sites/default/files/Merrill%20Final%20Research.pdf.

Merrill, M.C. (2012) "*Kasha* and Quality in Kyrgyzstan: Donors, Diversity, and Dis-Integration in Higher Education", *European Education*, 43/4: 5–25.

Merrill, M.C. and Dukenbaev, A. (2011) "Youth and Higher Education", in A. Warkotsch (ed.) *The European Union and Central Asia*, London: Routledge.

Merrill, M.C. and Ryskulova, C. (2012) "Kyrgyzstan's New Degree System", *International Higher Education*, 68, Summer 2012: 18–20. Online. Available: https://htmldbprod.bc.edu/pls/htmldb/f?p=2290:4:0::NO:RP,4:P0_CONTENT_ID:118279.

Munson, Z. (2001) "Islamic Mobilization: Social Movement Theory and the Egyptian

Muslim Brotherhood", *The Sociological Quarterly*, 42: 487–510. Online. Available: www.jstor.org/stable/4121130 (accessed on 30 November 2009).

Najibullah, F. (2009) "Turkish Schools Coming under Increasing Scrutiny in Central Asia", *Radio Free Europe/Radio Liberty (RFERL)*, 26 April. Online. Available: www.rferl.org/content/Turkish_Schools_Coming_Under_Increasing_Scrutiny_In_Central_Asia/1616111.html (accessed on 25 July 2009).

Namatbaeva, T. (2008) "Kyrgyzstan: No Work for Madrassah Graduates", *Institute for War and Peace Reporting (IWPR) Central Asia*, 528, 24 January. Online. Available: www.iwpr.net/index.php?apc_state=hen&s=o&o=l=EN&p=rca&s=f&o=342190 (accessed on 29 November 2009).

Office of Licensing and Registration, Department of Professional and Financial Regulation, State of Maine (2009) *Certified Public Accountant*. Online. Available: www.maine.gov/pfr/professionallicensing/professions/accountants/cpa.htm (accessed on 29 November 2009).

Official Bologna Process, 2010–2012 (2010) "History". Online. Available: www.ehea.info/article-details.aspx?ArticleId=3 (accessed on 16 January 2011).

"Path to Europe: State Program of Kazakhstan", *IncrEAST* (16 October 2008) Online. Available: www.increast.eu/en/392.php (accessed on 29 November 2009).

Pomfret, R. (2007) "Lessons from Kyrgyzstan's WTO Experience for Kazakhstan, Tajikistan, and Uzbekistan", *Asia-Pacific Trade and Investment Review*, 3/2. Online. Available: www.unescap.org/tid/publication/aptir2470_richard.pdf (accessed on 25 July 2009).

PRB (Population Reference Bureau) (c. 2007) "Kyrgyzstan". Online. Available: www.prb.org/Countries/Kyrgyzstan.aspx (accessed on 21 July 2009).

Quigley, J. (2004) "Kyrgyzstan's Accession to the WTO", *EurAsia Bulletin* 8/1 and 2. Online. Available: www.eias.org/publications/bulletin/2004/janfeb04/ebjanfeb04p11.pdf (accessed on 25 July 2009).

Ranking Forum of Swiss Universities (2009a) "Times Higher Education Supplement". Online. Available: www.universityrankings.ch/en/methodology/times_higher_education.

Ranking Forum of Swiss Universities (2009b) "Shanghai Jiao Tong University". Online. Available: www.universityrankings.ch/en/methodology/shanghai_jiao_tong (accessed on 25 July 2009).

Reeves, M. (2004) "Academic Integrity and its Limits in Kyrgyzstan", *International Higher Education*, 37. Online. Available: https://htmldbprod.bc.edu/pls/htmldb/f?p=2290:4:396327834974583::NO:RP,4:P0_CONTENT_ID:100650 (accessed on 18 January 2011).

Reeves, M. (2006) "Schooling in Ak-Tatyr: A Shifting Moral Economy", in A. DeYoung, M. Reeves and G. Valyayeva (eds) *Surviving the Transition? Case Studies of Schools and Schooling in the Kyrgyz Republic since Independence*, Greenwich: Information Age Publishing.

Roope, J. (2009) Class presentation, Comparative Education, Kent State University, Spring semester.

Salmi, J. (2009) *The Challenge of Establishing World-Class Universities*, Washington, D.C.: The World Bank.

Saxenian, A.L. (2002) "Brain Circulation: How High-Skill Immigration Makes Everyone Better Off", *The Brookings Institution*, Winter. Online. Available: www.brookings.edu/articles/2002/winter_immigration_saxenian.aspx (accessed on 29 November 2009).

Sharma, Y. (2009) "Small States Share Higher Education Costs", *University World News*,

12 July. Online. Available: www.universityworldnews.com/article.php?story=2009071
0113541922&mode=print (accessed on 22 July 2009).

Smirnitsky, A.I. *et al.* (1971) *Russian-English Dictionary*, 9th edn, Moscow: Soviet
Encyclopedia Publishing House.

Steiner-Khamsi, Gita and Stolpe, Ines (2006) *Educational Import in Mongolia: Local
Encounters with Global Forces*, New York: Palgrave Macmillan.

Tasbulatova, S. and Belosludtseva, V. (2007) *Skills Development and Poverty Reduction:
Kazakhstan*. Online. Available: www.etf.europa.eu/pubmgmt.nsf/(getAttachment)/0AF
C88130388A04FC125739B00564477/$File/NOTE797LEE.pdf (accessed on 1 October
2009).

Umland, A. (2005) "Teaching Social Sciences at a Post-Soviet University: A Survey of
Challenges for Visiting Lecturers in the Former USSR", *European Political Science*,
4(2). Online. Available: www.palgrave-journals.com/eps/journal/v4/n2/pdf/2210025a.
pdf (accessed on 23 July 2009).

UNDP (United Nations Development Programme Kyrgyzstan) (2010) "Kyrgyzstan: Successful Youth – Successful Country", *National Human Development Report*, Bishkek,
Kyrgyzstan.

University of Central Asia website. "One University, Three Campuses". Online. Available: www.ucentralasia.org/campus.htm (accessed on 23 November 2009).

Uzenbayev, R.A. (2009) (Dean of the Accounting, Tourism, and Management Faculty,
Osh Technical University) Interview with the author, Osh, Kyrgyzstan, 29 June 2009.

Vollebaek, K. (2010) Statement by Knut Vollebaek, OSCE High Commissioner on
National Minorities, to the 837th Plenary Meeting of the OSCE Permanent Council.
Vienna, 18 November. Online. Available: www.delegfrance-osce.org/IMG/pdf/hcnm-
gal0005r1_hcnm_837pc.pdf (accessed 23 January 2009).

Weitz, R. (2008) "Central Asia: Looking at Language Politics", *EurasiaNet*, 28 January.
Online. Available: www.eurasianet.org/departments/insight/articles/eav012808a.shtml
(accessed on 27 July, 2009).

WHO (World Health Organization) (2007) "Kyrgyzstan". Online. Available: www.who.
int/hrh/wdms/media/Kyrgyzstan.pdf (accessed on 22 July 2009).

WTO (World Trade Organization) (c. 2005) "Kyrgyz Republic – Trade Policies by
Sector".   Online.   Available: www.wto.org/english/tratop_e/tpr_e/s170–04_e.doc
(accessed on 25 July 2009).

Conclusion

Pınar Akçalı[1] and Cennet Engin-Demir[2]

Post-Soviet Kyrgyzstan is challenged with several tensions between the old and the new on the one hand, and domestic and international on the other. In many areas of political, economic and social life, the legacy of the past meets with the requirements of the post-Soviet transition, and the domestic conditions and priorities of Kyrgyzstan are shaped or influenced to some extent both by the necessity of adaptation on the part of the people to post-Soviet era conditions and to certain international actors and their priorities.

One major conclusion of this book is related to the regional, tribal and kinship ties in Kyrgyzstan which are among the basic traditional identity factors in the country, the roots of which go back to the pre-Soviet era. These markers of identity that continued to be influential during the Soviet era, however, are now being reconstructed and put into practical social use in order to meet the numerous challenges of the economic, political and cultural arenas in Kyrgyzstan. In other words, in order to cope with these challenges, these ties are used as either tools/instruments or as justifications for adaptation to the new economic, political and cultural challenges and for solving various problems arising from them.

This pattern can be very clearly observed in the rural economy of Kyrgyzstan, which continues to be the largest sector, employing most of the Kyrgyz people. Since the native Kyrgyz still tend to live in rural areas dealing with agriculture, the post-Soviet challenges in terms of shifting to a market economy based on private property could be most clearly observed in the former *kolkhoz* structures. The *kolkhoz* of the Soviet era is the private farm of the post-Soviet era, in which the traditional identity patterns such as kin preference, clan association, nepotism and male dominance are clearly observed. However, these identity patterns are put into practical use only if they provide a benefit to the relevant actors. In other words, as long as they are feasible and mutually beneficial, the patrons and their clients utilize these ties to meet personal interests. As Svetlana Jacquesson's chapter shows, the discourse over officially acknowledged descent lines are either reflected or not reflected depending on the practical use of such lines. Social intercourse may therefore take different patterns that may or may not be shaped by descent lines. In other words, as Aksana Ismailbekova suggests in her chapter, patrons and their clients may or may not promote descent depending on the manipulation of various strategies that are used within the circles of trust that are justified by kinship ties. The former *kolkhoz*, while making the shift to a private farm in the post-Soviet era, becomes a new arena of patron–client relations that are neither forced nor voluntary. In this new context, disorganized management and unspecified division of labour among the actors in the farm are shaped to a large extent by manipulative strategies to meet one's own economic interests that are justified by kinship or descent ties.

One rather interesting issue that needs to be taken into account is related to the unique situation of the Kyrgyz *mashayakche* that is analysed in David Radford's chapter. As mentioned by Radford, these people have opted to reconstruct "Kyrgyzness" by converting to Christianity, justified on the grounds that these two are much more compatible with each other, as compared to Islam. Thus, these converts challenge the centuries old assumption that "to be Kyrgyz is to be Muslim", as they do not see themselves any less Kyrgyz than their Muslim co-nationals. This major shift in the definition of Kyrgyzness further complicates the post-Soviet identity building attempts in the country by challenging one of the basic identity markers of the Kyrgyz people as being Muslims. As the case of the Kyrgyz *mashayakche* indicates, depending on the specific conditions and/or preferences of the people, certain identity factors may or may not be put into social use. In other words, they may or may not be adopted in the process of social construction of Kyrgyz identity.

Another such similarity can be observed for patterns of political leadership and constitutional reform in Kyrgyzstan. As the chapters of Irina Morozova, Seçil Öraz and Anita Sengupta indicate, political leaders in Kyrgyzstan, both during and after the Soviet era, have utilized the same identity markers in order to adapt to new conditions. According to Morozova, in sharing economic and political benefits, clan/tribe or regional ties are always utilized within the specific general framework and/or conditions of the era. The rivalry and consolidation of elites may take the constant form of shifting alliances shaped to a large extent by the competition over resource distribution. The same could be observed in the leadership patterns of post-Soviet Kyrgyzstan, as analysed in the chapters of Öraz and Sengupta. Based on the general traditional patterns of authoritative patriarchic and tribal structure of Kyrgyz society, political leaders have turned out to be the major actors in post-Soviet Kyrgyzstan. The political developments have indicated an endless construction and reconstruction of the political system in which the political actors have played the most important roles in introducing constitutional reforms as well as determining the trajectory of the regime type. As put forward by both authors, the post-Soviet political transformation was neither democratic nor smooth, but rather shaped to a large extent by the actions of the presidents and their major concern of being the dominant power as compared to the legislative and the judicial bodies. Here again we see the role of traditional identity factors, such as clan/tribal affiliations surrounding both Akaev and Bakiev shaping the constitutional reform process to a considerable degree. In other words, utilization or at least consideration of these affiliations could very well shape the political trajectory of Kyrgyzstan.

Post-Soviet Kyrgyzstan has also faced a myriad of issues and problems in the field of education, which mostly resulted from challenges in socio-cultural, political and economic upheaval in the transition. New trends and policies that aim to develop post-Soviet curricula and to promote necessary attitudes and values in order to cope with the socio-cultural, political and economic changes taking place both in the domestic and international spheres are emerging. The curriculum challenges of all societies in transition (including Kyrgyzstan) fall into three categories: the challenge of pedagogy, the challenge of introducing the new subject matter and the challenge of teaching civics, social studies and history. As the main actors of educational systems, Kyrgyz teachers, too, need to be equipped with the necessary knowledge, understanding and skills to cope with the challenges of post-Soviet transition in the country. In his chapter, Düishön Shamatov argues that newer teachers, in addition to the typical personal and institutional challenges (adjusting to school culture, rules and regulations, children with various needs and interests or classroom management problems), now also face those challenges that have emerged after the collapse of the Soviet Union. Insufficient resources, inadequately qualified and experienced colleagues, high student drop-out rates, a constantly changing curriculum, lack of textbooks and low salaries with frequent delays and deductions are additional sources of distress that new teachers now have to deal with. In addition, the teaching of history became more difficult in the early post-Soviet years. As in many countries in transition, the teaching of history is expected to provide means to promote the new national ideology with concepts such as nation building, construction of identity and protecting and strengthening Kyrgyzstan's independence (Ibraimov 2001). Kanybek, the participant history teacher in Shamatov's case study, had faced serious challenges in planning, conducting and evaluating his lessons because of insufficient knowledge and skills developed regarding different pedagogical approaches during pre-service years, and lack of textbooks and materials with clear goals and objectives in history teaching in transition. Therefore, Kanybek's teaching approaches follow the usual patterns of those during Soviet times with great emphasis on imparting textbook knowledge to pupils through lecturing and retelling. However, a student-centred approach where learners are active critical thinkers rather than passive receivers and where teachers are facilitators rather than authoritarian experts needs to be integrated in classroom practices, particularly in the instruction of history to develop the concepts of democracy, liberty and market economy in Kyrgyzstan.

Higher education was also challenged by broad changes in social, political and economic life in post-Soviet Kyrgyzstan. Alan DeYoung argues that expansion of the higher education sector is among the most visible changes brought about by educational reforms in Kyrgyzstan. Although the Kyrgyz Republic has experienced, over the past two decades, a substantial decline in quality both at the secondary and higher education levels, university enrolment has dramatically increased. Higher education institutions have increased from fewer than 10 to about 50. The systemic decline in financial support for state universities has significantly undermined their quality. Serious deterioration in faculty quality, few material resources, crumbling state university buildings and minimal student support services are the other factors that decrease the quality in higher education. De Young sees a serious "gap" between expressed aims for higher education in the country at the official level, including the education ministry and university presidents, and what is actually happening. Official proclamations embrace a call to improve academic quality and prepare students for the world of professional practice. However, there is a "tremendous surplus of college educated graduates who were unemployed and also that employers were dissatisfied with the skills of their new college educated workers" (Drummond and DeYoung, 2004: 229). Internationalization of programmes is put forward as one of the most important ways of raising academic quality by almost every major university in Kyrgyzstan. Several inter-governmental and private universities provide opportunities to build academic skills and international exchange programmes for their students.

Internationalization of higher education is considered to be unavoidable because of the globalization of various political, social and economic spheres of life. However, internationalization in transition countries has some unique dimensions that are not found in many other countries. Martha Merrill argues in her chapter that for a dozen different reasons in the field of higher education, Kyrgyzstan cannot isolate itself from the demands, priorities and pressures of international actors. On the one hand, Kyrgyzstan's ability to act in some realms is limited by factors such as its size, its geographic location, its economic situation and restrictions of General Agreement on Trade in Services. On the other hand, the spheres over which Kyrgyzstan does have control, such as the language of academic materials, financial support for reform in higher education, labour migration and "brain circulation", international rankings of universities, attracting international faculty, the globalization of quality assessment materials, degree structures, high degree of ministerial control over the content and structure of university curricula, and corruption in academic integrity needs more attention to increase the quality of higher education in the country. Flexibility and innovation, academic integrity, curricular independence and transparency in operations are what Kyrgyzstan needs to strengthen its own higher education system to cope with the challenges resulting both from local and international changes.

As can be observed in all of the three specific areas that are analysed in this book, Kyrgyzstan is under the pressure of balancing the legacy of the past with the challenges of the present on the one hand, and the demands of domestic and international actors on the other. This pressure should be seen as one of the major determining factors of this post-Soviet country that may have even more of a powerful influence in the long run, as the country's resources in major areas of life are quite limited. The challenges of recent years in terms of ethnic clashes and political instability may add to the problems of this strategically located country, putting it more in the spotlight of the international community.

Notes

1 Middle East Technical University, Department of Political Science and Public Administration.
2 Middle East Technical University, Department of Educational Sciences.

References

Drummond, T. and DeYoung, A.J. (2004) "Perspectives and Problems in Education Reform in Kyrgyzstan", in S.F. Heyneman and A.J. DeYoung (eds) *The Challenges of Education in Central Asia*, Greenwich, CT: Information Age Publishing, 225–242.

Ibravimov, O. (2001) *Kyrgyzstan Encyclopedia*. Bishkek: Center of National Language and Encyclopedia.

Index

Page numbers in *italics* denote tables, those in **bold** denote figures.